THE NEW HUMAN REVOLUTION

VOLUME 14

THE NEW HUMAN REVOLUTION

VOLUME 14

DAISAKU IKEDA

ILLUSTRATIONS BY
KENICHIRO UCHIDA

World Tribune
—*Press*—

Published by World Tribune Press
606 Wilshire Boulevard
Santa Monica, California 90401

©2007 by Soka Gakkai
Printed in the United States of America

Complete Set   ISBN: 978-0-915678-32-7
Volume 14   ISBN: 978-0-915678-46-4
Interior and cover designed by Gopa & Ted2, Inc.

10   9   8   7   6   5   4   3

Contents

Editor's Note

The citations most commonly used in this book have been abbreviated as follows:

♦ GZ refers to the *Gosho Zenshu*, the Japanese-language compilation of letters, treatises, essays and oral teachings of Nichiren Daishonin.

♦ LS refers to *The Lotus Sutra*, translated by Burton Watson (New York: Columbia University Press, 1993).

♦ OTT refers to *The Record of the Orally Transmitted Teachings*, translated by Burton Watson (Tokyo: Soka Gakkai, 2004).

♦ WND refers to *The Writings of Nichiren Daishonin*, vol. 1 (WND-1) and vol. 2 (WND-2) (Tokyo: Soka Gakkai, 1999).

Wisdom and Courage

O N MAY 3, 1969, some twenty thousand members gathered for the Soka Gakkai's Thirty-second Headquarters General Meeting held at the Nihon University Auditorium in Ryogoku, Tokyo. The hope-filled azure sky stretched out above, the sun shining like a golden crown over the heads of these champions of Soka. A decisive struggle was about to begin and the wheels of history were being set in motion.

The members listened in anticipation as Shin'ichi Yamamoto's dignified voice rang out: "May 3 of next year will mark the tenth anniversary of my becoming Soka Gakkai president [in 1960]. In that respect, these next twelve months will be a period of putting the finishing touches on this decade. At the same time, we are now at the start of a decade that will culminate with the completion of the Seven Bells[1] in 1979. I therefore hope you will have the awareness that this year will be a powerful starting point for victory."

After announcing that the Soka Gakkai membership in Japan had reached 7,027,296 member-households, Shin'-ichi said: "I would like to propose that we aim to achieve 7.5 million member-households by May 3 of next year. What do you think? Those who agree, please raise your hands!"

The members' hands shot up as they cheered in a show of approval and then broke into enthusiastic applause—applause that represented their determination to spread Buddhism in accord with Nichiren Daishonin's statement, "The 'great vow' refers to the propagation of the Lotus Sutra" (OTT, 82).

Shin'ichi continued: "Propagation is the lifeblood of religion. A religion that does not propagate its teachings is dead. I recall how President Toda, amidst criticism and ridicule, achieved his lifelong dream of 750,000 member-households (in 1957). With the same spirit, let us adorn the thirteenth memorial of Mr. Toda's death on April 2, 1970, as well as my tenth year as Soka Gakkai president, with the accomplishment of the goal of 7.5 million member-households by May 3 of next year. I believe this is the way for us as disciples to repay our debt of gratitude to our mentor."

Once again applause reverberated throughout the auditorium. The great spirit of Soka is to courageously and resolutely stand up for kosen-rufu, always filled with fresh determination. Those who do so experience the tremendous life force of the Bodhisattvas of the Earth surging within them, and they are able to transform their state of being. This is the way to forge open the path to victory and prosperity.

SHIN'ICHI THEN SPOKE about the student protest movement that was sweeping Japan at the time, as well as the purpose of Soka University, preparations for which were proceeding smoothly toward its scheduled opening in 1971.

He said: "At present, conflict is raging on university campuses throughout Japan. It has become a serious social problem. I regard this troubled state of affairs as a sign that the times are calling for a completely new kind of university, based on fresh ideals and a fresh philosophy. The most distinctive characteristic of Soka University will be the faculty, a core of people who embrace a youthful passion for learning and who will, whether they are well known or not, dedicate themselves wholeheartedly to education. In addition to such a faculty, I would like to invite many leading scholars from both within and outside Japan, who are sympathetic with the Soka University's founding ideals, to lecture on specific topics for the students.

"I myself intend to study as well and, if the university administration permits, offer some lectures on literature." The audience applauded excitedly. "My guess is that there will be little chance of that, though!" Shin'ichi added to the members' joyous laughter.

Shin'ichi believed that at the heart of the student uprisings was the alienation and antagonism students felt from their authoritarian and spiritually enervated teachers. It was his conviction that education needed the presence of passionate and inspiring teachers, as exemplified by the youthful nineteenth-century Japanese educator Yoshida Shoin.[2] At his private academy in Hagi, Choshu (present-day Yamaguchi Prefecture), Yoshida fostered many talented young people who later came to play a pivotal role in ushering Japan into the modern age.

"Teachers and students should not be in opposing positions," Shin'ichi said. "By rights, they are partners walking the path of learning together. In other words, their relationship must be nurturing and democratic. I would like Soka University to be an ideal model of an educational community in which students are actively involved in the institution's operation."

Shin'ichi also discussed his future plans to establish a correspondence course, thereby opening the university to the general public. From the earliest planning stages, Shin'ichi focused on the idea of such a program.

The Russian author Leo Tolstoy once observed, "No one has ever thought of establishing universities based on the needs of the people."[3] Shin'ichi was determined to rise to that challenge.

SHIN'ICHI SPOKE of other plans he had for Soka University, including sponsoring a research expedition to the Silk Road, the route along which Buddhism spread eastward to Japan, and promoting the study of humanistic economics. He then announced Soka University's fundamental guidelines as: (1) Be the highest seat of learning for humanistic education; (2) Be the cradle of a new culture; and (3) Be a fortress for the peace of humankind.

He said: "In contrast to the present educational environment, which reduces people to mere cogs in the social mechanism and ignores their humanity, the first of these three guidelines points to the need to make Soka University one that fosters well-rounded individuals richly endowed with wisdom and creativity who can take the lead in society.

"The second guideline calls on Soka University students to champion the creation of a great new culture that promotes the infinite flowering of human potential based on the Buddhist philosophy of life during these times when modern civilization is deadlocked.

"The reason the third guideline advocates peace for humankind is that without peace, neither the creation of a new culture nor society's future development can be realized. We absolutely mustn't allow the world to lapse into a state of war, plunging humanity into the depths of suffering. Indeed, the greatest challenge facing the human race today is how to attain and preserve a peaceful world.

"I wish to declare that the Soka University we are constructing must be a citadel of learning that stands on the side of the people and works for human happiness and peace."

The French philosopher Alain wrote, "Our entire future depends upon education."[4] The future of Japan and the world will ultimately be determined by the kind of universities that are established and the kind of leaders those institutes foster. For example, the purpose of the establishment of the University of Tokyo (originally Imperial University), a leading Japanese institution of higher learning, was to produce people who would work for the nation, enabling it to catch up and rapidly become assimilated with the West after the end of its isolationist period in the late nineteenth century. Many other universities founded in later years followed suit and adopted the same ideology. This, Shin'ichi felt, was the source of the limitations of contemporary Japanese universities.

WHILE IT IS only natural for universities to foster capable people who will contribute to society and the progress and development of the nation, Shin'ichi firmly believed that the age had arrived wherein a broader perspective of university education was necessary. The twenty-first century, he felt, must be an age when the focus of humanity shifted from the pursuit of national interests to the pursuit of human interests, from division to unity, from war to peace. Universities, too, needed to move from producing people to work for the sake of the nation to producing people who work for the happiness, peace and prosperity of all humankind. A new leadership model was also essential, one that not only called for the mastery of a body of knowledge and skills, but for integrity and upholding the high ideal of striving for human happiness, as well as the creativity to fully utilize the potential of technology and scholarship.

Fostering such people required universities with firm educational principles that served as a strong spiritual foundation. Indeed, the world was waiting for the establishment of Soka University, founded on Nichiren Buddhism's humanistic philosophy of life.

Shin'ichi then spoke about the student uprising, saying: "I am well aware that the current student movement has come about not only in protest to the status quo at our established universities, but also to the contradictions and injustices of society in general. At the same time, however, certain student agitators and politicians are exploiting the pure spirit of these young people and causing them to veer from their original aim of reform.

"One indication of this is the manner in which the movement continues to divide into splinter groups, giving rise to unnecessary confusion and unrest. It pains me to see this happening. I shudder to think what will transpire if the situation persists and devolves into a vicious cycle of division and upheaval. I believe I am not alone when I say that, for the sake of the student movement's sound development, as well as for Japan's future, we need to find another way to proceed. Do you agree?"

The Nihon University auditorium shook with the members' applause.

"I would like our student division members to ponder this issue carefully, and then take action in the fashion that you think best."

BEFORE BRINGING his speech to a close, he went on to address the significance of Nichiren Buddhism in the history of human civilization as well as the relationship between propagation and compassion.

Shin'ichi's main concern at this time was the direction in which the student protest movement was heading. By the end of June 1969, demonstrations had erupted at 103 universities across Japan. Their causes varied from campus to campus, and included such issues as tuition hikes and the management of student centers.

The movement was originally spearheaded at each university by students unaffiliated with any particular political group. They formed what were known as All-Campus Joint Struggle Committees and conducted numerous activities such as strikes to demand accountability and solutions to problems. Many other students became involved and the movement spread broadly across campuses throughout the country.

Through their efforts, the students exposed the chronic ills of Japan's modern universities, including the privileged nature of these institutions and their feudalistic ways and traditions, as well as their exclusion of student input in the universities' operation. They also questioned the inherent contradictions within the university system whereby the schools' ties to the state were rendering them a part of a mechanism that was inevitably contributing to environmental pollution and the oppression of ordinary people. Their activities were a rejection of established values, as well as an exposé of the postwar power structure and the egoism of the authorities.

The students further realized that, as individuals who were studying at these universities and participating in the system, they themselves were supporting the authorities in their oppression and control of the people. They were not merely victims but also an active part of the problem.

Thus, in addition to dissolving the universities, their purpose became to engage in self-criticism and self-transformation. In other words, a distinguishing feature that helped spread the All-Campus Struggle Movement was the students' inward focus and their fundamental exploration of what is the best way for human beings to live.

As the movement progressed, however, the students were ultimately unable to realize this aim, for the term *self-criticism* came instead to be used when attacking others and forcing them to engage in the act themselves.

STUDENTS AT UNIVERSITIES throughout Japan occupied and barricaded school buildings. But the university administrations made no serious attempt to find fundamental solutions to the issues the students raised. Some in fact called in riot police to drive students out by force.

The emergence of student power movements was not unique to Japan. In March of the previous year, 1968, radical students occupied classrooms at the University of Paris X-Nanterre campus, demanding changes in university policies and improvements in campus facilities. In response, the university authorities eventually shut down the campus. Then, on May 3, students gathered at the Sorbonne in Paris's Latin Quarter to protest the closing of Nanterre.

The university again called in the police to have the students removed, an act that only inflamed the students' anger. In turn, the latter built barricades in the Latin Quarter and hurled Molotov cocktails that exploded amid the fresh greenery of the trees lining the avenues, sending flames and clouds of black smoke into the sky. Tear gas launched by the police filled the air as a bitter struggle was waged in the city's streets.

In the end, some six hundred students were arrested, and the Sorbonne was also closed. This event marked the start of the May crisis, a series of incidents that shook the administration of French President Charles de Gaulle[5]. This was followed by a number of protest demonstrations, including a gathering of some thirty thousand students at the Arc de Triomphe. Major French labor unions, such as the General Workers Confederation, allied themselves with the students, and a nationwide strike ensued. Workers throughout France occupied factories as the protest grew into a massive general strike involving more than eight million people.

In the United States as well, student demonstrations against the Vietnam War were actively taking place.

The global rise of student power was, on the one hand, an explosion of the frustration and anger young people felt toward social structures that oppressed and controlled people, and, on the other, a declaration of their rejection of society's established values.

THE PURE SPIRIT of youth exposes the distortions of society like a clear lens and launches uncompromising criticism at its foes.

In Japan, as in other parts of the world, young people revolted against the willingness of older generations to avert their gaze from such problems as people's growing sense of alienation in society, environmental destruction and pollution, in exchange for the comfort of fleeting prosperity. But eventually student power in Japan would be crushed by the force of the government.

Its ultimate decline was symbolized by a two-day clash between riot police and students who had occupied the University of Tokyo's Yasuda Auditorium in January 1969, a confrontation that ended in the students' removal from the building.

The struggle at Tokyo University had begun in January 1968 with an indefinite strike initiated by medical students against the implementation of a new registration system following the abolition of the internship program. During the strike, an incident occurred in which a group of students forced their way into the University of Tokyo Hospital chief of staff's office and held him hostage overnight. The university took disciplinary action against seventeen students as a result.

The fact that one of the students disciplined had not been involved in the confrontation outraged the entire medical student body, which in turn initiated a series of protests. Seeking the repeal of the disciplinary action against the seventeen students and negotiations with the faculty, they first occupied a part of the medical school, and then in June, seized the Yasuda Auditorium, the symbol of the university. In response, the university lost no time calling in riot police and had the students forcibly removed.

The students' anger exploded, and the struggle spread throughout the rest of the university. The Yasuda Auditorium was once again taken over by students, and it was there that the Tokyo University All-Campus Joint Struggle Committee was formed. The students barricaded themselves inside several other campus buildings, including the Exhibition Hall of the Engineering School and the Law Research Center. This was the situation as 1969 began.

The entrance examination for the new school year was

approaching. At eleven in the evening on January 17, the university administration ordered the students to evacuate the buildings, but the students had no intention of complying. The university therefore asked the Tokyo Metropolitan Police Department to send in the riot police again.

At seven in the morning on January 18, some eighty-five hundred uniformed and plainclothes police officers began to pour through the gates of Tokyo University.

A THIN LAYER of ice covered Sanshiro Pond on the University of Tokyo campus and the police officers' breath came out in white puffs. Helicopters flew noisily overhead as the police moved in about one hundred vehicles that included armored cars and water cannons. Anticipating fierce student resistance, they had brought ten thousand tear gas canisters, and some officers were armed with guns.

Among the groups involved in the uprising were two rival factions—a group affiliated with the Japan Communist Party and another comprised of the core members of the All-Campus Joint Struggle Committee. When the riot police were summoned, the JCP activists, who had been occupying the medical and education buildings, fled their posts and left the struggle to their rivals, who remained in control of the Yasuda Auditorium and other campus facilities.

The attack began. The riot police, clad in navy blue uniforms, helmets and combat boots, stormed the buildings, removing one barricade after another. They were nearly the same age as the students they were fighting against. Five hundred riot police laid siege to the Engineering School's

Exhibition Hall, where they met the intense resistance of the fifty student occupiers. The police launched canisters of tear gas en masse and fired water cannons at the students, who shielded themselves with plywood sheets and retaliated by throwing the canisters back at them, along with Molotov cocktails and chunks of concrete.

There were injuries on both sides. On one part of the campus, a brief truce was called to evacuate the wounded students.

On the roof of the Engineering Building, a student was badly hurt by a tear gas canister that struck him directly in the face. Just then, a student leader picked up a megaphone and shouted down to the police: "One of our comrades has been hit, and he may lose his eyesight. We ask your commanding officer to allow him to be brought down for treatment."

The immediate reaction of the police was one of anger and incredulity. Here they were risking life and limb in the line of duty because of these students. To them, the fact that the students could make such a request was an indication that they were not fully committed to their cause and that they were extremely self-centered.

The commanding officer responded through a loudspeaker, "Surrender and come out!"

"Is that your answer?" the student yelled back several times.

SILENCE FELL over the area. Then, after taking a moment to compose himself, the student announced, "For the sake of our comrade, we surrender unconditionally."

A little after one in the afternoon, the students occupying the Engineering Building raised a white flag. The riot police surrounded and arrested more than thirty of them.

Meanwhile, a bitter struggle was continuing at the Yasuda Auditorium. The students kept up their resistance, fending off the police. The police dropped tear gas on the roof of the auditorium from helicopters and shot it through the barriers on the ground level. They also used the water cannons to spray liquid tear gas into the building.

Tokyo University acting president Ichiro Kato observed the scene gravely, his arms folded and his brow deeply furrowed.

By the evening of January 18, the barricades had been removed from twenty-three classrooms and study rooms in the Engineering Building, the Law Research Center and other locales, but students remained in the Yasuda Auditorium. Night fell, and with the darkness came an increased possibility of danger, so the police postponed their final operation until the following day. They spent the night on campus, and from early morning on January 19 resumed their efforts to remove the students from the auditorium.

Supported by water cannons, the riot police used chainsaws to cut their way through the barricades made of lockers, desks and chairs. More tear gas was shot inside the building. The students resisted with Molotov cocktails, stones and bamboo lances, but gradually their barricades were removed from the second, third and fourth floors, and they were driven to the rooftop.

A little after four in the afternoon, the students on the

roof stopped throwing stones and began to sing the social-ist anthem, "Internationale," waving a red banner, the sym-bol of their movement, as they did so. Through a megaphone, a student leader called out in an anguished voice, "We want you to consider the reason why we can-not give up our struggle."

DUSK WAS FALLING. The riot police advanced to the roof of the Yasuda Auditorium and then to the clock tower. They arrested students one after another and removed the red flag from the roof. This finally brought to an end the student occupation of the Yasuda Audito-rium, which had continued for roughly six months from July of the previous year, 1968.

It was reported that a total of 375 students were arrested for trespassing and other offenses that day. Meanwhile, in the environs of nearby National Railways Ochanomizu Station, a confrontation between riot police and student activists belonging to anti-Japan Communist Party groups, who were demonstrating in support of the student strug-gle at Tokyo University, had been going on since the pre-vious day, January 18. In an attempt to create a liberated zone, the students had barricaded themselves behind mounds of desks and chairs they had piled up in the streets, and were vigorously throwing stones at the police. The conflict wreaked general havoc in the area, stopping trains and leaving many shop signs destroyed and windows of buildings and parked cars broken.

Shin'ichi watched these events on television, and from the morning of January 18, he had been praying earnestly that there would be no casualties among either the students or the police. One evening several days before the riot police entered the Tokyo University campus, Shin'ichi went to observe the situation at the school, making his way to the Yasuda Auditorium. He was very concerned about the students, who had been occupying the building for nearly half a year.

Students were gathered in small clusters here and there on campus, many of them holding long wooden sticks. A number of students could also be seen peering out from the auditorium, wearing helmets and with hand towels tied around the lower half of their faces.

Shin'ichi stood looking at the building for several minutes. He wondered how the students were eating and bathing, what their vision for reform was and what hopes they had for their own futures. All sorts of thoughts raced through his mind.

When a couple of students came outside, Shin'ichi made a move to speak to them. But a Soka Gakkai leader accompanying him tugged on his arm to stop him. Shin'-ichi paused and, not wanting to cause any trouble, decided to remain silent.

JANUARY 19, the day the riot police ended the Yasuda Auditorium student occupation, was a Sunday, and a Soka Gakkai study department entrance examination was being held from one in the afternoon at various locations throughout Japan. Shin'ichi visited two exam sites in Tokyo—at the Soka Gakkai Sumida Community Center in Sumida Ward and the Aoto Community Center in Katsushika Ward—to encourage the members taking the exam. Following that, he went to another community center in Adachi Ward, which was being remodeled, and then headed to Bunkyo Ward for a ceremony inaugurating the Soka Gakkai's Meiji University Group.

Shin'ichi listened to the events unfolding at Tokyo University over the car radio. He asked the driver to take a route from the Ochanomizu area that would lead them around the campus, or to at least get as close to the school as possible. But the students, in their attempt to turn the Ochanomizu Station area into a liberated zone, had barricaded the road, so the driver had no choice but to take a detour. The streets in the Hongo area, where Tokyo University was located, were also closed to traffic and filled with crowds of students and the general public.

According to the news reports, a large number of both students and riot police had been injured. The thought of this pained Shin'ichi deeply. All of them were precious young people who would shoulder the future. In addition, student division members and children of Soka Gakkai members might be among those holed up on the campus. But there was nothing he could do.

If a new path for the student movement isn't opened in order to prevent such a situation from reoccurring, everyone will suffer, he thought to himself.

At about this time, silence fell over the Tokyo University campus. The students on the roof of the Yasuda Auditorium who had been throwing stones stopped their resistance and began lining up to make their final statement. The moment of the fall of the Yasuda Auditorium, the citadel of the student struggle, had arrived.

Shin'ichi reached the venue where the Meiji University Group inaugural meeting was being held just after four.

Some fifty members had assembled. Addressing them, he said: "Thank you for gathering today! The situation is dire not only around Tokyo University but also in the Ochanomizu area, where Meiji University is located. I just came from there, and it seems the movement is floundering in confusion."

After leading the members in reciting the sutra, Shin'-ichi held a discussion with them. A student asked, "How can we best lead our lives as people dedicated to realizing a better society?"

ALL THOSE PRESENT felt the need for social reform in order to put an end to the oppression of the people by the government authorities. They firmly believed that this was the correct path and the proper attitude for all people of conscience. But they didn't think that society could be reformed through student demonstrations or by barricading university campuses.

They were also aware that though students might advocate social reform while in school, once they graduated and entered the work force, they would have no choice but to toe the company line. This meant there was a strong possibility of them becoming part of the social structure that maintained the oppression they opposed. In this sense, many student division members were deeply concerned about how best to carry out their reformist ideals.

Shin'ichi responded to the member's question: "There is no need to conceive of revolution based solely on such historical examples as the French Revolution or the Russian Revolution. It is superficial to think that a new society can be built following the same methods of past revolutions, and it is simply unrealistic to imagine that society can be reformed by waving sticks or using violence of any form. The image of a revolutionary as someone who employs such tactics is completely antiquated. And, personally, I do not wish to see a single young person come to harm!" he said emphatically.

Shin'ichi's words conveyed his true sentiments to the members.

He continued: "During the time of the Russian Revolution and the old regime in France, the structure of society was relatively simple, with a handful of rulers controlling all the wealth. But today society in general has developed to a greater extent, becoming much more pluralistic. The distribution of society's benefits and burdens is also extremely complicated.

"A vast majority of people, while being aware of society's contradictions and inconsistencies, enjoy a considerable degree of comfort from the established social order. A violent revolution cannot work in such an atmosphere."

Shin'ichi looked directly at the member who had asked the question and said: "I think that the most important issue raised by the student-led All-Campus Joint Struggle Committees is how to surmount the egoism of those in power, as well as that in our own lives. In other words, they are searching for a sure way to triumph over the devilish nature inherent in power and human life."

"ONLY NICHIREN BUDDHISM can defeat human egoism and its devilish nature, and create an age in which true humanity prevails. For doing so is a struggle to overcome the fundamental darkness inherent in life.

Nichiren Daishonin writes, 'The sharp sword that severs the fundamental darkness inherent in life is none other than the Lotus Sutra' (WND-1, 1038). Indeed, the solution lies in carrying out kosen-rufu, a movement in which each individual reveals the great life-state of Buddhahood through Buddhist practice and fundamentally transforms his or her life.

"Kosen-rufu is a comprehensive revolution based on the revolution of the individual. It is the process of actualizing the Buddhist spirit of compassion and the philosophy of the sanctity of life in the realms of government, economics, education, art and every area of human endeavor. The purpose of kosen-rufu is to build a society in which science, medicine, law and all other disciplines and systems created by human beings contribute to the happiness of humanity and produce genuine value. That is why, as Buddhists, we must never turn a blind eye to the reality of society."

The member who had asked the question nodded in understanding.

Shin'ichi continued: "In short, the effort to introduce Buddhism to a single individual and thereby transform his or her life is the most gradual and certain path of nonviolent revolution. Furthermore, to live dedicated to kosen-rufu is the best way of life for a genuine reformer.

"It is also by demonstrating your abilities in society and gaining the trust of others that you can introduce Buddhism to others. We are attempting to carry out a new kind of revolution that no one has ever attempted before. And you are the ones who will actually achieve it and build a new age."

Shin'ichi looked at the face of each member present. They were aglow with the determination to create such an age.

On January 20, the day after the riot police had cleared the Tokyo University campus, Acting University President Ichiro Kato met with Minister of Education Michita Sakata about the university entrance examinations for 1969. The university strongly insisted that the exams be held, but the government, which placed priority on the school's resumption of classes, did not agree. As a result, the 1969 entrance exams were canceled.

THE REMOVAL of the students from the Tokyo University campus by riot police had a tremendous impact on the student movement in general. The students who had been directly involved in the struggle, as well as those on other campuses who had supported the activities of the All-Campus Joint Struggle Committees, were made painfully aware of just how formidable the power of the government could be.

Arrested, many of the young people were overwhelmed with feelings of despair and frustration. Some were tortured by a sense of emptiness and loss of purpose. Others, realizing that sticks and Molotov cocktails were no match for the highly trained and well-equipped police, decided to arm themselves and start organizing paramilitary groups.

Deeply concerned about the present and future state of Japan's universities, Shin'ichi continued to think about the best way to resolve the problem.

With pure intentions, the students had sharply pointed

out society's injustices as well as the contradictions inherent in the university system. This was an expression of their youthful sense of right and wrong. How many university professors, however, responded to their pleas by seriously going over the issues with them and looking for a solution? Before the students resorted to holding demonstrations and calling for negotiations, shouldn't the university presidents, department heads and professors have laid aside their positions of authority to listen open-mindedly to their message and engage them in dialogue? But, sadly, they lacked the courage to do this. They had neither the desire nor the will to take such action. Instead, they brandished their authority and did nothing but treat the students with disdain. This fanned the students' distrust.

Before the riot police were sent in to quell the struggle, Shin'ichi wrote an article for the February 1969 issue of a leading Japanese women's magazine called *Shufu no Tomo* (The Homemaker's Friend), titled "My Thoughts on the Student Movement." In it, he stated, "I believe that a lack of love and trust for the students is the fundamental reason the conflict has spun out of control."

Shin'ichi felt it was absolutely inappropriate to use police force to suppress the students, fearing that the intervention of the national government would compromise the autonomy of the universities.

SHIN'ICHI ALSO clearly expressed his thoughts about the hard-line stance of some within the government that the police should be sent in to deal with the campus protests. He wrote: "Such is the government's folly to turn a blind eye to its incompetence in administering its own educational policies. Using force will only aggravate the situation."

Touching on the point that certain radical elements aiming to incite a class struggle were behind the expansion of the student protest movement, he stated: "These activists have been able to mobilize and instigate the general student population precisely because our society does indeed have such failings and injustices. In order to resolve the conflict, therefore, it is of crucial importance that these issues be addressed, corrected and eliminated at their root."

Denouncing all forms of violence, he also asserted that the reason why students with pure motives could take part in violence and destruction was that their movement lacked a solid foundation of ideals. "In fact," he wrote, "the vast majority of citizens disapprove of the outbreak of violence on university campuses and are angered by radical activism off campus. This means that the movement is losing sight of its aim to trigger a mass revolution. No revolution can be accomplished if ordinary citizens are alienated."

Shin'ichi then described the revolution appropriate for the times, saying: "It must be a revolution of the spirit of each person through philosophy and high ideals, based on the idea of respect for human dignity. How can a movement that cannot even convince and transform a single individual transform society as a whole?

"Destruction and violence are the methods of the inhumane who lack the ideals and philosophy that speak to the sensibility of others and can convince them. Nothing is more regrettable."

The aim defines the methods. The instant violence is used, even the noblest ideal is defiled. Any inhumanity or contradictions that arise in the pursuit of reform reflect the kind of society that will emerge after the struggle is done.

Shin'ichi wrote his article with heartfelt concern for the students, all of whom he regarded as his own children, his own siblings.

A FTER RIOT POLICE brought the student occupation of the Tokyo University campus to an end, the student movement evolved from an on-campus struggle to a broad-based political protest movement, with its activities becoming more radical.

On May 24, 1969, three weeks after Shin'ichi had proposed a new approach for the student movement at the Soka Gakkai Headquarters general meeting, the ruling party submitted a bill in the Diet for new university legislation, officially titled Bill of Temporary Measures Regarding the Operation of Universities. The alleged main purpose of the bill was to support the universities' autonomous efforts to address the campus conflicts, but in actuality it was a bid for direct government intervention in the operation of institutions of higher learning.

For example, it empowered the minister of education to halt all educational and research activities at national universities where conflicts had continued for a period of more than nine months. If the problem remained unsettled an additional three months after that, the minister was authorized to take other measures, including closing the institution permanently. These provisions were to be applied to public and private universities alike. Attempting to resolve the campus upheaval through strengthening government control, however, was to ignore the essential causes of the problem and likely only to exacerbate the strife.

When he learned of the proposed legislation, Shin'ichi immediately sat down and wrote an article titled "On University Reform." It was published in the July edition of the Soka Gakkai-affiliated monthly magazine *Ushio,* which went on sale in early June, as part of a series of his essays on culture. In the essay, Shin'ichi argued that a new vision was urgently needed for the rebuilding of Japan's universities, a vision that offered a clear response to the question of the purpose and meaning of human existence, and he called on his readers to seek a genuine philosophy of life.

He concluded the essay by stating: "It seems that there are elements within the political community moving to achieve the reconstruction of our universities through government intervention, but that is like pouring oil on the flames. The present situation can only truly be resolved by respecting the sanctity of education and insuring its autonomy from government control.

"By rights, education should be a solemn endeavor to foster the citizens and culture of the next generation. As such, it must have clear independence that will not be compromised by the political forces of the day. From that standpoint, I propose adding to the three independent branches of government—the legislature, the judiciary and the executive—a fourth independent branch, that of education.

IN HIS EXPLORATION of the nature of education, one conclusion Shin'ichi had arrived at was the importance of securing the independence of educational institutions. In order to realize education that truly contributed to human happiness, it was crucial to establish educational principles based on deep insight into humanity, as well as to conduct research on different pedagogical methods. This necessitated open and free discussion involving teachers, scholars, students and parents, as well as recognizing the autonomy of teachers with regard to research and educational practice.

In Japan, however, school education was an administrative matter of the government, supervised by the Ministry of Education. Under such circumstances, it was impossible to escape the interference of government in education. That is why, for the sake of securing an autonomous and independent education system, Shin'ichi proposed that education be established as a fourth branch of government, on a par with the legislative, judicial and executive branches.

In stark contrast to the government's new university legislation, his position called for a fundamental reform of universities and the educational system as a whole. His response to the issue was prompt, and his proposal was timely.

No matter how good one's intentions, if one does not speak out at the crucial moment, one may as well be asleep. The struggle of words is a struggle to clearly distinguish when to speak out and take action; it is struggle against time.

Shin'ichi's proposal that education be established as a

fourth, independent branch of government struck a responsive chord in the hearts of the Soka Gakkai student division members, who saw the new university legislation as a powerful threat to the freedom and independence of higher learning. They found Shin'ichi's idea very eye-opening. On campuses throughout Japan, these members could be seen holding copies of the *Ushio* article and excitedly discussing the originality of the concept. They felt that the new law was sure to lead to the universities' demise, but also believed that simply opposing it would not result in actual reform. A constructive plan for education was necessary, they thought, and Shin'ichi's proposal gave a clear indication of that direction.

S PEAKING ENTHUSIASTICALLY with her fellow student division members, one young woman

remarked: "In his essay, President Yamamoto has unobtru-
sively offered this idea of education as the fourth branch
of government, but I think it's truly ingenious. Doing so
is the only way to prevent the government from abusing
its power in the realm of education and to win education's
freedom. It is a great innovation, comparable to the idea
of the tripartite separation of powers articulated by Locke
and Montesquieu."

Another coed chimed in: "I agree completely. I really
feel this is a historic proposal, crucial to opening the way
to an age of genuine humanism. We must make certain
that it does not go unnoticed. But only a limited number
of readers will be exposed to it in a monthly magazine, and
they are sure to forget about it eventually. We need to bring
this proposal to the attention of everyone throughout
Japan and stir up public opinion. I think we should start by
making all our fellow students and our professors aware
of it."

As Plato said, "We should never shrink from speaking
the truth as we see it."[6] This was indeed the determination of the student division members.

A young man then spoke up: "Yes, let's do that. I also
think we should initiate a movement against the university legislation with the aim of establishing a new, independent education branch in the government."

"I agree," said another. "Until now, we have devoted our
energies to spreading Nichiren Daishonin's teachings as
the fundamental way to change society. If we fail to oppose
a law that threatens the autonomy of our universities,
which defines our existence as students, then we would be
neglecting our responsibility. So let's take action!"

Student division members throughout Japan stood to promote the idea of the independence of education and to oppose the university legislation. As Buddhists committed to the mission realizing a peaceful society based on Buddhist ideals, they could not sit idly by and do nothing.

At the urgent request of the student division members, Shin'ichi's essay "On University Reform" was reprinted in the student division newspaper. The members handed out the publication on their respective campuses as well as on the street, calling out for the defeat of the university legislation.

REQUESTS FOR the promotion of a broad-based movement to stop the adoption of the university legislation poured into the Soka Gakkai student division secretariat from members studying at universities throughout Japan. The secretariat agreed, and volunteers began making preparations for a nationwide network of members working for the cause. The National Liaison Council Against the University Legislation was thus formed, and its inaugural meeting was held on June 26, 1969, at the Suginami Public Auditorium in Tokyo.

Many student division members eagerly looked forward to the start of this new movement, and Masaharu Nakayama, a representative from the Kyushu region, was one of them. He was in his third year at a private university in Fukuoka Prefecture. Having begun practicing Buddhism while a junior high school student, he had been raised in the Soka Gakkai. After entering the university, he joined the school newspaper. At his university, the school newspaper and the student council were the pillars of the student movement.

When the university unilaterally announced a tuition hike, students belonging to these two groups requested a meeting to discuss the matter with university representatives. They logically articulated their reasons for opposing the increase, speaking with utmost respect and politeness. Nevertheless, their pleas were met with contempt, with one of the university professors declaring: "There is no need for us to bring this up with students. The matter isn't open for discussion. There's simply nothing to talk about."

Nakayama, who was in attendance, was shocked by the professor's attitude, and he found himself retorting, "Is that the way for a rational-minded professor to speak to students?"

The professors showed no indication whatsoever that they were willing to discuss the issue with the students. Angered by their authoritarian behavior, which implied that students had no say in their university's operation, Nakayama's fighting spirit was ignited.

We cannot tolerate such an unreasonable state of affairs! We must change this situation! he thought. From that moment on, Nakayama took the lead in the movement against the tuition hike. His actions were born from the sense of justice he had learned through his involvement in the Soka Gakkai. As he waged his campaign against the increase along with other student activists, he couldn't help but ponder the question of how, as a Buddhist, he should deal with not only this problem, but with wider social issues such as the Vietnam War.

N AKAYAMA THOUGHT: *Radical student activists are throwing themselves heart and soul into the student protest movement. But the more they experience clashes with riot police and witness their comrades being beaten and arrested, the stronger their animosity toward state power grows and the more extreme and destructive their actions become. What we need is a new, constructive mass movement based on Nichiren Buddhism.*

President Yamamoto has issued many important proposals, calling for the normalization of Japan-China relations and an immediate halt to the hostilities in Vietnam, and addressing the problem of nuclear weapons. In order to put those proposals into action, a new movement needs to emerge from within the Soka Gakkai, one that is grounded in the people. This is our mission as President Yamamoto's youthful successors.

Having arrived at that conclusion, Nakayama was deeply struck by Shin'ichi's proposal at the Headquarters general meeting that the student movement take a new direction. Thus, when he heard about the student division's establishment of the National Liaison Council, he enthusiastically attended the inaugural meeting. Many other student division members as well had been involved in the All-Campus Joint Struggle campaign and other student activities, wanting to resolve the contradictions and injustices they saw taking place in the university system. A number of them felt that, as Buddhists, they should initiate a new kind of movement to oppose war and address various social problems.

Religion cultivates character, which in turn enables people to empathize with the suffering of others. This leads the individual to an awareness of his or her social responsibility to work for people's happiness and to correct such problems as injustice and inequality. The National Liaison Council became the starting point of a new humanistic movement of students awakened to their social mission.

The stage at the Suginami Public Auditorium, where the inaugural meeting was held, was adorned with banners proclaiming "June 26 Inaugural Meeting of the National Liaison Council Against the University Legislation" and "Protect Freedom of Learning!" The event opened with cheers and chants by more than a thousand representatives from universities across the country, who held signs and waved flags. This was followed by opening remarks, a progress report, the introduction of council officers, a keynote address and determinations by representative members.

Tadayuki Tsunoda, a first-year graduate student at the University of Tokyo, was appointed council chairperson.

IN HIS SPEECH, Tsunoda denounced the university legislation, saying: "The fact that the law has an effective term of only five years clearly shows that it is a security measure on the part of the government to counter the intensifying student demonstrations against the renewal of the US-Japan Security Treaty next year (1970). What's more, through this legislation, the government is trying to assert direct control over the universities, a move that seeks the unjust interference of state power in the education system and jeopardizes the free pursuit of learning."

Pointing out that the act also threatened the livelihoods of both faculty and students with its proviso for the possible closure of universities, he declared: "In response to calls from Soka Gakkai student division members and other students opposed to the university legislation, we have established this National Liaison Council Against the University Legislation to expand our protest movement in a more unified fashion on the national level and bring this issue to the attention of all citizens.

"If the government takes a hard-line stance against us, let us rise up resolutely and carry out a mass outdoor protest rally!" The more than one thousand assembled students conveyed their approval with vigorous applause.

The government, however, was desperate to enact the university legislation. The Sixty-first Ordinary Diet Session that had begun at the end of December of the previous year, 1968, was originally scheduled to last one hundred fifty days, coming to a close on May 25. But the ruling Liberal Democratic Party extended the session to an extraordinary 222 days, until August 5. They were determined to pass the legislation during this period, rail-roading it through the Diet if necessary.

The National Liaison Council thus held a rally on July 10 at the Kokumin Kaikan Hall in Osaka as well as an outdoor demonstration by some ten thousand of its members in Tokyo's Meiji Park on July 23. At the latter event, a statement of protest was read, announcing, "We, the members of the National Liaison Council Against the University Legislation, are adamantly opposed to the new law, which gives the government the power of life and death over our universities, and we are determined to keep up our fight until we bring an end to this tyranny of the state."

However, as if mocking the students' call, the following day, July 24, the university legislation was forced through the Lower House Education Committee.

THE LDP'S RAILROADING of the legislation enraged the minority parties, but on the evening of July 29 it was approved at the Lower House plenary session and then sent to the Upper House for ratification. Soka Gakkai student division members were angered and embittered at the forced passage of the bill, which a vast majority of students strongly opposed. At the same time, they were made keenly aware of the importance of election results and representation in the Diet.

Two annual summer training sessions, each lasting three days and two nights, were held for the young men's student division members at the head temple Taiseki-ji, running from July 30 through August 3. On the evening of July 31, the second day of the first session, members from around Japan gathered for a meeting on one of the temple's open fields. Since the university legislation would be enacted if approved during the current session of the Upper House, this would be the student division members' final opportunity to protest it en masse.

The students poured forth from their lodgings and formed a line as they made their way to the field, carrying banners and placards.

When he heard that the student division members would be holding a rally, Shin'ichi, who was also at the head temple to offer guidance and encouragement to participants in the various summer training sessions taking place there that month, decided to attend so that he could watch over his wise and courageous youthful fellow members. He understood well the sentiments of the students who were standing up to fight against the university legislation. He, too, felt it was crucial to preserve the autono-

my of the universities as well as the freedom of education. On his way to the field, Shin'ichi came upon the
marchers.

"Thank you for your efforts!" he said to the young people. "Where are you from?"

"Tokyo," the students replied.

"I will fight alongside you," Shin'ichi continued. "Let's
work together to open the way to the future!"

With that, he picked up one of the students' flags and
stood at the front of the line. Wanting to encourage them,
he borrowed a whistle from another student and began to
march proudly with them, holding his flag high and blowing the whistle. The students followed after him, chanting
in time to the whistle: "Down with the university legislation! Victory will be ours!"

MOST OF THE members were already on the field,
marching in formation when Shin'ichi arrived with
the others. To students at the entrance wearing helmets
and with towels covering the lower half of their faces, he
remarked, "You look like radical activists!"

"These helmets are a symbol of our opposition to
authoritarianism," a student replied.

"I see," Shin'ichi said. "Then I'd like to wear one, too.
May I borrow one? The Soka Gakkai will always carry on
its fight against the devilish nature of authority." Shin'ichi
put on a helmet, using its chin straps to secure a towel
under his chin like the other students, and once again
hoisted his banner high. The young people cheered as he
did so.

At last, the start of the meeting was announced. Various

university group representatives, including from Kyoto and Tohoku universities, stood up and conveyed their determinations to change the times. Throughout the meeting, the field echoed with the students' vigorous cheers.

The National Liaison Council chairperson then took the stage, reporting on the all-out efforts of the students involved in the campaign to halt the passage of the university legislation. He declared: "The time has come for us to rise up with fresh resolve! The outrageous actions of the LDP-led government, exemplified by the railroading of the university legislation, are a fundamental perversion of parliamentary democracy that causes me to tremble with anger.

"Under these circumstances, our efforts mustn't stop with our protests against the legislation. We need to act on an even broader scale to protect democracy and human rights and put an end to such authoritarianism. I therefore propose that we expand and develop the National Liaison Council and create a new student alliance this fall. What do you say?"

Cheers and applause rang out across the field. The faces of the seventy-five hundred assembled students shone with a fighting spirit. Shin'ichi leaned forward in the chair that had been prepared for him and applauded enthusiastically. In his heart, he said to the youth: "Kosen-rufu is a struggle based on love for humanity. I hope you will give your all to every challenge you feel promotes human happiness and freely endeavor to paint a magnificent picture of kosen-rufu. For you are the leaders who will shoulder full responsibility for the twenty-first century."

A STUDENT DIVISION leader picked up a microphone and called out: "My fellow students of Japan! Pledging to win in our struggle, let's raise our voices in protest!"

Shin'ichi energetically came to his feet and, along with the students, thrust his right fist high in the air and shouted: "We will fight! We will stop the university legislation!"

Shin'ichi trusted and respected the student division members. That is why he wholeheartedly supported their resolve and was determined to take action with them.

When remarks by youth division leaders were finished, the members began to chant "Sensei! Sensei!" urging him to speak. He thus took the microphone and said: "I am happy to be able to meet with you all today in such high spirits. The Soka Gakkai's foremost purpose is to protect justice and peace, and we have dedicated our lives to this cause while working for kosen-rufu since the time of first president, Tsunesaburo Makiguchi. Now, all of you, the heirs to that legacy, have stood up for the sake of the Japanese people and for world peace. The Soka Gakkai student division members are the most capable force in Japan for building a new society. Your endeavors signal a fresh dawn for Japan and the world.

"I hope that you will strive with courage and passion to blaze a new trail for the future of your fellow students and toward realizing happiness for the people. Please study even harder and advance together with your sights set five or ten years hence, always remaining united. I will continue to do my utmost to open the way for you, even just a little bit, so that you may take your place and valiantly carry out your struggles on the grand stage of society.

"I am happy to be your steppingstone. I hope you will surpass me and advance boldly and cheerfully for the sake of your own happiness as well as for that of others."

Shin'ichi then joined the students as they placed their arms around each other's shoulders and sang a favorite student division song.

Protecting young people is protecting the future. There are leaders who use young people, exploiting their dedication and selflessness to secure their own status and position. But no matter how crafty such leaders may be, in the end, youth will see through their deception and rip off their masks of shameless impudence.

ANOTHER NATIONWIDE outdoor rally was taking place on the same open field of the head temple on August 2, the second day of the second part of the young men's student division annual summer training session. The rain that had been falling from the previous night had stopped by afternoon, and the green of the trees sparkled in the sunlight shining through breaks in the clouds.

The student division members were gloomy and tense. The end of the extraordinary Diet session was drawing near, and they were concerned that the university legislation would be forcefully pushed through the Upper House education committee.

A little after four in the afternoon, Shin'ichi stood in front of the Sessen-bo lodging temple where he was staying and watched as the students headed for the field in demonstration formation. Eventually, a group of students from Okinawa marched past, holding placards with slogans such as "No more B-52s!" Shin'ichi waved with both arms as he stepped forward to greet them: "You're from Okinawa! It must have been a long journey for you to get here."

Falling into line with them, Shin'ichi borrowed the Ryukyu University flag that one of them was holding, and said: "I'll carry this. Let's wage a struggle to realize lasting peace, seeing it through together to the very end!" The thick bamboo flagpole was about ten feet long and rather heavy, but Shin'ichi lifted it up high and began to lead the procession, just as he had done with student division members a couple of days before. Shin'ichi's shout "Return Okinawa!" echoed into the sky. The students chanted these words with him as they continued to march.

Shin'ichi recognized several of the Okinawa members, having spoken with them at an inaugural meeting for university groups when he visited the islands in February that year. The group's chants were led by an intrepid and confident-looking young man shouting particularly loudly, his cheeks flushed with excitement. His name was Mitsuhiro Moriyama, and he was the Okinawa student division secretary.

Seeing Shin'ichi carrying their flag and marching along with them, Moriyama felt Shin'ichi's strong hopes for the Okinawa student division.

Around this time, the movement for Okinawa's reversion to Japan had been picking up momentum. But as students belonging to the Marxist so-called New Left became more and more involved, the struggle was growing increasingly radical.

OKINAWA STUDENT DIVISION members spoke to their extremist counterparts, telling them that it was wrong to advocate violence, and that people's happiness could not be secured through reformation that sacrifices their humanity. "Our struggle," they would say, "must always be based on dialogue, for it is a struggle to profoundly change the inner reality of the individuals making up society, while respecting the dignity of each person's life. Our aim is to transform society based on this idea of human revolution. Class struggle and changing social structures do not offer a fundamental solution to people's suffering. The movement being advanced by the Soka Gakkai is the most peaceful and quintessential of all revolutions."

Some student division members declared to the radical New Left students: "Eventually it will be clear whether the class struggle you advocate or the Soka Gakkai's movement is correct. Let us each dedicate our lives to finding out which it is!"

Shin'ichi was well aware of the efforts of the Okinawa student division members, who were dealing with the problem of the US bases on their islands. That is why, whenever he visited Okinawa, he always made time to meet with and encourage them. Also, when he learned earlier that year that members from Okinawa would be participating in the nationwide student division meeting in Tokyo at the end of March, he wrote messages in a number of his books to present to representatives. On that occasion, he gave Mitsuhiro Moriyama a book with the inscription, "I entrust Okinawa to you!"

Shin'ichi often thought: *The parents of the current Oki-*

nawa student division members suffered the bitter cruelty of World War II, confronting head-on the reality of life and death. After the war, they did their best to raise their children under the hardship of US occupation, entrusting them with their dreams for peace. Now, these young people have a mission and a duty to bring peace and prosperity to Okinawa for the sake of the happiness of their fellow citizens. In other words, they are the generation responsible for the happiness of Okinawa.

Shin'ichi was overjoyed to see these Okinawa student division members gathered, brimming with a fighting spirit. He began to perspire as he waved their flag high and chanted along with them. Eventually, Shin'ichi's chant changed from "Return Okinawa!" to "Okinawa, give it your all!"

THE NATIONWIDE OUTDOOR rally of the second part of the young men's student division annual summer training session began just before five with appeals from representatives of various university groups and the chairperson of the National Liaison Council Against the University Legislation. As the gathering was taking place while the university legislation was about to be railroaded through the Upper House education committee, the students' remarks were filled with outrage and sharp criticism of the government.

Just like at the outdoor demonstration held a couple of days earlier, on July 31, Shin'ichi was not intending to offer greetings or guidance at this event; he simply hoped to encourage the members by watching over them and supporting their efforts. But in the end, the students' thunderous applause convinced him to speak.

Shin'ichi stood up and, raising his right fist in the air, called out to the students, "We will fight for the people!" The participants repeated this chant, their high-spirited voices reverberating against the foothills of Mount Fuji. Together, they all then shouted, "We will win, for the sake of peace and happiness in the twenty-first century!"

Shin'ichi then said, "I look forward to your development!"

His words were filled with his greatest hopes for the student division members.

He then briefly remarked: "It is my firm belief that your growth as student division members who uphold the humanistic philosophy of Nichiren Buddhism, is the very force that can realize peace and lead Japan and the world out of confusion. I will give my life for you. You are my treasures. Witnessing your development is the greatest joy of my life. Let us fight for the sake of the people! Let us boldly and courageously advance toward the realization of our just cause!"

The happy cheers and applause of the young people echoed in the evening air. From the top of the hillock where he stood, Shin'ichi looked on as the participants moved into demonstration formation once again and exited the field. Seeing him standing there, students waved up at him, calling, "Sensei! Sensei!" He waved back energetically. The wind blew through the pink sky. There was no barrier between the hearts of Shin'ichi and the students.

WITH TEARS in his eyes, Takashi Morii watched Shin'ichi continue to wave to the young people exiting the field. A second-year student at a private university in Tokyo, he had joined the Soka Gakkai just two months earlier. He had been active in the student movement, which he had joined partly out of his disappointment in the lack of humanity displayed by his professors.

Morii was from Hakodate in Hokkaido. His father was a middle-level manager for the Japan National Railways (now Japan Railways), but with four children, the family struggled financially. When Morii started at the university, his eldest sister had just graduated. His two younger sisters also wished to receive a higher education. Not wanting to add to his family's burden, Morii joined a newspaper's scholarship program in order to pay his way through school and entered a private university in Tokyo.

But the newspaper job was harder than he had imagined. He had to get up at half past three in the morning every day to deliver the morning paper, after which he attended classes. He would then leave school at half past two in the afternoon to deliver the evening paper. In addition to that, he had to go around collecting payments and soliciting subscriptions. No matter how tired he was, he had to finish his daily tasks.

He also was disappointed in the mass-production education he was receiving at the university. There were so many people attending the entrance ceremony that it had to be held at the Nippon Budokan, a giant hall in Tokyo. The lecture auditoriums on campus were so expansive that professors needed to use microphones to be heard. And the teachers were neither passionate nor humanistic. On the crowded campus, Morii felt isolated and alone.

The following incident took place one day. In a relatively small class, there was a student who had to work part time to support himself and was therefore often absent. On this particular day, however, he was able to attend.

When the teacher noticed him, he said coldly, "So, I see you're still alive!"

The classroom rocked with laughter.

"Every year, we have at least one student who ends up dead somewhere or who just disappears," the instructor added.

The student just looked down silently at his desk. The teacher may have intended his remark as a joke, but he showed no sign whatsoever of possessing a desire to foster and educate young people.

ABOUT A MONTH after school began, Morii almost stopped attending classes altogether. He found nothing inspiring in the mechanically delivered lectures. Moreover, exhausted from his job, he was so tired that he was unable to absorb anything even when he did go to class. His days were spent in the demanding physical labor of delivering newspapers and the often-humiliating work of soliciting new subscribers. Rushing back and forth between the university and his job, he felt completely worn out.

I'm just a lowly worker slaving away in a tiny corner of the big city, he thought. At school, Morii saw students living in circumstances very different from his. Supported by their wealthy parents, many wore fashionable clothes, drove fancy sports cars and spent all their time enjoying leisure activities. They made Morii feel wretched and sorry for himself.

At about this time, a friend introduced him to the theories of communism, explaining that in a capitalist society a small bourgeois elite dominated, exploited and oppressed the working-class proletariat. Class struggle, he said, was necessary to liberate oneself and society from that injustice.

Facing such inequities in his own life, Morii was attracted to the ideas of "exploitation" and "class struggle." He joined the New Left group to which his friend belonged and began studying Marxism in earnest. The group was a radical faction that advocated violence. Morii participated in demonstrations, throwing stones and Molotov cocktails. He also went to other universities to support their protests. He was passionately committed to a cause that he believed in and that gave him a tremendous sense of fulfillment.

Eventually, he found himself under police surveillance. He decided to leave his job at the newspaper, figuring he would only cause trouble for the company if he stayed there, and that by quitting he would be free to devote all his time to the struggle. One day in the autumn of his first year at school, he went off to a demonstration and never returned to work.

He did, however, make a trip to see his family in Hakodate. Having left the newspaper, he was obligated to return the scholarship money the company had given him. Hoping his father would bail him out, he told him that it was impossible to study and work at the same time. His father believed this excuse and agreed to pay the money back.

AFTER RETURNING to Tokyo, Morii rented an apartment, which soon became a gathering place for the other members of his radical group. Dreaming of revolution, Morii supported himself through part-time jobs. He marched proudly in demonstrations, holding aloft his group's flag. In one clash with riot police, he barely escaped with his life after almost being crushed when a crowd of rioters fell on top of him.

During the Tokyo University uprising, prior to the time the riot police entered the campus, Morii supported the struggle by helping occupy the Yasuda Auditorium, the symbol of the students' liberation. The day the riot police were called in to end the occupation, he was among those setting up barricades in the environs of Ochanomizu Station in order to make the area a liberated zone.

Around this time, he received news from home that his father was having problems at work and that his health was poor. In late March 1969, just before starting his second year at the university, Morii went back to Hakodate. It turned out that his father was being held responsible for a misdeed committed by one of his subordinates and that this, compounded by a conflict he was having with some relatives, was causing him terrible emotional stress. His father appeared defeated and lifeless.

When the elder Morii saw his son, he began to unburden his feelings to him, declaring at last that he wanted to quit his job and move to Tokyo. But Takashi ignored him. As far as he was concerned, his father, as a middle manager of the railways that supported the capitalist system, was an unwitting member of the petty bourgeoisie. As long as he remained bound to such a family, he felt, he would be unable to carry out a socialist revolution. He wanted to have nothing to do with his father.

With the intent of disassociating himself from his family, Takashi announced: "I am involved in the student movement. I have decided to be an activist and dedicate my life to the revolution."

"What?" his father shouted, trembling with rage. He had been a member of the Special Attack Force (Kamikaze Squadron) during World War II and was a typical ultranationalist who hated communism. When he sent Takashi to Tokyo, he had repeatedly warned him, "You tend to get carried away with things, so don't get involved in the student movement."

A HEATED ARGUMENT ensued. Takashi yelled: "I knew you wouldn't accept this, so I have decided to live my own life! Just think of me as dead!"

His father's face fell in disappointment. That night, the

elder Morii was unable to sleep. He kept getting up, sitting restlessly for a while, then going back to bed. The next day, he jumped off a cliff into the sea in a suicide attempt. He was rescued and rushed to a hospital, but he remained unconscious. Several days later, he died.

Takashi was guilt-stricken and blamed himself for his father's death. After the funeral was completed, he returned to Tokyo, but his days were spent in deep depression. Rather than try to support or help his father in his time of need, he had treated him with cold indifference, thinking that was the proper behavior of a revolutionary. He hated himself for this.

He began to doubt whether his group, which placed itself in the vanguard of the proletariat movement while at the same time compelling its members to cut ties with their families, could ever truly forge an alliance with the people. If he continued in his activities, he felt certain that his mother would suffer the same fate as his father. Morii sank into a deep apathy. He lost all enthusiasm for life.

Noticing Morii's condition, his landlady, who was a Soka Gakkai member, tried to reach out to him in friendship and encourage him. She had spoken to him about Buddhism several times before, but Morii, subscribing to the Marxist doctrine that religion is the opiate of the people, had always turned a deaf ear. Now, however, being utterly dejected, he paid attention when she brought up the subject of faith again.

On occasion he would debate her vigorously, but each time she would listen to his views with a warm smile and then explain logically and clearly the importance of faith.

In her assurances that he could absolutely overcome his struggles, Morii keenly felt her genuine concern for him.

IN ADDITION TO the landlady, members of the Soka Gakkai men's and student divisions also visited Morii and talked to him about the Buddhist philosophy of life. Morii sensed a fresh and profound insight into human existence in such Buddhist principles as the "oneness of body and mind," the "oneness of life and its environment," "attaining a life-state of absolute happiness" and "human revolution." He was also moved by the members' experiences in faith, which conveyed how they had faced their diverse problems head-on, challenged and overcome them.

Marxism, he realized, offered no solution to the most important issue of human life: how people can surmount their inner suffering. But Buddhism did. Morii was particularly impressed by the words of second Soka Gakkai president Josei Toda, which a member shared with him: "We must fight with love for all living beings. Today, there are many young people who don't even love their parents, so how can they love others? Ours is a struggle of human revolution—a struggle to overcome our own lack of concern for others and awaken to the compassion of the Buddha." Morii agreed with this completely, and he was deeply interested in a philosophy that fused human ethics and the concept of revolution without contradiction.

Morii was also drawn to the warmth and sincerity of the Soka Gakkai members. There was a spirit of fellowship and camaraderie among the student activists as well, but the slightest ideological disagreement often led to people becoming bitter enemies. Though the extremely humanistic goal of liberating ordinary people from social injustice was the starting point of the student movement, warmth and consideration for others were hard to come by among its ranks. While in his heart Morii did his utmost to remain critical of religion, he found himself gradually attracted to the Soka Gakkai.

He also felt, however, that if he took faith he would somehow be betraying his activist friends. After pondering the issue for more than two months, Morii decided to join the Soka Gakkai in June 1969. Two weeks later, some fellow activists paid him a visit. They wanted to know why he hadn't been participating in demonstrations lately and pressed him to engage in self-criticism.

MORII BEGAN TO tell his fellow activists about the struggles he had been experiencing since his father's suicide, revealing that he had joined the Soka Gakkai out of a desire to find a new way of life. He said: "I couldn't give my father any encouragement or hope. Even if power is restored to the working class, people will never truly be free if they are unable to overcome their inner suffering. But the Buddhist philosophy upheld by the Soka Gakkai offers a means by which people can be liberated from their karma and spiritual suffering. I want to give this faith a try." He was firmly resolved.

Unable to respond, his visitors left, resigned to the fact that Morii was no longer one of them.

Morii exerted himself earnestly in learning to recite the sutra and chant Nam-myoho-renge-kyo, wanting to develop conviction in faith as quickly as possible. As he did so, the profound apathy he had felt since his father's death disappeared, and he experienced renewed life force welling forth from his being. It was as if the sun had risen in his heart and illuminated the darkness. He started telling everyone he could about Buddhism, and eventually succeeded in introducing many of his former newspaper dormitory friends and fellow students to Nichiren Daishonin's teachings. The proletariat warrior had become a champion of kosen-rufu.

And so it was that Morii came to participate joyously in the annual summer training session at the head temple. As he made his way to the rally, he came upon Shin'ichi carrying the Ryukyu University flag and heading for the field together with the members from Okinawa. This was a completely different Shin'ichi than the one Morii had imagined. He had thought that as the president of such a large religious organization, Shin'ichi would be an imposing and unapproachable figure, but what he discovered was an unpretentious individual without any attachment to position or status.

Seeing Shin'ichi perspire as he encouraged the members and chanted, "Okinawa, give it your all!" Morii felt he was observing true human sincerity. And when he heard Shin'ichi's words to the student division members at the rally—"I will give my life for you. You are my treasures. Witnessing your development is the greatest joy of my life"—an electric shock coursed through his body.

MORII WAS AMAZED to find a leader who so trusted and loved students, and who actually stood together with them. If politicians and the presidents and faculty of universities behaved that way, he thought, the student protest movement would never have happened.

But Shin'ichi was only doing what he felt needed to be done. He was resolved to devote his life to fostering young people with all his heart and being.

With tears in his eyes, Morii waved back energetically at Shin'ichi, who stood watching as the students exited the field. This encounter with Shin'ichi gave him tremendous conviction in faith.

Returning to Tokyo with fresh determination after the training course, Morii threw himself even more enthusiastically into sharing Nichiren Daishonin's teachings with others. He wanted to communicate the humanism of Buddhist thought to as many people as possible. Three months after joining the Soka Gakkai, he had introduced Buddhism to sixteen new member-households, including his mother and his two younger sisters.

His mother, who had been suffering from terrible grief at the loss of her husband, had grown very weak, but once she began practicing, her health grew stronger by the day.

Morii thought with a keen sense of realization: *The struggle to liberate people begins with lighting the flame of hope and courage within the heart of each suffering individual. It is when people acquire the power to live and then stand up as the protagonists of change that society will truly be transformed.*

Immediately after the second student division nation-wide outdoor rally had finished on August 2, the news was broadcast that the university legislation had been forced through the Upper House education committee. With the end of the extended Diet session fast approaching, the ruling LDP ignored the protests of the opposition parties and held a session of the education committee by order of the committee chairperson. At 6:20 PM, the legislation was railroaded into passage amid jostling and indignant shouts.

The entire process, from explaining the reasons for proposing the legislation to the actual vote, took no more than four or five minutes, and the bill was pushed through without any deliberation. Now, all it needed for enactment was approval at the Upper House plenary session.

Student division members were outraged by this high-handed action. The anger of youth at injustice is the force that changes society.

THE NATIONAL LIAISON Council Against the University Legislation immediately issued a statement in the name of its chairperson, proclaiming its opposition to the forced passage of the university legislation by the Upper House education committee. The document declared:

This is a violation of the principle of parliamentary democracy and is certain to add fuel to the flames of the university conflict. . . .

The attitude of the LDP-ruled government in railroading this legislation into passage can only be described as a form of fascism aimed at destroying not only the freedom of learning but culture in general. While pleading our case for the repeal of the university legislation with even stronger determination to the Japanese people, we intend to resolutely stand up against this oppression by the government.

The next morning, August 3, National Liaison Council members handed out leaflets denouncing the government's actions at seven major train stations in the Tokyo metropolitan area. The group then visited the Diet where they met with representatives of the LDP and other parties, presenting a petition for the withdrawal of the bill and strongly voicing their opposition to it. They also submitted the petition to the vice chairperson of the Upper House, the chief cabinet secretary and the minister of education.

But that evening, the LDP, taking advantage of the confusion in the Upper House plenary session, succeeded in getting the bill passed through a surprise motion by the house chairperson. Without any debate, it was approved instantly by a standing vote. It was a true example of the tyranny of the majority.

Yukio Ozaki,[7] regarded as an important contributor to the establishment of Japan's parliamentary system of government, once lamented that the Diet building, which should be a forum for deliberation, was nothing more than a voting hall. Indeed, the passage of the university legislation was a case in point.

On August 17, the legislation finally went into effect. At this juncture, the Ministry of Education identified sixty-six public and private universities as places of conflict, of which eighteen were designated as seriously troubled. Afraid of the consequences such a branding would generate, the designated universities quickly called in riot police and forced the resumption of classes.

The triumph of oppression is tantamount to the defeat of education.

The resumption of classes under the surveillance of riot police was a far cry from the normalization of university life. The issues raised by the student movement remained unresolved, while the autonomy of higher education and the freedom of learning were sacrificed.

WITH THE ENACTMENT of the university legislation, the argument came to the fore in the student movement that the only way to oppose the government's authoritarian actions was with even greater force. On September 5, a national federation was formed between the All-Campus Joint Struggle Committees of each university and the New Left groups, with the exception of the leftist Revolutionary Marxist faction.

Behind this unification, however, was the ulterior motive of the coalition's various leftist groups to mobilize the non-affiliated students for their own purposes. The movement thus became increasingly political as a fierce and violent power struggle ensued among the member groups for leadership of the national organization. As a result, more and more students began to feel alienated from the cause. While they continued to support the purity of the movement's goals on an emotional level, they questioned the inhumane and violent turn it was taking.

Soka Gakkai student division members, who had given their all to opposing the university legislation as part of the National Liaison Council, were deeply angered by the bill's forced passage, and they keenly felt the need for a mass movement to put a stop to the government's abuse of power. Above all, however, they were concerned about the student movement's acceleration toward violence, for it meant that a movement born from the sincere desire to right society's injustices had tragically degenerated into a mere force for destruction.

Feeling a strong and urgent necessity for the establishment of a new student alliance—an alliance that would champion a peaceful movement together with the people—they set themselves to the task of creating such a coalition. As had been announced at the outdoor rally of the annual summer training session the previous month, members of the National Liaison Council took the initiative. On September 25, a preparatory committee was formed and the name "New Student Alliance" was selected.

Open registration drives for the new group were held on university campuses across the country. The preparatory committee additionally decided that a regular bulletin would be produced, and they also drew up the group's platform. At last, a shining light of hope was beginning to pierce the darkness of the turbulent times. Wise and courageous young people were finally rising up in earnest to work for university reform and peace.

ON OCTOBER 19, Yoyogi Park in Tokyo's Shibuya Ward was filled with demonstrators wearing white helmets emblazoned with the words *New Student Alliance*. Some seventy-five thousand students from 368 universities had assembled, coming from as far north as Hokkaido and as far south as Okinawa. Behind the stage that had been set up in the center of the park hung a banner that read "Inaugural Meeting of the New Student Alliance," and colorful university flags in green, blue, red, yellow and white fluttered above the huge crowd.

A light rain had started falling before the rally began, but the park was brimming with the students' energy as their high-spirited voices sang:

Blazing a new path,
we are united to achieve victory
over the authoritarian system of old . . . .

The rain stopped around one in the afternoon, and the opening of the inaugural meeting of the much-anticipated New Student Alliance was announced.

Members of the press were surprised at the huge turnout. At that time, the largest number of students to be mobilized for a demonstration had been forty-seven thousand for JCP-affiliated groups and forty-two thousand for the anti-JCP New Left groups. This rally of seventy-five thousand for the New Student Alliance was the biggest yet.

After the presiding officers were introduced, Masaki Okayama, a member of the inauguration preparatory committee and a fourth-year student at Meiji University, reported on the developments leading to the formation of the New Student Alliance. Next came personnel announcements and an introduction of the group's bylaws and platform.

Tadayuki Tsunoda, chairperson of the National Liaison Council Against the University Legislation, assumed the equivalent position in the New Student Alliance. Masaki Okayama and Kyoto University second-year graduate student Hiroaki Otani were named vice chairpersons, while Koji Murata, a second-year Tokyo University student, became the chief secretary.

The group's platform stated: "Today, the established social structures and values are beginning to crumble on a global scale. This is an indication of the deadlock that has been reached by all systems of thought and philosophy that are based on the modern rationalism of Western civil society. The cause of this can be found in modern rationalism's lack of focus on the human being. Without a profound grasp of the true nature of human life, this approach cannot serve as a philosophy that enables people to change themselves on a fundamental level. As a result, society today is steeped in confusion.

"The New Student Alliance is initiating a fresh movement based on a philosophy of life that places utmost importance on respect for human existence and that upholds a correct understanding of the human spirit."

THE PLATFORM further highlighted the various types of alienation experienced by people in society as well as the loss of humanity brought about by modern rationalism. The most significant demand of the university reform movement, it stated, was "the creation of a new system of learning founded on a fresh view of humanity that takes as its standard a philosophy focused on human life."

The aims of the New Student Alliance were then outlined in four points: (1) to secure a peaceful society that rejects war through nonviolent reformation based on humanism; (2) to rally together and organize an extensive alliance of ordinary people, who are the true protagonists of the reformation effort, and carry out a powerful people's movement that will expose the current illusion of democracy and establish a genuinely democratic society;

(3) to realize university reform and create a new system of learning grounded in humanism that serves the people; and (4) to build a new movement structure to carry out these three goals.

The crowd was struck by the idea of "humanism" announced here, and the flame of nonviolent revolution informed by this concept was thus ignited. Thunderous applause erupted, signaling approval of the platform.

Newly appointed chairperson, Tadayuki Tsunoda, next made a declaration to commemorate the alliance's inauguration. Touching on such issues as the problem of American military bases on Okinawa, the US-Japan Security Treaty, the university legislation, and the Vietnam War, he said, "The 1970s are a historic turning point that will see either the finish or the continuation of state power that utilizes science and technology to control people as a means to an end, based on the philosophy of modern rationalism dominated by capitalist thought."

Proclaiming that their most urgent task was to rally a great force for change grounded in a new philosophy, Tsunoda then called out, "Awakened to our responsibility as the key players building a new age in human history, we hereby declare the establishment of the New Student Alliance with a membership of one hundred twenty thousand students from 368 university campuses as well as ordinary citizens throughout Japan!"

A blanket of clouds covered the sky, but the participants' applause pierced the gloom like thunder.

Following this declaration, representatives from Tokyo University, Waseda University and Osaka University delivered passionate and rousing determinations.

NEW STUDENT ALLIANCE chief secretary, Koji Murata, then took the podium. He began by announcing the slogans, "The Seventies—Anti-war, Pro-peace," "The Seventies—A New System of Higher Learning" and "The Seventies—Fighting Alongside the People." He went on to discuss the defects of the US-Japan Security Treaty and listed as goals of the Alliance the immediate and unconditional reversion of Okinawa to Japan, the return of Japan's northern territories from the Soviet Union, the complete elimination of American bases on Japanese soil, the signing of peace and friendship treaties with all the nations of the world and the restoration of diplomatic relations with China. The audience applauded energetically, signaling their agreement.

The event came to a close with the resonant chants of the seventy-five thousand participants echoing through the woods of the adjacent Meiji Shrine: "We will fight! We will bring about a new system of higher learning!"

This marked a fresh start for the student movement based on a concept of humanism that transcended and sublimated the notions of capitalism and communism. It was a unique and independent movement that went beyond the extant framework of the JCP Old Left and the anti-JCP New Left, and as such it offered a third way for student-power activities.

Just after the inaugural meeting of the New Student Alliance had begun, a car carrying Shin'ichi Yamamoto made a circuit around Yoyogi Park, where the rally was taking place. He was on his way to Yokohama to attend a Kanagawa Prefecture leaders meeting, but he asked the driver to go via the road near the park so he could catch a glimpse of how the event was proceeding.

Yoyogi Park was packed with students, and flags of various colors waved above their heads. Shin'ichi could hear the powerful speeches even from inside the car. He remarked to one of the leaders traveling with him: "What an incredible turnout! The student division has risen at last. One important aspect of religion is how it contributes to society. This gathering here represents the beginning of a new age. If the existing student movement that is becoming increasingly violent were to draw in more and more students, society would head in a very dangerous direction. Unless we create a new movement to put a stop to that trend, young people will suffer. That's why I have high hopes for the New Student Alliance."

PEERING UP AT the sky through the car window, Shin'ichi murmured: "It looks like it might rain at any moment. I hope no one catches a cold." He chanted softly, praying for the rally to be a success and to end without mishap. When the car had completed one circuit of the park, Shin'ichi asked the young man driving to go around once more. None of the rally participants noticed Shin'ichi riding in the car slowly circling the park.

The news of the formation of the New Student Alliance was immediately broadcast on television. Shin'-ichi was able to watch it with the leaders accompanying him when they arrived at the Kanagawa Headquarters building. "Everyone is in high spirits," he remarked joyfully. "It turned out to be a huge event."

Shin'ichi's thoughts remained with the students as he continued to inquire about their well-being, asking whether those who had journeyed from afar had accommodations for the night and about their travel and food expenses.

As both Shin'ichi and the student division members had feared, the student movement in Japan took an extremely violent turn. Activists raided police boxes to acquire weapons, and some groups used pipe bombs and carried out paramilitary training. On March 31, 1970, the Red Army Faction[8] hijacked a Japan Airlines plane and forced the pilot to take them to North Korea for military training.

There was also an acceleration of infighting within the movement itself. Old Left and New Left groups had clashed for years, but now various New Left groups were vying fiercely among themselves for leadership. In addition, differences of opinion and strategy led to further splintering and heightened antagonism between the groups, and scuffles erupted from among them almost daily. This set in motion a recurring cycle of attacks and counterattacks.

As such incidents grew more frequent, police surveillance and scrutiny also intensified, a reality that began to take a serious mental toll on the radical student activists. Paranoid about spies and being informed on, they became highly suspicious of each other, which resulted in witch hunts and beatings within the groups.

THE VIOLENT STUDENT movement was brought to a tragic end with a clash between the police and the United Red Army.

The United Red Army was formed in July 1971 when the Red Army merged with another radical group. Using weapons they robbed from gun stores, the group carried out military training while moving from place to place throughout the mountainous areas of Japan's Gumma Prefecture.

During that time, they tortured and killed fourteen of their own members on grounds of ideological deviation. In February 1972, the police combed the mountains and arrested two of the group's ringleaders along with numerous other members who were fugitives from justice. The United Red Army was thus driven into a corner. But on February 19, the five remaining members holed themselves up in a lodge owned by a musical instrument manufacturer in the neighboring Nagano Prefecture resort town of Karuizawa, taking the caretaker's wife hostage. During the next ten days, the police mobilized a total of thirty-five thousand officers to secure the area and carry out a rescue mission.

On February 28, the police finally decided to enter the building by force. They smashed through a wall of the building with a wrecking ball and, after a shootout, arrested the United Red Army members and freed the hostage. Two police officers were killed in the battle and twelve were wounded. It was senseless bloodshed perpetrated under the slogan of "revolutionary justice" by students who had studied at Japan's highest seats of learning.

In his novel *The Devils,* the Russian author Fyodor Dostoyevsky gives this thought to a youthful revolutionary, "A man and his convictions are two different things."[9] No matter how high-sounding the ideals we as human beings advocate, if they lack humanity, they will lead to disaster. By rights, ideology should inform our way of life and be the epitome of our humanity. Therefore, no matter what ideals we claim to uphold, no matter what fine phrases we spout, without undergoing an inner transformation, we cannot hope to actualize those ideals in society.

A large majority of conscientious students eagerly desired a humanistic movement that fought alongside the people. Some of those who joined the New Student Alliance had in fact formerly been involved with radical factions.

TETSUO UNNO, who had been a radical student activist, was a student at a private university in Tokyo. As the movement continued to take on a violent hue, he came to doubt its methods and recognized its limitations, and he eventually quit.

Unno was born in Osaka and grew up in a medium-sized city in the Chugoku region. The city was dependent on a large metal manufacturer that sustained its economy. With the mayor and many city council members in the company's pocket, the city was virtually run through a tight power structure involving affiliated companies and civic organizations with intimate ties to the manufacturer.

Ordinary citizens lived in poverty, and it was suspected that their health was being compromised by the metal factory pollutants, but no one complained. Rather than stand up and attempt to change their situation, the people had come to accept the status quo. Caught in a complex web of mutual obligations and personal feelings, they ended up trying to undermine each other. Some came to hold utterly irrational prejudices, venting their frustration at their downtrodden condition by behaving contemptuously toward those worse off than them.

Tetsuo Unno's father worked in Osaka until Tetsuo was three years old, but he lost his job when his employer went out of business. At the introduction of a friend, he took a job in the city where the dominant metal manufacturer was located, and the family moved there. He thus began working for a subcontractor of the metal business.

As newcomers, the Unno family was treated coldly by the community. When Tetsuo was in elementary school, they joined the Soka Gakkai, and the boy began reciting the sutra alongside his parents. He also attended discussion meetings regularly, where he came into contact with genuine human warmth. Those gatherings always made him feel at ease.

Growing up in a household that struggled financially, from childhood, Tetsuo experienced firsthand society's inequities and contradictions. In high school, partly due to the influence of his homeroom teacher, Unno became interested in socialism, which advocated a society free of economic inequality. Wanting to attend a university, he spent a year after graduating from high school preparing and was subsequently accepted to a prestigious private university in Tokyo.

WHEN UNNO MOVED to Tokyo to attend the university, he was reunited with a former high school classmate. It was this encounter that led him to join the student movement. For better or worse, friends are often the most powerful influences of our youth. Unno was astonished to see how his old friend had changed. During high school, he had been gentle and mild-mannered, but now he had the bearing of a radical student activist.

Their conversation covered such topics as the Vietnam War and Japan's industrial and political structures, and as they spoke, the friend continued to emphasize the importance of class struggle. Everything he said seemed new and revolutionary, and his arguments were extremely logical. Unno was overwhelmed. He was ashamed that until then he had not thought seriously about social issues.

Unno began to pore over books on Marxism. He felt very satisfied to have come across a new perspective. When he had first moved to Tokyo and entered the university, Unno enshrined the Gohonzon in his apartment and started participating in Soka Gakkai activities with local Soka Gakkai members and student division members who kept in touch with him. But now, he became more focused on the antiwar movement and the effort to democratize the universities than on his Buddhist practice. Eventually, at the invitation of his friend, he joined the on-campus struggle.

At Soka Gakkai meetings, Unno had heard about the concept of human revolution and how, by transforming oneself through the teachings of Buddhism, society would change as well. But that seemed like an incredibly indirect route, and he feared that it would ultimately be a confirmation of the status quo. Unno decided to quit the study group he had joined at school in order to prepare for the national civil service examinations. He wanted to overcome his self-centeredness, which is how he came to regard his desire to study for the sole purpose of gaining personal success rather than to fight against social contradictions.

Devoting himself to the struggle, he spent several days

on the barricaded campus. Living such a lifestyle wasn't easy, though, and he was weak from sleep and food deprivation. He nevertheless felt as if he was putting his beliefs into practice, which gave him a sense of deep satisfaction that he had not experienced in his university life until then. Under these tense conditions, he also felt a strong solidarity with his fellow student activists. Before long, Unno joined a particular radical group.

AS UNNO BECAME more involved in the student movement, his attitude about the experiences that Soka Gakkai members shared at meetings also changed. Though he had once found them moving, now the members' accounts of overcoming financial difficulties or illness, or being recognized on the job, sounded selfish and bourgeois. They also seemed to affirm and support the present social structure, with all its inequities and injustices.

Still, sometimes when he came back to his apartment to wash his clothes, he would sit down in front of his Buddhist altar and recite the sutra and chant Nam-myoho-renge-kyo. Once during a confrontation with riot police, Unno had been severely beaten with a nightstick. Thinking that this might be some sort of punishment for having almost stopped practicing altogether, he was deeply disturbed. He prayed to the Gohonzon to remain unhurt in his participation in the demonstrations, and then returned nonchalantly to the barricades.

Such are the subtle workings of the human heart. That is why it is important to enable people to forge a connection with Buddhism.

As the days went by, the students occupying the campus buildings grew more and more reckless, and there were increasing displays of wanton behavior. A great deal of drinking and carousing was also taking place.

Then, with the passage of the university legislation, the university administration called in the riot police. Unno and his fellow activists put up a vigorous resistance, but in the end they were forcibly driven from the buildings. When the final battle was occurring, many students not involved in the movement stood on the sidelines observing the struggle as if they were watching a ball game. Some of them even took photographs of the conflict. Unno was saddened by the fact that the movement hadn't been able to forge a greater solidarity even among the student body.

After the riot police had removed the barricades, the university administration instituted a lockout aimed at closing the universities to activists. The group Unno belonged to subsequently shifted the focus of their protest activities from the university to political issues. They devised a plan to carry out an armed struggle in order to prevent the visit of Prime Minister Eisaku Sato to the United States, a trip aimed at securing Okinawa's reversion to Japan in exchange for a promise to extend the US-Japan Security Treaty.

Unno opposed violence, but he was overruled by others who insisted that it was the only way to respond to the powerful force of the government.

JUST WHEN UNNO'S group had finished preparing for their armed struggle, the police raided their hideout and seized all their weapons. Someone had leaked their plan to the authorities. Several members of the group were arrested, but Unno managed to escape—though he hurt his arm in the process. As Unno sat catching his breath on a park bench, a middle-aged woman who noticed his bloody shirt approached him.

"Oh my," she said, "that looks bad. You need treatment right away. Just wait here." She went to the nearest pharmacy and came back quickly with some antiseptic. She treated his wound and then said with a smile, "You'll be fine now."

Unno was touched by her kindness. He then noticed a copy of the Soka Gakkai study journal, *The Daibyakurenge*, peeking out of her handbag. She was a Soka Gakkai member.

When he got home, Unno, suffering from the physical pain of his wound and the anguish of mental defeat, couldn't help but question the meaning of his protest activities. *While claiming to be working for the liberation of the people, the strategies conceived by our leaders are completely unrealistic,* he thought. *There is no way society is going to be changed through a military uprising. Somewhere along the way, we've veered off track.*

Unno thus separated himself from the group. Feeling empty inside, he holed himself up in his apartment and agonized over his past actions, asking himself: "I've been advocating struggle to my fellow students, but what philosophy do I possess myself? One reason the student movement has reached an impasse is that it has placed itself above ordinary people. I wonder if there is any such thing as a way of revolution that really advances together with the people? What is genuine revolution anyway, and what does it mean to be a human being? Can an ideal society actually be realized by overthrowing the government and changing its political and economic systems?"

His thoughts just went around and around in circles, never reaching any conclusion.

He casually picked up a Soka Gakkai publication from a pile of such books that were on his desk. Among them were lectures on Nichiren Daishonin's writings and compilations of guidance by Josei Toda and Shin'ichi Yamamoto. His parents had given him the materials, but he had never felt like reading them before. Looking for something to pass the time, he began to leaf through the volumes. Many of them dealt with the issue of human revolution.

THE WORDS *human revolution* first attracted attention among the general public when University of Tokyo president, Shigeru Nambara, spoke of the need for such a revolution at the university's graduation ceremony in the autumn of 1947, two years after Japan's defeat in World War II. At the ceremony, Nambara said that while society was currently undergoing a political and economic revolution, as well as a second industrial revolution, each of those revolutions must be for the sake of human beings and contribute to their well-being.

In order for these changes to serve humanity, he argued, first a transformation of the lives of people themselves—a human revolution—was needed. He described such a transformation as a spiritual revolution taking place in the realm of ethics and religion, and a cultural revolution, without which democratic political revolution and

socially oriented economic revolution would be meaningless and ultimately end in failure. It was a remarkably keen
insight.

When second Soka Gakkai president Josei Toda learned
that President Nambara had spoken of the importance of
human revolution, he could not conceal his joy. It was a
concept that Mr. Toda, who was then working to rebuild
the Soka Gakkai, had continuously stressed in his lectures
on the Lotus Sutra and Nichiren Daishonin's writings.
Both he and his predecessor, Tsunesaburo Makiguchi, had
concluded that the fundamental transformation of the
individual was the basis for the achievement of human
happiness, social prosperity and world peace.

Furthermore, after reading the Lotus Sutra with his life
and deeply pondering its meaning while in prison during
World War II, Mr. Toda awakened to the profound realization that Nichiren Buddhism elucidates the great principle by which human beings can change the inner reality
of their lives. He became firmly convinced that it was only
through such a transformation based on Buddhism that
people could achieve their human revolution, and he left
prison with an unshakable determination to stand up by
himself to actualize kosen-rufu.

President Makiguchi had originally promoted educational reform because he believed that the only way to
change society was to foster human beings through education. In an article entitled "Introduction to Value-
Creating Education" that Mr. Makiguchi contributed to
the November 1930 edition of the educational journal
Environment—the same month that the Soka Kyoiku
Gakkai (forerunner of the Soka Gakkai) was founded—he

wrote: "The world is awaiting fundamental reform and advancement in the fields of politics, economics and the arts through the power of education. The solution to society's contradictions and problems is to be found in a basic transformation in humanity itself, and bringing about this fundamental change in human nature is ultimately the role of education."

IN DECEMBER 1935, Soka Gakkai founding president Tsunesaburo Makiguchi, writing about social reform, declared, "In the end, the reconstruction of the human spirit at the core through religious revolution is the lasting solution to the chaos of human affairs." President Makiguchi was steadfast in his belief that the key to social reform was the fundamental transformation of humanity through Nichiren Buddhism—in other words, human revolution. The human revolution that Tokyo University President Shigeru Nambara advocated was thus quite similar to that which President Makiguchi and his disciple Josei Toda had consistently articulated and called for. But Mr. Toda strongly wished to make the case to the university president that such a revolution could only be carried out through Nichiren Buddhism.

Buddhism ultimately teaches that it is through the transformation of the inner self that the world can be transformed. Nichiren Daishonin stated: "If the minds of living beings are impure, their land is also impure, but if their minds are pure, so is their land. There are not two lands, pure or impure in themselves. The difference lies solely in the good or evil of our minds" (WND-1, 4). *Land*, here, refers to the social and natural environment in which we live. According to Nichiren Daishonin, the key to social change is a change or revolution in our minds.

Tetsuo Unno had often heard the phrase *human revolution* at Soka Gakkai meetings, but he had never really thought in depth about its significance. As he read the Soka Gakkai publications his parents had given him, however, he was astonished at the profundity of the ideas presented in them. For the first time he was able to grasp that such Buddhist concepts as "three thousand realms in a single moment of life" and "the oneness of life and its environment" elucidated the meaning of life itself and provided the philosophical basis for the principle of human revolution.

Based on his own experience in the student movement, he also firmly understood that if people are self-centered and lacking in compassion, then even if they were to succeed in carrying out their proposed revolution, society would not improve in the least. This confirmed for him the importance of human revolution in the present circumstances.

BUDDHISM TEACHES THAT the three poisons of greed, anger and foolishness inherent in human life are the primary causes of our unhappiness. Buddhahood is the fundamental power of the universe that enables us to overcome these poisons; it is the highest and noblest state of life. And Buddhism explains that such a life-condition exists in all people.

In short, Buddhahood is a function of supreme compassion and wisdom, and the source of all life activity. The manifestation of Buddhahood empowers us to transcend the self that is dominated and motivated by suffering and desire, and to establish our true selves. Summoning forth and establishing this state of being in our lives is the path to attaining Buddhahood in this lifetime, or the path to realizing absolute happiness. It is the ultimate goal of human revolution.

What is the method for achieving this? Nichiren Daishonin embodied the great life-state of Buddhahood, which is one with the fundamental Law of the universe, in the form of the Gohonzon for the sake of all people of the Latter Day of the Law. It is by believing in the Gohonzon and dedicating ourselves to the mission of working for the happiness of humanity that we are able to bring forth the Buddhahood within our own lives.

Tetsuo Unno spent several days studying the Soka Gakkai publications. They seemed to bring a ray of light into the personal spiritual darkness that was causing him to feel deadlocked. He thought to himself excitedly: *The idea that Buddhahood is universal to all people is a principle that promotes respect for the dignity of life and the equality of all human beings, transcending such differences as ethnicity and nationality. Furthermore, Buddhism's emphasis on transforming the self, our inner state of being, is far more profound and sophisticated than merely trying to change our moral code, engage in self-development or reform our consciousness. This is it! The philosophy I've been looking for has been right here all along!* Unno was so overcome with joy that he wanted to shout out loud.

Around this time, a member visited him. Shortly thereafter, he attended a meeting—his first in a long while—and was struck by how bright and cheerful everyone was. The members welcomed him warmly. From then on, Unno began to actively participate in Soka Gakkai activities, and in the process he made many wonderful discoveries.

UNNO REALIZED THAT the Soka Gakkai itself was a great and unprecedented people's movement. Within the organization, people of different professions, ages and social positions worked earnestly side by side, day and night, for kosen-rufu—that is, for the realization of world peace and happiness for all humanity. The members came from various walks of life—there were company owners and directors of major firms, factory workers and clerks, homemakers and students. They did not oppose each other, but advanced in unity toward a shared goal. There was no separation between the leadership and the masses.

In fact, full-time homemakers, who tended, in Japanese

society, to be conservative, dependent and influenced by the opinions of others, were usually on the front lines of Soka Gakkai activities. Unno was surprised to observe that the women's division members were the ones who inspired and galvanized the other members.

In addition, the Soka Gakkai's movement was centered on the lives of ordinary people, always taking the problems and sufferings of actual individuals as its starting point. Until now, Unno had thought that the members' experiences of having their prayers for personal success or recovery of their health realized were somehow selfish. But he came to understand that those desires served as the driving force for the revolution that is kosen-rufu, and were the reason that the movement spread among the people. He had previously regarded personal happiness and dedication to a cause as contradictory. Buddhism, however, teaches building happiness for oneself and others at the same time.

Soka Gakkai members also frequently spoke of the principle that "earthly desires are enlightenment." Nichiren Buddhism does not reject desire; rather, it teaches that as we earnestly carry out our practice and dedicate ourselves to the goal of kosen-rufu, our desires become the motivating force for our attainment of enlightenment, our perfection as human beings. This is eloquently borne out by the fact that members brim with joy and hope as they devote themselves each day to striving for the happiness of their friends and the well-being of society while accumulating great benefit.

In other words, the Soka Gakkai movement links the pursuit of individual happiness and the ideals of revolution, harmoniously and without contradiction, just as the earth rotates on its axis while at the same time revolving around the sun.

THE EXPERIENCES Tetsuo Unno heard related by Soka Gakkai members at discussion meetings were genuine accounts of human revolution. On one occasion, a young man shared how, having lost his ability to trust other people and his desire to work, he had shut himself in his apartment for a time, but after joining the Soka Gakkai, he felt courage and a renewed sense of purpose and was now engaging in his work with enthusiasm. Another person told how she had decided to try chanting because of the difficulties she always had getting along with others, and that, through her practice, she had come to realize that her self-centered nature was the cause. As she chanted to change that aspect of her personality, she explained, she began to feel greater compassion and consideration toward others.

Unno was deeply moved by these stories, which he found to be fresh accounts of self-reliant individuals transforming their lives. What is more, these members possessed a firm conviction that they were the protagonists who would change society, and as such, they were striving hard for the happiness of their friends and the prosperity of their communities, with a strong desire to realize peace for Japan and the world.

Unno could see that the driving force for the members' actions was a powerful sense of religious mission, an understanding that they had been born to carry out kosen-rufu as Bodhisattvas of the Earth.

The members knew that the only way to achieve kosen-rufu, to realize happiness for all humanity, was to spread the life-affirming and compassionate philosophy of Nichiren Buddhism, while at the same time personally embodying and putting that philosophy into practice in their own lives. Furthermore, in order to eliminate such causes of human pain and suffering as war, poverty, illness and discrimination, they had to work for reform in every arena of society, including education, politics and economics. In other words, an awareness of their religious mission was inextricably linked to an awareness of their social and humanitarian mission.

Mahatma Gandhi, the leader of Indian independence, declared: "I do not know any religion apart from human activity. It provides a moral basis to all other activities which they would otherwise lack, reducing life to a maze of 'sound and fury signifying nothing.'"[10]

Unno sensed that the Soka Gakkai's movement was causing the mighty earth of the people to stir. In contrast, he realized that although he and his fellow student radicals had believed they were engaged in a great struggle, in reality they were barely scratching the surface.

WHEN UNNO heard that the New Student Alliance was being formed in order to open a new path for the student movement, he enthusiastically joined it.

With the impending expiration of the US-Japan Security Treaty in June 1970, the Alliance initiated a movement to oppose the treaty's automatic extension, as well as to call for peace and friendship treaties to be signed with every nation of the world and Okinawa's immediate and unconditional reversion to Japan. In this way, the group was searching for a way to establish lasting peace.

The security treaty was nevertheless extended in 1970, and the student movement in general subsequently experienced a rapid decline. The New Student Alliance, however, expanded its efforts and began addressing such problems as pollution and environmental destruction, taking action from a standpoint of humanism and protecting human rights. As the times changed, however, so did the role of the Alliance, moving from its promotion of a mass protest movement to functioning as a think tank with the mission of creating new age.

In the early 1980s, the New Student Alliance was dissolved, having spent more than a decade fulfilling its important role as a pioneering group advancing humanistic causes. Through their involvement in the Alliance, Soka Gakkai student division members were given the opportunity to seriously ponder and explore how, as Buddhists, they should approach various social issues. And it was these members, young people who also received direct training from Shin'ichi, who would go on to serve as the impetus for the broad range of peace activities that the Soka Gakkai organization itself would eventually promote, such as refugee support and antiwar publications. In that sense, the New Student Alliance helped blaze the trail for the Soka Gakkai's full-fledged movement of peace, culture and education.

Nichiren Daishonin declared, "If you care anything about your personal security, you should first of all pray for order and tranquillity throughout the four quarters of the land, should you not?" (WND-1, 24). In other words, if we wish to be happy, we need to pray above all for the peace and prosperity of the world. Since Buddhism is manifested in society, those who practice it must illuminate society with the light of their personal human revolution and continue to strive earnestly to construct a new age.

The fact that the name of our organization contains the word *Soka*, or *value creation*, is itself a declaration of its mission to contribute to society. That is why the Soka Gakkai is a religious movement unprecedented in human history.

NOTES

1. Seven Bells: The term given to the seven seven-year periods marking the history of the Soka Gakkai's development from its founding in 1930 through 1979. Shin'ichi introduced this concept (which second Soka Gakkai president Josei Toda had developed) on May 3, 1958, shortly after President Toda's death. He was then youth division chief of the general staff.

2. Yoshida Shoin (1830–59).

3. Leo Tolstoy (1828–1910), *Tolstoy as Teacher: Leo Tolstoy's Writings on Education,* translated by Christopher Edgar and edited by Bob Blaisdell (New York: Teachers and Writers Collaborative, 2000), p. 193.

4. Translated from French. Alain (1868–1951), *Propos sur l'education suivis de Pedagogie enfantine* (Paris: Presses Universitaires de France, 1986), p. 54.

5. Charles de Gaulle (1890–1970).

6. Plato, *The Laws* (London: Penguin Books, 1970), p. 261.

7. Yukio Ozaki (1858–1954).

8. Red Army Faction (Sekigunha): Radical student group formed

in 1969 within the student dominated New Left movement. Advocating world revolution through armed violence, throughout the 1970s the group gained worldwide attention for acts of terrorism and violence both within Japan and abroad.

9. Fyodor Dostoyevsky, *The Devils,* translated by David Magarshack (London: Penguin Books, 1971), p. 580.

10. Mahatma Gandhi, *All Men Are Brothers: Autobiographical Reflections* (New York: Continuum, 1958), p. 63.

Mission

ACH OF US has a noble mission. When we awaken
to that mission, the door to our inner life force is
unlocked and immeasurable strength and wisdom well
forth. Our fundamental mission is the realization of the
sacred and unprecedented undertaking of kosen-rufu, the
attainment of happiness and peace for all humanity.

On June 6, 1969, the ninety-eighth birthday of first
Soka Gakkai president Tsunesaburo Makiguchi, weather
forecasters announced the beginning of the rainy season
in the Tokyo area. That evening, after a day of rain, young
women's division representatives energetically made their
way to the Soka Gakkai Young Women's Center in

Minami Motomachi, Shinjuku Ward, not far from the Soka Gakkai Headquarters. They were all registered nurses. Some had rushed there from work immediately after changing out of their uniforms into street clothes, their cheeks flushed and their eyes sparkling with pride to be fulfilling their mission.

Just before seven that evening, more than forty members had gathered. After the start of the meeting was announced, Young Women's Division Leader Yumie Fujiya stood up to speak. Smiling broadly, she said: "I have some wonderful news to share with you today. I have been informed that President Yamamoto has decided to form a special nurses group, and he has given it a name as well: the White Birch Group. Our meeting today is the inaugural ceremony. Congratulations!"

The young women cheered and applauded resoundingly.

During his many visits to Hokkaido, Shin'ichi had been struck by the pure and elegant beauty of the birch trees growing there and decided that they were a perfect symbol for nurses, in their pristine white uniforms. The birch is a pioneer tree species, meaning that it is one of the first trees to appear in areas cleared by fire or logging. As such, it is said to have a strong life force. It is also called a nurse tree, because of its role in protecting the tree species that grow later.

Shin'ichi felt that White Birch Group was an ideal name for an assembly of nurses, people who dedicate themselves to caring for others.

SHIN'ICHI HIMSELF had an encounter with a nurse that he would always remember. The incident took place after he had completed his compulsory education and was working at a steel manufacturing plant that produced munitions for the military. The labor at such factories during World War II was very harsh. Though Shin'ichi had tuberculosis, he still had to work. His four elder brothers had all been drafted, and it was up to him to support the family.

Shin'ichi consistently pushed himself beyond his capacity. There were days when he went to work running a fever of 102 degrees Fahrenheit. And there were even occasions when he collapsed during the military training drills conducted by the factory. It was a time when people regarded taking a rest as a sign of spiritual weakness.

One day, in addition to his high fever, Shin'ichi coughed up blood, and so he went to the factory infirmary. Seeing his haggard appearance, the nurse quickly took his pulse and temperature. She was a woman of small stature in her mid–forties. With concern in her eyes, she said: "My, my! You are really ill! I'm afraid we don't have the proper medicine here, nor can we take an X-ray, so let's go to the hospital right away."

Shin'ichi was hesitant, but the nurse accompanied him to the hospital herself, supporting his weak frame as they walked. On the way there, she recommended that he go somewhere to convalesce. Then she plainly remarked: "War is awful, isn't it? I hope it ends soon. I know the times are hard, but you're young. Please don't allow anything, including illness, to defeat you."

After his examination at the hospital was finished, Shin'ichi bowed repeatedly and thanked the nurse with all his heart. "Don't worry, that's all right," she said. "I'm only doing what anyone would do."

It was a dark period when society and people in general were cold and uncaring. The nurse's dignified kindness therefore gave Shin'ichi tremendous strength and hope. For him, her words were the best medicine of all. Her courage to speak out against war at such a time and her consideration for him were no doubt two sides of the same coin. Having the compassion to care for another person's life itself becomes a powerful desire for peace.

SHIN'ICHI HAD PROPOSED the formation of a nurses group a month earlier. In recent years, the heavy burden carried by nurses had become a major social issue. There were not enough of them to tend to the growing number of hospital beds, and the shortage problem was increasing by the year. Hospital nurses typically worked a three-shift schedule divided into day, evening and night, but it had reached the point where most were working more than ten evening or night shifts a month, and some were doing as many as twenty.

The nursing staff of every hospital was exhausted. Because their labor was not adequately compensated, and because of the toll it was taking on their own health, many were considering changing professions.

In 1965, the Japan National Hospital Workers Union called on the National Personnel Authority to implement an administrative measure improving the working conditions of nurses. The NPA handed down a decision to limit the number of night shifts to eight per month and requiring that a minimum of two night nurses be on duty, but in reality, there was little change. A nationwide nurses strike was subsequently initiated to demand various improvements, including limited night shifts.

In May 1969, the workers union at Keio University Hospital in Shinano-machi, the location of the Soka Gakkai Headquarters, implemented a policy of self-regulation whereby nurses would work no more than eight night shifts per month according to a time schedule drawn up by the union. The new policy received wide media coverage, and the union found itself the target of criticism. People questioned what would happen to patients on nights when no nurse was on duty, and accused the nurses of sacrificing the patients' welfare for their own interests.

Shin'ichi knew that there were many nurses among the young women's division. In Tokyo alone, some seven hundred members were in the profession, but because of the demands of their work, many were unable to participate in Soka Gakkai activities as much as they would have liked. Even so, they gave their all to the activities they did attend and also served as first-aid staff at various Soka Gakkai events when their hectic schedules allowed.

Shin'ichi wished to show his support for these young women and to give them courage and hope. He wanted them to be aware of their noble mission as guardians of life and to become the greatest contributors to their respective workplaces. That is why, upon conferring with the young women's division leaders, he decided to form the White Birch Group.

SHIN'ICHI WAS KEENLY aware of the important mission that nurses had. Though remarkable advances had been made in the field of medicine, people were increasingly voicing concern that it was becoming too impersonal. In addition, with the excess number of prescription medications, many patients were complaining that they did not know if they were being treated or being used for experiments. People were no longer the central focus.

Given these circumstances, Shin'ichi wondered about the care that hospital patients were receiving—did they feel at ease and were they well looked after? He was also concerned about whether they were able to maintain their dignity and pride as human beings. Thinking about these issues, Shin'ichi could not help but have certain reservations about the current state of the health-care system in Japan.

Nurses play an extremely crucial role in bringing a human touch to the medical arena. Through their direct contact with patients, they experience every aspect of life. Their behavior and actions, therefore, have a tremendous impact on those in their care. Even the seemingly simple tasks of taking someone's temperature or giving an injection reflect a nurse's character and attitude, and patients are extremely sensitive to such factors. In addition, a nurse's view of life and humanity—in other words, their faith—is closely related to their personality and the way they interact with their patients.

Florence Nightingale remarked that whatever is a person's motivating force, that is their religion.[1] Truly dedicated nursing no doubt requires such a powerful motivating force, an almost religious conviction.

Buddhism teaches compassion, to "relieve suffering and impart joy," as well as the way to realize that ideal. It also holds that life is eternal across the three existences and teaches the principle of the sanctity of life—that is, that all people are worthy of the highest respect as beings who equally possess the Buddha nature. Buddhism is indeed the ideal philosophy to support the spirit of nursing.

Shin'ichi firmly believed that if Soka Gakkai members in the nursing profession made a continuous effort to polish themselves and become indispensable to their workplaces, they would form a powerful driving force in establishing patient-centered nursing care based on the concept of true humanism.

AT THE INAUGURAL meeting of the White Birch Group, plans for such future activities as the holding of monthly meetings on a local level were announced, followed by determinations by representative members.

One young woman who stood up to speak was Toshie Komori, who had begun teaching at a nursing school in spring of that year. In an energetic voice, she said, "Through my own actions and example, I will teach my students about compassionate nursing."

Next, Chizuru Yamaki, who would be going to work at a hospital in West Germany that August, inspired the members with her declaration: "President Yamamoto has said that the twenty-first century will be a century of life. As caregivers who are directly responsible for people's lives, I believe it is up to us to be pioneers in the effort to actualize that vision.

"What kind of nurses does the world need today? Of course, we should possess broad and deep professional knowledge and skill, but more important, we must have shining character that imparts comfort and hope to patients. Our mission is to create an ideal style of nursing for the twenty-first century. I'll be going to West Germany in August, but there are no borders when it comes to medical treatment or religious faith. As White Birch Group members, let us work together to become Florence Nightingales of the Mystic Law and build a century of life!"

Aiko Yonemitsu, who worked at a university hospital, also spoke, expressing her feelings about the nurses strike taking place nationwide. She said: "The strike began as a way to find a solution to the continuing nurse shortage and the subsequent heavy labor that is making it impossible for us to provide the care our patients deserve. I am fully aware of the need to improve our working conditions, but I think it is a mistake for nurses to leave their workplaces and abandon their patients. Saving and protecting patients' lives is the essence of our profession. The patients are not there for our benefit; we are there for theirs."

AIKO YONEMITSU felt that it was absolutely wrong for nurses to make their patients pawns in an effort to improve their own working conditions. To do so went against all reason, and it would ultimately render their struggle meaningless. She continued: "It's true that we are salaried workers, but I still think we mustn't forget our responsibility as guardians of life. I therefore feel that we should continue to look after our patients while at the same time carrying out tenacious efforts to urge the hospitals to increase their nursing staff so that adequate care can be provided."

Yonemitsu was from Kurume City in Fukuoka Prefecture. Deeply moved by a biography of Florence Nightingale she had read when she was in junior high school, she had decided to become a nurse and devote herself to the welfare of others. After graduating from junior high, she left home and entered a practical nursing school, where she lived in a dormitory. Two years later, she became a licensed practical nurse and began working at a hospital in Kurume City while also taking high school evening classes.

During that time, one of her seniors at work who had been ill with a kidney ailment became a Soka Gakkai member and soon regained her health. What impressed Yonemitsu even more than her co-worker's recovery, however, was the transformation in her personality. She had been a rather blunt and unfriendly type who rarely smiled, but since joining the Soka Gakkai she had begun to address her fellow nurses cheerfully and acknowledge their efforts. She also started taking more initiative in her work, and her constant complaining and carping stopped altogether.

At about that time, Yonemitsu also began to notice that patients who were Soka Gakkai members generally tended to recover more quickly and experience less side effects and complications from their treatment. She came to think that there must be some connection between the Buddhism taught by the Soka Gakkai and overcoming illness, and that led her to have a strong interest in the organization. As Nichiren Daishonin states, "Nothing is more certain than actual proof" (WND-1, 478). Possessing a strong inquiring mind, Yonemitsu could not ignore what she had witnessed with her own eyes.

"What kind of religion is practiced by the Soka Gakkai?" Yonemitsu asked her co-worker. But because the woman had just joined herself, she didn't really know how to reply.

"I CANNOT EXPLAIN it very well," Yonemitsu's co-worker said, "but if you come to one of our meetings, I think you'll gain an understanding of what the organization is all about."

Yonemitsu thus attended a lecture on Nichiren Daishonin's writings held at a local civic hall. The room was filled with people of all ages who were in high spirits, and the lecturer spoke with conviction, presenting the topic in a logical, clear and convincing manner. Yonemitsu decided that she, too, would try Nichiren Buddhism and joined the Soka Gakkai soon after.

As she began chanting, participating earnestly in Soka Gakkai activities, and studying Buddhism, the young woman realized that faith is the source that gives rise to strong life force. She was also impressed by Buddhism's profound insight regarding such concepts as the connection between mind and body, as well as by the Buddhist teaching of compassion, and she resolved to become a nurse who truly embodied that quality.

After graduating from high school, she moved to Tokyo to study at a nursing school. Once she became a registered nurse, she took a job at a university hospital. The nurses union there was quite active, but Yonemitsu found herself questioning the way it prioritized improving working conditions above caring for the patients.

Amid these circumstances, she continued to insist to her colleagues that, as nurses, their main focus should always be on their patients. Her actions, however, only made her the target of criticism. Her being a member of the Soka Gakkai also roused antagonism, but Yonemitsu refused to compromise her convictions. She believed that it was wrong to turn patients into pawns, no matter what the reason, and that the basic spirit of nursing was to place the highest priority on protecting the patients' lives at any cost. It was these views and feelings that she shared at the inaugural meeting of the White Birch Group.

Young Women's Division Leader Yumie Fujiya delivered the final words at the inaugural gathering, speaking of the mission of the newly formed group: "I personally had an unpleasant experience being treated like an object when I was in the hospital battling illness. I believe it is your mission as members of this group to bring a human touch to the medical arena by upholding the philosophy of compassion.

"The Lotus Sutra teaches the principle of lotus flowers

blooming in muddy water. No matter how difficult the situation, I hope you will bring flowers of trust and actual proof to bloom in your lives."

The participants nodded in agreement as they listened, their eyes shining with determination.

YUMIE FUJIYA reported on the White Birch Group inaugural meeting to Shin'ichi.

"This meeting may have been a small one," Shin'ichi remarked, "but in time, its significance will become clear. The group's members are all striving earnestly to practice Buddhism amid trying circumstances. Some of them are living in dormitories, no doubt sharing rooms with co-workers who don't understand their faith. I imagine they feel inhibited even just to recite the sutra and chant Nam-myoho-renge-kyo, facing ridicule from their peers.

"What is more, not only do they keep irregular hours working a three-shift schedule, but they are constantly dealing with the reality of life and death. It must be exhausting work that causes them enormous tension and stress. I'm sure they do their best to attend meetings, but there must also be times when emergencies prevent them from doing so.

"However, it is in continuing to exert themselves to fulfill their mission for kosen-rufu, even amid such harsh conditions, that correct Buddhist practice is found. In the process, they will cultivate their own humanity and be able to empathize with the pain and sorrow of others. They will develop the bodhisattva spirit, the spirit of compassion. As Nichiren Daishonin writes, "A hundred years of practice in the Land of Perfect Bliss cannot compare to the benefit gained from one day's practice in the impure world" (WND-I, 736).

Spring does not come without the passage of winter, and flowers bloom after a long period of endurance. Likewise, there is no victory or happiness in life without struggle. In order for the members of the White Birch Group to triumph together, it is important that they encourage, support and inspire each other to devote themselves to their mission."

Smiling, Shin'ichi then lifted his gaze as if looking into the future and said: "The seed has been planted now. In twenty or thirty years, this group will grow into a mighty tree. The fact that its members have chosen the nursing profession in order to help those suffering from illness means that they possess the bodhisattva spirit. If they awaken to their mission and endeavor to win over their own weaknesses, the White Birch Group will become a gathering of the purest, strongest and most trusted and respected women—women whose lives overflow with good fortune and benefit. I'm really looking forward to their development!"

Fujiya's eyes filled with tears as she listened to President Yamamoto share his profound hopes for the White Birch Group.

THE ESTABLISHMENT OF the White Birch Group infused its members with boundless courage and pride. Renewing their awareness as pioneers of the century of life and determined to manifest real humanism in their work, each initiated her own struggle.

Aiko Yonemitsu, who had expressed her feelings about

the nurse's strike at the inaugural meeting, had been studying the current criterion used for calculating the necessary ratio of nursing staff to patients. The standard system of nursing in effect at the time deemed that a ratio of one nurse to four patients was appropriate. Yonemitsu, however, felt that there was something wrong with a ratio set merely on a uniform calculation of patients without taking into consideration the content of the work involved.

Wishing to contribute to the realization of patient-centered nursing care, she decided to conduct a detailed survey looking at the actual duties of nurses, which she would use to establish a new guideline for calculating a sufficient nurse-patient ratio. Yonemitsu and a colleague joined forces and after completing the survey and the research, wrote up their findings in a dissertation. Able only to work on the project when they were off duty, they lost many hours of sleep in the endeavor. The paper was finally finished at the end of May, just before the formation of the White Birch Group, and the two women entered it in a contest held by a publisher specializing in medical topics.

The title of the paper was "The Present State of Nursing Standards Analyzed on the Basis of Nurse-Patient Ratios and the Content of Nursing Care." Reflecting the results of the two women's careful investigation, the document demonstrated that the workload of nurses was extremely heavy, and that so much of the nurses' time was taken up with assisting during medical examinations and other miscellaneous tasks that they were unable to give proper attention to treating individual patients. It also concluded that the current nurse-patient ratio ignored the reality of the situation and needed to be reconsidered based on a clear understanding of the actual content of the work involved. The report was extremely valuable in that it objectively and academically illustrated the urgent need to increase nursing staff in the health care industry.

That autumn, the paper was awarded a prize for excellence from the publishing company, and it also received considerable attention from the Japanese Society for Nursing Research. Yonemitsu then decided that, as a member of the White Birch Group, she would continue conducting research into various topics toward achieving more humanistic nursing care.

THE NEXT CHALLENGE that Aiko Yonemitsu took up was conducting research on treating pulmonary encephalopathy, a neurological disorder. In addition, papers she wrote jointly with other White Birch Group members on various topics, including the meaning of nursing and the necessary qualifications and abilities of nurses, were also awarded prizes. In time, her work as a nurse and her practical research efforts would be recognized, and she would go on to become a nursing instructor at a two-year college of medical technology and eventually a full-fledged professor.

Members of the White Birch Group, based on a belief that an understanding of the fundamental Law of life was vitally important to nursing, diligently studied Nichiren's teachings. The year after the group's establishment, they initiated a series of study sessions that they called the White Birch Study Group.

Learning Buddhist teachings helped them deepen their

awareness of their mission and became the driving force in their efforts to humanize the nursing profession. As they came to understand such concepts as three thousand realms in a single moment of life, the oneness of body and mind, the oneness of life and its environment, and the nine consciousnesses, as well as the mystic principle of responsive communion[2] that reveals the interconnectedness of all life, the members' interactions with their patients changed dramatically.

One member had an experience of caring for an eight-year-old girl who was in a coma after being badly injured in a traffic accident. Praying earnestly for the girl's recovery, the nurse held her hand and encouraged her every day, saying: "You're going to recover, so don't give up!" "Get well soon so that you can go back to school." But there was no response. One, then two, weeks passed without any change in her condition. From the third week, however, she began to show signs of improvement and eventually she began to move her eyes.

One day, while the nurse was giving her a sponge bath, the little girl suddenly spoke. "Thank you so much," she said. "I'm going to get well and go back to school." The nurse was completely taken aback. She realized that she had been communicating with the girl on the most profound level of life.

Many other White Birch members had similar experiences, which made them keenly aware of the importance of their frame of mind in caring for others. As a result, they began to chant sincerely for their patients and to approach their work with a firm determination to protect their patients' lives no matter what.

A S THEY CONTINUED to study Nichiren's teachings, the nurses' attitudes toward serving as first-aid staff at Soka Gakkai events also changed. One such member was a young woman named Chieko Satake, a native of Yamagata Prefecture who worked at a hospital in Shinjuku Ward, Tokyo. Her spirit had always been to give prompt and appropriate treatment to anyone needing first aid at a Soka Gakkai meeting.

As her understanding of Buddhism deepened, she began to think: *Of course I must do my best to aid the sick or injured, but is that my only responsibility? Buddhism teaches that all phenomena are encompassed in a single life-moment. Doesn't this mean that our prayers and determination as first-aid staff can actually prevent accidents from happening at the outset? Perhaps this should really be our spirit.*

She shared her thoughts with the other White Birch members, and everyone agreed with her. From then on, praying wholeheartedly beforehand for there to be no accidents became the tradition of those serving as medical staff at Soka Gakkai events.

The members also realized that many of those who fell ill at meetings did so for relatively simple reasons: they might have rushed to the venue without eating a proper meal, or they kept their overcoat on during the meeting even though the room was quite warm. The nurses dealt with this by having the leaders in charge remind the members to eat before coming or take off their coats inside if they felt hot.

The White Birch members also pondered the most effective nursing methods from a Buddhist perspective. Expanding on Florence Nightingale's idea that the purpose of nursing is to minimize the expenditure or depletion of the patient's "vital energy,"[3] they looked into methods that would actually draw forth their patients' life force.

The White Birch members noticed that a presence of hope and joy contributed to an increase in life force. Some tried to give their patients hope by helping them establish practical goals toward overcoming their illness and then supporting them in the process. In particular, they did their utmost to give their patients encouragement, determined to keep them from giving up out of a sense of frustration and loneliness at being ill.

Other members tried to make the hospital environment more friendly and comfortable by doing such things as decorating the dreary rooms and corridors with flowers.

CHIEKO SATAKE was appointed the first leader of the White Birch Group in August 1970 at the group's first general meeting, held at the Tokyo Third Headquarters building in Tabata. It was more than a year after the group's founding. On that occasion, she announced her determination, "*The Record of the Orally Transmitted Teachings* states, 'Nichiren declares that the varied sufferings that all living beings undergo—all these are Nichiren's own sufferings' (OTT, 138). I believe that the great compassion to share the suffering of others is the ultimate spirit of all health care and nursing professions.

"In order to manifest this spirit of Nichiren Daishonin, to carry out genuinely compassionate nursing and to be a source of hope that gives courage to all, we as nurses must be strong. Let us forge a state of life that can win over arrogance and that will not be defeated by sadness or swept away by karma.

"Toward that end, let us exert ourselves wholeheartedly on the front lines of kosen-rufu, never compromising our efforts as we strive to achieve our personal human revolution." Satake was convinced that this was the key to actualizing humanistic nursing.

A Buddhist scripture teaches that because of the "three forms of pride"—the pride of youth, the pride of health and the pride of life—people have an aversion to the old, the sick and the dead. But people must realize that they, too, will grow old, become ill and die.

Satake had observed that there was even a tendency among physicians and nurses to think of themselves as being in an advantageous position because of their health and to therefore condescend to their ailing patients. This attitude would become manifested in their expressions and speech, hurting the feelings of patients and causing a general atmosphere of mistrust. Such arrogance is one cause of medical treatment that lacks a human touch and looks at patients as mere physical objects.

When we awaken to the fact that we will also grow old, fall ill and die, we see that the elderly or ill person before our eyes is no different from us. That is the beginning of genuine empathy.

In her speech, Satake was asserting that the first step toward realizing compassionate nursing was a change in nurses' resolve as well as their own human revolution. In this way, the White Birch Group raised the banner of humanism and boldly set forth into the century of life.

FIFTY THOUSAND spectators lined both sides of Ocean Avenue in the Los Angeles, California suburb of Santa Monica to watch the Min-On–sponsored Japan–America Fife and Drum Corps Parade. Held to commemorate the Soka Gakkai's Sixth All-America Convention, the parade began in high spirits at ten in the morning on July 27, 1969. The hope-filled melody of the young women's division Fife and Drum Corps, emissaries of peace, soared into the heavens.

Starting at the intersection of Ocean Avenue and California Avenue, the grand parade made its way along the one-mile route to the Santa Monica Civic Center, the musicians playing joyously as they went. A total of two thousand performers put on a spectacular show that included musical performances by one hundred forty members of the Fuji Fife and Drum Corps from Japan and members of the US Fife and Drum Corps and Brass Band, as well as dance performances by groups from throughout the nation.

Receiving the full support and cooperation of the local municipal authorities, the parade was led by a police motorcycle escort, behind which followed the mayor of Santa Monica in an open car. With American history as its theme, the parade also featured a number of costumed performers, including a group of cowboys and someone dressed as first US president George Washington astride a white horse. There were also performances of Scottish dancing and the Hawaiian hula, as well as floats representing the US Capitol in Washington, D.C., and the Apollo 11 spacecraft, which had recently returned from a successful landing on the moon.

The crowd was especially dazzled by the spirited Fuji Fife and Drum Corps, whose members wore orange uniforms patterned with gold chrysanthemums. As they performed the "Stars and Stripes Forever," the young women moved perfectly into a star formation. This evoked enthusiastic cheers from the spectators. The crowd's response gave the members a tremendous sense of pride and satisfaction.

When we finally achieve success and victory, in that moment, all the struggles we went through to reach that point are transformed into glorious memories.

THE PARADE ADVANCED slowly down the avenue under the gently waving fronds of the palm trees lining the street. Off to the right lay the vast Pacific Ocean, whose waves breaking on the shore seemed to cheer the performers on. People inside the buildings to the left waved and applauded. Everyone appeared to be enjoying the spectacle immensely. Some even climbed trees to get a better view, while others stood atop telephone booths to take photographs.

The street had been blocked off in one direction for the parade, and traffic in the open lane often became congested as drivers slowed down to catch a glimpse of the parade as well. A large number of media representatives were on hand, with one television station even using a helicopter to film the procession from the air. Local papers also covered the event widely, printing headlines the next day that read: "50,000 Spectators Watch Buddhist Parade" and "Parade of Unprecedented Splendor Held in Santa Monica." Some people remarked that it was the best parade the city had ever seen, while others asked about the Buddhist organization that had sponsored it.

When the Fuji Fife and Drum Corps reached the civic center, an elderly Japanese-American man approached corps leader Fumiko Takamura and said excitedly, "That was a wonderful performance!" Wiping tears from his eyes, he then added: "About one hundred fifty Japanese-American families live in my community, and we have suffered greatly in the past because of our ethnic background. It has been very difficult.

"But your invigorating performance has inspired me with confidence and pride. I feel tremendous courage. You are the hope of Japan. By rights, I should be treating you all to a feast to express my gratitude, but at the very least I wanted to take this opportunity to thank you." He bowed repeatedly, his face aglow with emotion.

THE FUJI FIFE and Drum Corps had arrived at the Los Angeles International Airport at half past seven in the morning on July 25. In addition to the parade, they were to participate in the various events taking place in conjunction with the Soka Gakkai's Sixth All-America Convention being held at the Shrine Auditorium in Los Angeles at six in the evening on the following day. Some ten thousand members from throughout the United States, Canada and Mexico also gathered for the joyous occasion. The members attending the meeting wore graduation caps and gowns as a symbol of their pride as "professors of happiness and peace" studying and putting into practice the great life philosophy of Buddhism.

At the meeting, Shin'ichi's message was read in English and Japanese: "On board Apollo 11, a brilliant product of modern science, humankind has finally reached the moon. I wish to express my profound respect to all of you of the United States of America, the nation that has realized this long-cherished dream of humanity and thereby opened the door to an age of space exploration."

Apollo 11 had landed on the moon on July 20, and two astronauts aboard it had become the first to set foot on the lunar surface. On July 24, their command module splashed into the Pacific Ocean and was safely retrieved. This news thrilled not only the United States but the entire world.

In his message, Shin'ichi further remarked, "One point I would like to make, however, is that even though travel to the moon is now possible, solutions to such urgent problems confronting humanity as hunger, poverty and disease have yet to be found."

In order to solve those problems, Shin'ichi believed that

people needed to transcend divisions of nationality, ethnicity and ideology to work together in the shared awareness that we are all members of the same human family. It was crucial for people to overcome feelings of hatred and discrimination and to transform the world from one of conflict and opposition to one of trust and harmony. Toward that end, Shin'ichi was convinced that the Buddhist principles of equality and respect for life had to be established in the hearts of every individual.

He therefore declared to the members, "Let us deeply recognize that now is the time to spread Nichiren Daishonin's philosophy of life to every corner of the world!"

"NICHIREN BUDDHISM is a world religion from which people of all walks of life everywhere can practice and receive benefit. I firmly believe that by awakening people's humanity and enabling them to tap their powerful inner creativity through the teachings of Nichiren Daishonin, we can revitalize our deadlocked society and realize a great century of life. The attainment of happiness by each of you as individuals is inextricably linked to the happiness of America as a whole. Your endeavors will surely serve as an example for the rest of the globe. Brimming with youthful vigor and hope as you carry out your Buddhist practice, you are pioneers in the effort to construct a peaceful world."

With a final call for everyone to be champions of peace and suns of hope for humanity, Shin'ichi's message concluded. The Shrine Auditorium shook with thunderous cheers and applause.

If bonds of trust and friendship could be forged among

the vastly diverse people of the United States, the country would become a model of global peace. As a starting point, Shin'ichi earnestly hoped that the American members would hold a convention that epitomized that goal.

Peace is not simply the absence of war; it is a state in which people come together through mutual trust and their lives overflow with joy, energy and hope. This is the polar opposite of war—a condition in which people are plagued by hatred and a fear of death. With this awareness, Shin'ichi offered the meeting organizers advice on how to make the convention a success and chanted for it to be a dynamic and lively event. He also sent the Fuji Fife and Drum Corps to participate in the gathering as an expression of his desire to build a bridge of friendship linking Japan and the United States through music.

After announcements that included progress reports on the previous year's activities, new personnel appointments and plans for upcoming activities, greetings were delivered by Soka Gakkai Young Women's Division Leader Yumie Fujiya and General Administrator Yasushi Morinaga, who were both visiting from Japan.

The high-spirited meeting came to an end at 7:20 PM, and was followed by a joint performance by the Japanese and American Fife and Drum Corps.

A POWERFUL DRUMROLL echoed through the darkened auditorium. A spotlight moved over the audience and came to rest on the Japanese and American Fife and Drum Corps members standing in formation at the back of the auditorium's ground level. The American corps marched down the left and right aisles to the stage, with the Fuji Fife and Drum Corps, large feathers waving atop their white hats, coming down the middle. The entrance of these emissaries of peace who had crossed the Pacific to participate in the gathering was greeted with vigorous applause.

When the performers had all taken their places on the stage, each group addressed the audience in the other's language. Speaking in English, Fuji Fife and Drum Corps leader Fumiko Takamura said with a broad smile: "Thanks to the prayers of the Fife and Drum Corps members in Japan, we have been able to visit this great country that overflows with the frontier spirit! With today's meeting as our point of departure, let us advance together in unity, determined to play an important role in the actualization of world peace."

The Fife and Drum Corps performance began. As the lights dimmed, images from the Japan-US Fife and Drum Corps friendship exchange meeting held in Japan the previous year were projected on a large screen spanning the back of the stage. That gathering, with the participation of thirty-five hundred Fife and Drum Corps members from throughout Japan and two hundred from the United States, had taken place on August 16, 1968, at the Tokyo Metropolitan Gymnasium.

The screen showed Shin'ichi smiling as he watched the drum majors from both countries exchange batons. It was an unforgettable scene that conveyed the young women's determination to link the world through music as well as their shared commitment to work for peace.

The stage was illuminated again, and the American and Japanese drum majors ascended a platform in the shape of

Mount Fuji. There they exchanged batons once more in a symbol of praise for each other's dedicated efforts during the past year and their determination to initiate a fresh advance. A joint performance of the "Stars and Stripes Forever" ensued. The corps members played with all their hearts, resolved to open the path to peace.

Sincerity moves people's hearts. When the young women had finished, a men's division member in the audience stood up and shouted: "Bravo! Let's give them another round of applause! And let's do our best to carry out our mission as well!"

JULY 27, the day after the All-America Convention and the Japan-US Fife and Drum Corps joint performance, was the day of the parade in Santa Monica, the location of the Soka Gakkai's America Headquarters office. It was a parade of peace, fully conveying the joy and hope that were born from faith.

The members of the Japanese and American Fife and Drum Corps were welcomed at the civic center by applause and cheers. Entering the building, they embraced each other and celebrated their great success, their eyes wet with happy tears.

Before leaving Japan, the Fuji Fife and Drum Corps members had made a pact that they wouldn't cry, but now that the parade was finished, their tears flowed freely. They were all overjoyed to have challenged themselves and won.

One of the young women, Yoshimi Tachikawa, clutched her flute as she wiped her eyes. In her heart, she called out: "Grandma! I did it! It was a huge success!" Yoshimi's grandmother had died just two months earlier. Though she had been confined to bed in her last days, she had done her utmost to raise Yoshimi. And it was thanks to her that Yoshimi had joined the Fife and Drum Corps.

Yoshimi had lost her father to cancer at the age of seven. He had opened his own electrical appliance shop in Katsushika Ward, Tokyo, and things were starting to pick up when he suddenly fell ill and died. He left behind his wife, her parents, Yoshimi, her six-year-old sister and three-year-old brother. Yoshimi's mother had been in poor health since the birth of her son, and she was constantly in and out of the hospital. Then, a year after the death of her father, Yoshimi's grandfather died, effectively leaving her grandmother to support and raise three young children because her daughter was too ill. With neither mother nor father at home, the family atmosphere was gloomy. Overwhelmed by a deep sense of loneliness, Yoshimi never smiled.

In December of the year Yoshimi's grandfather died, her grandmother was introduced to the Soka Gakkai, and the whole family joined. When Yoshimi entered junior high school, a classmate who was a member of the Fife and Drum Corps invited her to watch a rehearsal. She also attended a young women's division leaders meeting at the Taito Ward Gymnasium together with her friend where the corps was performing. The brilliant smiles of the Fife and Drum Corps members and their powerful perform-ance made a deep impression on Yoshimi.

SHE DECIDED that she wanted to join the Fife and Drum Corps, but was told that first she needed to be reciting the sutra regularly and that she had to obtain a rec-ommendation from a local young women's division leader. She therefore began to practice regularly and to attend meetings with other young women's division members.

Yoshimi's biggest concern was financial. If she joined the Fife and Drum Corps, she would need the train fare to travel to and from rehearsals. But her mother was in the hospital and there was no extra money in the family budget for such an expense.

One day, she broached the subject with her grand-mother, who said: "If that's what you want to do, then do it. I hope you'll not only learn to play music, but strive to deepen your faith in Buddhism as well. We don't have a lot of money, but I will do my best to support you. After all, the only real treasure I can leave you with is faith in the Gohonzon."

Yoshimi thus joined the Fife and Drum Corps. Rehearsals were very demanding. Her leaders constantly presented her with challenges, such as learning the fife and various pieces of music. Wanting to show her grandmother her appreciation, however, Yoshimi was determined to do her best.

She also learned about unity and responsibility in the Fife and Drum Corps. On one occasion, when she was having trouble with a particular piece, a leader said to her: "You may think that it's OK if you're the only one who doesn't master this piece, but it's not. The performance will only be a success if each of us hits our notes perfectly to create a harmonious blend of sound. If you cannot play correctly, you'll ruin it for everyone else."

When Yoshimi finally succeeded in mastering the piece after diligent effort, her leaders were genuinely delighted for her.

The training was strict, but it was also filled with warmth. Before she realized it, Yoshimi had begun to smile again. *I'm not alone,* she thought. *I have all these sisters in the Fife and Drum Corps!* Through her experience in the corps, she developed a bright and cheerful disposition and began to tackle her endeavors with enthusiasm.

Human relations that are bound by trust and enable both parties to grow and learn are one of the greatest treasures of youth.

YOSHIMI'S GRANDMOTHER, who was the mainstay of the family, had a stroke in the March of Yoshimi's second year in high school. Yoshimi prayed earnestly to the Gohonzon. Her grandmother survived, but she was paralyzed on one side of her body. As the eldest child, Yoshimi now bore full responsibility for taking care of her family, including running the appliance store and performing all the household chores.

In order to allow Yoshimi to manage the store after school each day, her younger sister enrolled in evening classes when she graduated from junior high. At the time, Yoshimi was also looking after about twenty young women's division members as a group leader. Because of her family obligations, however, she was unable to participate in either young women's division or Fife and Drum Corps activities for a time. She felt left out and began to resent her situation.

Recalling the tremendous joy and vigor she experienced when she was actively working for kosen-rufu, she was keenly reminded of the greatness of Soka Gakkai activities. She chanted wholeheartedly each day that she would eventually be able to participate in such activities again and devote her life to kosen-rufu to her heart's content.

After graduating from high school, Yoshimi conferred with her family and they decided to close the store and rent out the space. Yoshimi thus took on a regular job and was able to start participating in Soka Gakkai activities and the Fife and Drum Corps once again.

The great Indian poet Rabindranath Tagore[4] said that glory is to be found in one's travails.[5] No life is without its ups and downs. The more hurdles we overcome in life, the greater degree of happiness we savor.

When the Fife and Drum Corps' trip to the United States was announced, Yoshimi resolved that she would participate somehow. But however she looked at the situation, she realized it was going to be very difficult to come up with the airfare. Even so, she was determined to go, and she prayed with all her might to make it happen.

Then the Chinese restaurant that had been renting the family's shop space decided to move out after completing less than two years of their five-year lease, which they had already paid in full. The restaurant owner said that since he was breaking the contract, the Tachikawas could keep the remaining three year's worth of rent. No sooner had that happened than a clothing store took over the space and paid the contract fee, so the money the family received from the previous tenant was a genuine windfall and Yoshimi was able to buy her plane ticket to America.

SOON AFTER the rehearsals for the trip to America began, Yoshimi's grandmother died. She was seventy-seven. Addressing her grandmother, who seemed to be sleeping peacefully in her coffin, Yoshimi said: "Thank you, Grandma, for taking care of us all those years. Because of you we were able to encounter the Soka Gakkai. Though things were difficult, with your encouragement I was able to join the Fife and Drum Corps. You gave me the greatest gift of all. Thank you, thank you so much, Grandma!"

On the morning of her departure for the United States, Yoshimi bowed to a framed photograph of her grandmother and said: "I'm going now. I'll do my best. I know we'll be a big success. Please watch us!" Yoshimi sensed her grandmother's support.

Having reached America at last, Yoshimi marched energetically down the avenue in Santa Monica, calling out silently to her grandmother: "Look at me! Look at

Yoshimi!" And when the parade was completed, an image of her grandmother smiling and nodding in approval rose in her mind's eye.

Noriyo Sada, the leader of the accordion players, had overcome illness to make the journey to the United States. In June, a month before the trip, she felt a sudden pain in her right knee during parade rehearsal and was unable to walk normally. She went to see a doctor, who told her that, in addition to having injured her tendon, her spine was curved. "You've strained yourself carrying something that's far too heavy for you," the doctor said. "You need to rest. Please don't put any strain on your back for a while."

The accordion weighed about twenty-two pounds, and for the last two months Noriyo had been toting it and a bag on an almost daily basis to various rehearsal locations. For a girl of her slender build, the load had been too much. The unnatural posture she had adopted to compensate for the weight on her lower back and shoulders seemed to be the root of the problem.

If she couldn't carry her accordion, however, there was no point in going to the United States.

NORIYO FELT as if she had been cast from the heights of joy to the depths of despair. She chanted in tears every day, asking the Gohonzon why such a thing had to happen to her. She was sad and angry, but as she continued chanting, she began to think: *There must be a reason for this. It may well be a test so that I can develop an invincible self. Even if I cannot play the accordion, there must be something I can do as a member of the Fife and Drum Corps.* And with that, her tears stopped.

After considering what she could do to help ensure the success of the Fife and Drum Corps' trip to the United States, she volunteered to work behind the scenes in ways that wouldn't strain her physically, such as copying the sheet music by hand for the other members.

When we encounter an obstacle, our first reaction is often to think that it's all over and there is no way we will succeed. We lose the spirit to challenge ourselves. The true cause of defeat in life, however, is not the obstacles we meet, but the fact that we give up in the face of them.

The pain in Noriyo's leg gradually subsided and she recovered much sooner than expected. She consulted with her doctor regarding the trip to America, and he advised her against marching in the parade, but said that she could play her accordion as long as she was seated. Noriyo thus played joyfully in the joint concert of the US and Japan Fife and Drum Corps at the Shrine Auditorium, and during the parade, she took pictures of her friends' smiling faces for the corps' records.

People of various ethnic backgrounds participated in the US Fife and Drum Corps. Deeply moved to see such a diverse group of people embracing each other and shedding tears of joy after their performance, Noriyo continued snapping photos. She thought to herself: *The United States has had serious problems with racial discrimination, but in the Soka Gakkai, members respect one another as children of the Buddha and are linked by bonds of trust. This organization is the epitome of human harmony. I will definitely devote my life to worldwide kosen-rufu!* This was a dream that Noriyo Sada had actually cherished for many years.

ASPIRING TO WORK for global kosen-rufu, when she graduated from high school, Noriyo enrolled in an English conversation school. Her trip to the United States with the Fife and Drum Corps further solidified her commitment to that goal.

Six years later, she met and married a Soka Gakkai member who was visiting Japan from Micronesia and she became Noriyo Rodriguez. She returned with her husband to his home on the island of Ponape (now Pohnpei). In the village where they lived, there was no electricity, natural gas or plumbing. The couple used water from the nearby stream for cooking, doing laundry and bathing. They spent their evenings by the light of oil lamps. Though they were not well off materially, they were surrounded by a rich natural setting and the beautiful hearts of the local people. Noriyo chanted earnestly and strove to share Nichiren Buddhism with her fellow villagers, determined to make her new home into a land of genuine happiness.

The Rodriguezes eventually had children, who also grew up strong and healthy. In time, Mr. Rodriguez founded a bank in order to establish a sound financial base for his family in Micronesia. It collapsed, however, when a Japanese friend defrauded him and made off with the bank's funds. In 1984, her husband died of a heart attack while she was in Japan to give birth to their youngest child. She returned to Micronesia with her infant and raised her family on her own, living on her husband's pension. Her in-laws also supported her in any way they could.

Whenever she felt that grief might overwhelm her, Noriyo would pick up her accordion and play Soka Gakkai songs. Their melodies had penetrated deep into her heart, and as she played them, courage surged from within her being. Remembering the trip she had made to the United States with the Fife and Drum Corps, she thought to herself: *At that time, I also overcame tremendous hardship through chanting Nam-myoho-renge-kyo. As long as I have the Gohonzon, I can surmount any sadness. After all, I'm a proud member of the Fife and Drum Corps! I can never be defeated!* Such moments reignited her fighting spirit.

A Soka Gakkai chapter was finally established in Micronesia in 1992, with Noriyo Rodriguez as its leader. Having triumphed over some of life's greatest trials, the former Fife and Drum Corps member had become the mother of kosen-rufu in Micronesia.

The spirit of a person tested and trained in youth is strong, and such a spirit emits a golden brilliance that can never be obscured.

NORIYO WAS ALWAYS thinking about how she and her fellow Soka Gakkai members could contribute to their community as Buddhists, and she took action herself to do so. Wanting to share the joy of music with the local children, she taught them to sing and play musical instruments and organized concerts for them. As a result of such persistent, steady efforts, trust in the Soka Gakkai International spread widely throughout Micronesia.

In March 2001, the Federated States of Micronesia conferred an honorary citizenship on SGI President Shin'ichi

Yamamoto and his wife, Mineko. FSM President Leo A. Falcam personally established the honor—the first of its kind in Micronesia—in order to present it to the couple, having learned of their international efforts for peace, culture and education through the local members.

In July of the same year, the Pohnpei Traditional Supreme Council of Chiefs awarded SGI President and his wife Pohnpei's traditional highest titles of honor. The award's conferral ceremony took place in Japan with the eldest son of Noriyo Rodriguez acting as interpreter. He and two of his siblings studied at Soka University in Japan, and all five of Noriyo's children grew into fine, capable adults. Looking back, she knew that the first step in her journey of global kosen-rufu was her trip to the United States as a member of the Fife and Drum Corps.

On the evening of July 27, the day of the Santa Monica parade, the Fuji Fife and Drum Corps visited a hospital in Los Angeles and performed for the patients in its central courtyard. The musicians' schedule in America was quite packed, but thinking of their mission to contribute to fostering good relations between Japan and the United States, they were not the least bit fatigued. An awareness of one's mission is a source of energy.

The hospital patients enthusiastically applauded the Japanese tunes the young women played, as well as their impressive drill formations. During the performance, some of the young women stepped forward and presented the audience with leis made of paper origami cranes that had been created by Fife and Drum Corps members who were unable to go to the United States. Tears filled the eyes of many patients as they conveyed their gratitude for the warm encouragement of these emissaries of peace from Japan. The concert was very well received, with many people remarking that it had given them new hope and energy.

O N THE EVENING of July 28, the day after the parade, a friendship exchange gathering was held for the US and Japanese Fife and Drum Corps members on the beach at Playa Del Rey in Los Angeles. Standing around a bonfire, the emissaries of peace from both countries talked while enjoying rice balls and barbecued fare prepared for them by local women's division members. The Pacific Ocean stretched out before them, but in the darkness the only sign of its presence was the sound of waves echoing in the night air.

A member of the American Fife and Drum Corps remarked: "Japan is on the other side of this ocean, and so are the Soka Gakkai Headquarters and President Yamamoto. That means we are directly connected to President Yamamoto by this body of water. President Yamamoto has come to the United States many times to teach us about Buddhism, and we, the members of the young women's division here, consider him to be our mentor in life. Therefore, whenever I'm struggling or having difficulties, I come to the ocean. I call out: 'Sensei, I won't be defeated! I'll do my best.' There is no barrier separating me from my mentor. I am communicating with him all the time." Tears shone in her eyes as she spoke.

Yoriko Kida, the only Fuji Fife and Drum Corps member who made the trip from Akita Prefecture,[6] was deeply moved by her American counterpart's words. Because her hometown was a long distance from Tokyo, she had always felt that President Yamamoto was somehow far away from her and her fellow members in Akita. The young woman's remark, however, brought her to her senses. *America is much farther from Tokyo than Akita,* she thought. *Compared to the United States, Akita is right next door to Sensei. But this member is much closer in spirit to Sensei than I am. Physical distance or one's position in the organization doesn't determine the mentor–disciple relationship. It's completely a matter of one's attitude, one's seeking spirit.* With this realization, Yoriko Kida renewed her determination to strengthen her bond with President Yamamoto.

The Japanese and American Fife and Drum Corps members learned much about faith from each other and together reinforced their eternal vow to carry out kosen-rufu. The light of the bonfire illuminated the friendly gathering.

REPORTS ON THE All-America Convention and the events in which the Fuji Fife and Drum Corps was participating were conveyed to Japan on a daily basis by telephone. When Shin'ichi learned of the great success of both the joint Japan-US Fife and Drum Corps performance that followed the convention and the parade the next day, he smiled broadly and said: "That's wonderful. It's a historic achievement. I'm so happy to hear that both the members and people in the community at large enjoyed the performances immensely.

"The Soka Gakkai Fife and Drum Corps is unrivaled in the world. It is the pride of our organization. The young women really did their best. Please convey my profound appreciation to them." As the founder of the Fife and

Drum Corps, Shin'ichi was filled with joy and emotion to know that it was serving as a wonderful bridge of friendship between the two countries.

The Fuji Fife and Drum Corps was founded on July 22, 1956. A few months prior to that, Shin'ichi, then youth division chief of the general staff, had met with several young women's division leaders at his home to discuss the future development of the young women's division. As they talked, the idea of establishing a fife and drum corps was brought up. This had been a goal cherished by the young women ever since the formation of the young men's division Brass Band.

The Brass Band had been inaugurated two years earlier, in May 1954, at Shin'ichi's suggestion. Not a single Soka Gakkai senior leader had demonstrated any understanding for the proposal; rather, they opposed it out of hand, saying it had nothing to do with faith and that he should forget about it. But the idea was based on Shin'ichi's belief that an outstanding religion invariably gave rise to brilliant art and culture, and that the realization of a humanistic culture was the Soka Gakkai's mission. It was also his conviction that the fostering of art and culture would demonstrate the greatness of Buddhism.

Knowing that music transcended national and ethnic barriers and was a language that could bring people together, Shin'ichi was certain that a brass band would make a huge contribution to the creation of peace. Moreover, uplifting music would inspire and encourage members in their efforts for kosen-rufu. After giving the matter careful consideration, Shin'ichi reached the conclusion that a brass band was indispensable.

O F ALL THE Soka Gakkai leaders, only President Toda supported Shin'ichi's idea and encouraged him to go ahead with it, saying, "If that's what you want to do, Shin'ichi, then do it."

The Brass Band was officially established on May 6, 1954, following a young men's division leaders meeting at the Shibuya Public Hall in Tokyo. Assembling members who played an instrument or were interested in learning, the new group embarked on its activities.

The band's first performance was on May 9, just three days after its inauguration, during a youth division general pilgrimage to the head temple. None of the sixteen performers had their own instruments, so they had to borrow them for the band's sudden debut. It was raining that day, but the members were excited, saying to each other: "The start is crucial. Our first performance will determine whether we come out triumphant!" "We mustn't be defeated by adversity. If we win in the face of difficulty, then we will make a truly historic achievement!" Burning with a fighting spirit, the young men played valiantly amid the pouring rain.

Despite the minor setback of one of the borrowed drums becoming damaged by the rain and the potential trouble this might cause, the musicians' performance inspired the pilgrimage participants tremendously.

Shin'ichi wanted to at least be able to equip the Brass Band with its own instruments, and so he raised the money himself to do so. The Brass Band members practiced intensely and improved steadily, and Shin'ichi encouraged them at every opportunity. Eventually, the Brass Band became an integral part of the Soka Gakkai,

stirring members' spirits with their rousing renditions of
Soka Gakkai songs.

The success of the Brass Band made the young women's
division eager to start its own fife and drum corps as soon
as possible. When Shin'ichi learned of this from the young
women's division leaders, he smiled and said: "All right,
let's establish a fife and drum corps, too. But providing
instruments for the corps may be difficult. I promise to
buy them somehow or another, but please give me a little
time." Filled with hope, the young women nodded in
understanding.

At that time, the Soka Gakkai did not have the funds to
purchase instruments for the new fife and drum corps.
Shin'ichi was planning to buy them out of his own

pocket. When he had saved up the necessary amount, he asked Brass Band Leader Takeshi Arimura to make the purchase. Arimura selected secondhand fifes and drums that were in good condition from among instruments being sold by the US Army.

ON JULY 22, 1956, THE day of the Fife and Drum Corps' establishment, young women who wished to join the corps gathered at the Soka Gakkai Headquarters. None of them, however, had ever held a fife or drum before. The fife players eagerly lifted their instruments, ready for their first instruction from young men's division Brass Band Leader Takeshi Arimura. But when they put the fifes to their lips and blew, no sound came out. When they blew even harder, they became dizzy and winded. Though most of them also couldn't read music, they tried their best.

From that day, the Fife and Drum Corps members embarked on a bold challenge. They were inexperienced technically, but unrivaled in spirit and determination. The drummers, for example, were constantly vocalizing the rhythm to the music they were learning in an effort to master it. When they returned home at the end of the day, they would practice with chopsticks on a makeshift drum pad, which they fashioned by wrapping a dishcloth over a cutting board.

Rehearsals were carried out amid the members' busy schedules of work, study and Soka Gakkai activities, but no one ever complained. They all knew that starting any new endeavor required patience and effort.

The first performance of the Fife and Drum Corps

took place during the young women's division leaders meeting held at the Nakano Civic Hall in Tokyo on September 3 of the year the group was formed (1956). On that occasion, Mieko Koga, an elementary school teacher who was taking night courses at a music college, was appointed leader of the corps. There were a total of thirty-three members—ten drummers and twenty-three fife players. With Koga conducting, they played the well-loved Japanese song "Moon Over the Ruined Castle" and other favorites of the young women's division.

They had all practiced very hard, but nearly half of the fife players were still inaudible. Not yet able to read music, some of them wrote out the notes syllabically on a piece of paper and taped it to the back of the person standing in front of them. In addition, there weren't enough drum straps, so the front row of drummers rested their drums directly on the stage, which muffled the sound.

THE FIFE and Drum Corps members were all extremely nervous before their debut performance. Their hands trembled as they held their instruments and their legs shook. Though they did their best, it was far from a first-rate performance. Some of the audience humorously dubbed them the "breath band" because all that could be heard was a blowing sound as they played.

When Shin'ichi learned of this from the young women's division leaders, he smiled and said: "What people say about them now doesn't matter. The important thing is that they become the best in the world. And I know they will. I am convinced of it. The reason I am so certain is that in order to become the best, one must have a lofty goal and a strong sense of purpose. Without a clear goal, one cannot reveal one's full potential. The Soka Gakkai Fife and Drum Corps exists for the sake of kosen-rufu, for the happiness of humankind and world peace. What could be loftier?

"Therefore, if the corps members are aware of their goal and mission, they will be able to demonstrate talent greater than they ever imagined. At the same time, however, they must practice in earnest and make tremendous effort. In any undertaking, success is another word for effort. If our Fife and Drum Corps wants to surpass other groups, it has to practice harder than any other. Faith is the driving force for rising to such a challenge."

On September 23, twenty days after its debut performance, the corps participated in the youth division's third sports meet, the Festival of Youth, held at the Nihon University athletic field in Shimotakaido, Tokyo. It was their first performance in front of President Toda and Shin'ichi. Having heard of the jokes about the "breath band," Mr. Toda approached the Fife and Drum Corps before they went on and asked with genuine concern, "How is it going? Do you think you can play?"

"Yes!" the members replied enthusiastically.

"That's great," President Toda said with a smile, nodding approvingly. He then suggested they take a photograph together. He, too, had high hopes for the Fife and Drum Corps.

THE FIFE AND Drum Corps members wore cream blouses, black skirts and white sneakers for their performance in the Festival of Youth. It had rained the day before, so when they rehearsed on the wet field, both their shoes and socks became soaked with muddy water. Nevertheless, covering up the dirt on their shoes with white chalk or toothpaste, the young women played in the highest of spirits.

Compared to their debut performance, they had all made tremendous progress, but they still had some ground to cover before redeeming their "breath band" nickname. Shin'ichi praised them wholeheartedly, saying: "It was a powerful performance and I could really feel your enthusiasm. You have come a long way in a short time." He also presented each member with a pair of clean white socks.

Warm and sincere encouragement is the secret to enabling those striving to do their best to reveal their potential.

The musical skills of the Fife and Drum Corps improved

at an astonishing pace as it continued performing at various Soka Gakkai events, including a Headquarters general meeting and a young women's division general meeting. Six months after its foundation, jokes about the "breath band" had ceased completely and the Fife and Drum Corps had become the hope of the organization. Whenever Shin'ichi met with corps members, he encouraged them in earnest to become the best of its kind in the world. He would also tell them that the time would arrive when they would perform with members from other countries.

To the young women, that seemed like a far distant goal, but none of them thought it was impossible. Rather, making that aim their shared determination, they poured their entire beings into practicing each day.

The seed of determination contains within it the fruit of accomplishment. "If you want to understand what results will be manifested in the future, look at the causes that exist in the present" (WND-1, 279). Where there is true resolve, there is unremitting effort and a strong spirit of challenge. Without action, one's goals are nothing but empty dreams.

IN OCTOBER 1957, the year after the Fife and Drum Corps was formed in Tokyo, a branch was also established in the Kansai region. That same month, the first Fife and Drum Corps training session was held at the head temple. There, Shin'ichi encouraged the young women to be "as bright as the sun and as pure as the moon." And in discussions with them, he praised them as Bodhisattvas Wonderful Sound.

Bodhisattva Wonderful Sound is described in the

twenty-fourth chapter of the Lotus Sutra as residing in a land in the eastern direction called Adorned with Pure Light. He is depicted as being enormous in height with a face more beautiful than "a hundred, a thousand, ten thousand moons put together," having "a body pure gold in color, adorned with immeasurable hundreds of thousands of blessings," and possessing "splendid dignity and virtue" (see LS, 290–93).

The sutra explains that when Bodhisattva Wonderful Sound learns that Shakyamuni Buddha will be preaching the Lotus Sutra in the *saha* world, he says to Buddha Pure Flower Constellation King Wisdom, "I must journey to the saha world to do obeisance, wait on, and offer alms to Shakyamuni Buddha and to see many other bodhisattvas there" (see LS, 291). Before he leaves, Buddha Pure Flower advises him, saying, "You must not look with contempt on that land or come to think of it as mean and inferior." He informs the bodhisattva that although the *saha* world is "full of dirt, stones, mountains, foulness, and impurity," and "the Buddha is puny in stature and the numerous bodhisattvas are likewise small in form" (LS, 291), he must nevertheless respect them.

This is because those who preach the Law amid the most difficult of circumstances deserve the highest respect. Such people, this teaching says, should not be judged based on appearances, but regarded with the highest esteem. Shin'ichi wanted the members of the Fife and Drum Corps to likewise accord utmost respect to all the Soka Gakkai members working quietly and diligently for kosen-rufu, and to touch them with the music of hope and courage.

As Bodhisattva Wonderful Sound made his way to the *saha* world, the lands he passed through quaked and trembled, "seven-jeweled lotus flowers rained down and the instruments of hundreds and thousands of heavenly musicians sounded of themselves without having been struck" (LS, 293). This symbolizes the benefits and blessings of the Lotus Sutra.

Though we may proclaim the correctness of Buddhism, if proof of this is not demonstrated in society, then such claims are mere self-righteousness. Shin'ichi firmly believed that the members of the Fife and Drum Corps would communicate the greatness of Nichiren Buddhism to the entire world through their exquisite music, just as Bodhisattva Wonderful Sound had done.

SHIN'ICHI'S ENCOURAGEMENT profoundly awakened the Fife and Drum Corps members to their mission. At the time, there were about one hundred members in the corps. With some of them studying music professionally, the group's general level steadily improved, and eventually its performances became an indispensable part of all major Soka Gakkai events.

In 1958, the Fife and Drum Corps uplifted Soka Gakkai members with its performances at both the March 1 completion ceremony for the head temple's Grand Lecture Hall, which had been built and donated by the organization, as well as the ceremony on March 16, in which President Toda transferred the mission of kosen-rufu to the youth. Then, after President Toda's death on April 2, the Fife and Drum Corps led the funeral procession together with the young men's division Brass Band, their dignified music conveying the vow of disciples to carry on the mentor's legacy.

In the following month of May, a Fife and Drum Corps branch was formed in Hokkaido, followed by the establishment of one in Tohoku in July and in Kyushu in August. That December, the first nationwide Fife and Drum Corps general meeting was held in Tokyo's Shinagawa Ward, with Shin'ichi, who was then youth division chief of the general staff, in attendance. A total of 260 members participated—152 from Tokyo, 55 from Kansai, 20 from Tohoku, 17 from Kyushu and 16 from Hokkaido.

With the wish that the Fife and Drum Corps would become the best in the world, Shin'ichi spoke to the members about the true meaning of art. After the gathering, he met with representative members and encouraged them wholeheartedly as he listened to each of their reports.

Shin'ichi knew that many of the members were having difficulty finding the time and money to participate in corps practices on top of their work, studies and Soka Gakkai activities. Nevertheless, they devoted themselves earnestly to inspiring others with their hopeful melodies. Shin'ichi was touched by their wonderful sincerity. He therefore continued to encourage them as if he were paying his respects to Bodhisattva Wonderful Sound.

Encouragement is a warm breeze imparting hope to others. The word itself means to give courage. Encouraging others can help dispel their suffering and sadness and plant the seed of courage in their lives. It is an action filled with the power of regeneration. Leader is another name for one who encourages others.

O N MAY 3, 1960, AT the Headquarters general meeting where Shin'ichi was inaugurated as the third president of the Soka Gakkai, the Fife and Drum Corps played a fanfare to herald the beginning of a new age. Wearing a uniform of white blouses, skirts and socks, as well as red bow ties, they marched in their first real street parade from Tokyo's Ryogoku Municipal Hall to the Nihon University Auditorium, where the meeting was taking place.

Aiming to be best in the world, the corps never ceased to take on new challenges. In November 1961, it presented its first drill performance at the Ninth Young Women's Division General Meeting, in front of a gathering of eighty-five thousand members at the Mitsuzawa Stadium in Yokohama. This kind of performance entails moving into a variety of formations while playing music.

The young women faced many challenges in preparing for this event. Until then, they had only experienced marching in parade formation, but now they sought to create a number of moving patterns. Having never seen a drill involving more than a few dozen performers, their task of making a show with hundreds was no easy feat. They had to come up with their own ideas and plan them from scratch.

The members in charge of doing this thought of nothing else. They looked for hints in lacework patterns and the city's neon signs. When they went for a meal together, their tableware became models for drill designs. They were uncompromising in their efforts, ever striving to make the patterns more complex and exciting.

It is by challenging ourselves that we realize fresh

advancement and open the path to a glorious future. Once we stop doing so, we become deadlocked.

Finding a place where they could practice their formations with so many people was also difficult. But all of their struggles paid off, blossoming into a beautiful performance at the Ninth Young Women's Division General Meeting. In their red-and-white uniforms, the seven hundred twenty members of the Fife and Drum Corps filled the athletic ground with various patterns, including a checkerboard, and "V" and "X" formations. Amazed and impressed, the spectators applauded them vigorously.

THE FIFE AND Drum Corps came to be highly regarded by society at large, and began receiving invitations to perform at non-Soka Gakkai events, such as the opening ceremonies of a Japan-France rugby match in 1962. The young women's refreshing and tremendously skilled performances, along with their brilliant smiles, fostered greater trust in and understanding of the Soka Gakkai. In time, the corps started to function as more than a forum where young people could polish their musical talents—it became a sort of youth school where they could cultivate friendships and the spirit of teamwork, as well as forge their characters.

Shoko Odano, who would go with the corps to America and later be appointed the third Fife and Drum Corps leader, was one young woman who learned the Soka Gakkai spirit and a humanistic way of life through her involvement in the music group.

Odano had joined the corps at the encouragement of her older sister when she was in her first year of high school. Not long after doing so, she was given the responsibility of contacting several other members about rehearsal times and locations. She found that there were some people on her list who didn't show up even though she had called them. This didn't particularly bother her, however, because she felt that she had done her job by letting them know, and if they didn't attend, it was their problem. Independent and self-sufficient by nature, she didn't like to interfere in the business of others or have them interfere in hers.

But when she noticed how other members handled the same responsibility, she was surprised. When someone they had contacted failed to show up for rehearsal, they were deeply concerned. They would chant about it, receive guidance from their leaders in the corps and even go to the member's home to encourage her.

When Odano asked a fellow member why it was necessary to go to such lengths, the young woman replied: "If those members attend rehearsals and improve their skills, they'll be able to perform with us, which will be a wonderful memory of their youth. Nothing beats the feeling of creating a beautiful and inspiring performance. I think that everyone who joins the Fife and Drum Corps has that aspiration, and I really want us to be able to achieve our goal together. That's why I will never give up. Even though no one would say anything if I made less effort, I know I would be doing myself a disservice."

Odano was embarrassed. She realized that the true Soka Gakkai spirit was to care more for others than for oneself.

ODANO WAS DEEPLY moved by the earnest efforts of her leaders who, though none were professional musicians, strove to make the Fife and Drum Corps the best in the world. Inspired by their spirit, she thought about how she, too, could contribute to achieving that dream. The conclusion she reached was that perhaps what the corps needed most at that point was to acquire a higher level of technical knowledge and expertise. As a result, despite being somewhat unsure of her own talent, she decided to enroll in music school in order to be of greater use to the Fife and Drum Corps.

Each person has a mission. True unity is born when each person stands up and carries out his or her personal mission to the fullest. That is also the way to create a new history.

Shin'ichi was happy to see the Fife and Drum Corps gradually becoming more technically sophisticated. He wanted to support the young women in taking their place on the world stage and wished that, as they engaged in exchanges with the Soka Gakkai Fife and Drum Corps being established in other countries, they would fill the world with the music of hope. It was with that desire that, after the Japan-US Fife and Drum Corps friendship exchange meeting held in Tokyo in August 1968, he proposed that the Fuji Fife and Drum Corps go to the United States in July 1969.

In March 1969, after the one hundred forty members who would make the trip to America were confirmed, the Fife and Drum Corps performed at a Headquarters leaders meeting held at the Tokyo Metropolitan Gymnasium. Many of the meeting participants, however, felt that there was something lackluster about the performance, which was meant to celebrate the forthcoming trip. The young women had improved technically, but somehow their music wasn't stirring.

Shin'ichi expressed his true sentiments to the youth division leaders: "Today's Fife and Drum Corps performance seemed devoid of the spirit that the young women conveyed on that day when, covered with mud, they were so eager to inspire the members. That's a pity."

When Shin'ichi's remarks were passed on to the Fife and Drum Corps members, they understood what he meant. Caught up in the idea of going overseas, they had been concentrating on superficial techniques in order to impress people with their skills. Their focus had been solely on making themselves look good. They had also felt that because they had worked so hard in the past, they must be good enough now. But this was just complacency and negligence. In the end, their attitude had been transmitted through their performance.

THE FIFE AND Drum Corps members decided to go back to their starting point of faith, and challenged themselves afresh with sincere chanting. As the great composer Beethoven wrote, "Music must make the fire of the human spirit blaze."[7]

The members of the Soka Gakkai Fife and Drum Corps and Brass Band have a mission to set alight the flame of joy and courage in people's hearts through their inspiring music. Toward that end, their own spirits must burn brightly with the light of faith.

The Fife and Drum Corps members who would be traveling to the United States practiced almost every day from April through July. When they met, they studied Nichiren Daishonin's writings and guidance from Soka Gakkai publications to reconfirm their mission for kosen-rufu. They were also strict and uncompromising with each other as they strove to maintain a high musical standard. One passage in particular became their shared guidance: "My followers, . . . you had better cut short your sleep by night and curtail your leisure by day, and ponder this! You must not spend your lives in vain and regret it for ten thousand years to come" (WND-1, 622).

Though the trumpet or string players, who would be playing in the orchestra for the joint Japan-US performance, might split their lips or cut their fingers, they never slackened their efforts. In addition, everyone gave their all at their jobs so that they could receive time off for the trip. Some arrived at their workplaces an hour or more early each morning, while others cut their lunch hours short.

In mid-July, having heard about the intense efforts the Fife and Drum Corps members were making, Shin'ichi dropped in on one of their meetings taking place in a facility near the Soka Gakkai Headquarters so that he could encourage them. When he arrived at the entrance to the building, he called out, "Thank you all so much for your hard work!" The members standing nearby gasped in surprise and the others hurried to join them. "You're really doing your best," Shin'ichi said. "I hope you will perform once more at the July Headquarters Leaders Meeting." The members' eyes lit up with determination.

On July 20, the Fife and Drum Corps orchestra, wearing the new uniforms they had acquired for their upcoming trip, performed the march "Le Pere de la Victoire" by the French composer Louis Ganne under the direction of Fife and Drum Corps Leader Fumiko Takamura. Their music was powerful and resonated with fresh spirit, its beautiful and stirring sound captivating the audience.

WHEN THE FIFE and Drum Corps performance at the July Headquarters Leaders Meeting finished, the Nihon University Auditorium fell momentarily silent before erupting in thunderous applause. Assured that the corps' upcoming US performance was going to be a great success, Shin'ichi leaned forward in his seat and applauded vigorously. He wished to sincerely commend the members' hard work and diligence.

There can be no victory without earnest and strenuous effort. Those who have had the opportunity to truly temper and forge themselves in their youth are fortunate. That is because genuine happiness lies in possessing a brilliant spirit that can never be defeated, no matter what hardships we may face. It is not others, nor our fate or the times we live in, which make us unhappy; it is our own weaknesses.

Inner weakness is the ultimate cause of unhappiness. It is what prevents us from rousing hope or courage and leads us to give up. It is what makes us fall into apathy and self-destructive patterns of behavior, what causes us to hold grudges against others and fills us with self-loathing. That is why, in order to lead a happy life, the most important thing of all is to forge and develop our inner strength when we are young.

When Shin'ichi heard of the Fife and Drum Corps' tremendous success in America, he thought: *If the Fife and Drum Corps members can maintain the determination, spirit and sense of mission with which they went to the United States, as well as keep up their hard work, they are certain to be unrivaled in the world. I'm sure they will all become great victors in life.* Cheering them on in his heart and visualizing each of their faces, Shin'ichi continued to pray for their growth.

With their performance in the United States as a springboard, the Fife and Drum Corps advanced proudly toward their lofty goal of achieving unsurpassed musical excellence. They were given many opportunities to perform overseas, including traveling to the Soviet Union together with Shin'ichi in a trip that surmounted the barriers of ideology, in 1974. They would also go on to repeatedly win top prizes in Japanese national marching band competitions.

Today, there are more than twenty thousand Fife and Drum Corps members in Japan alone, and corps have been formed in twenty-six countries and territories around the world. The hope-filled melodies of these emissaries of peace are echoing vibrantly into the skies of the twenty-first century.

A TOTAL OF one hundred thousand members participated in the Soka Gakkai's 1969 summer training course at the head temple, which was held from July 30 through August 28 in thirteen three-day, two-night sessions. Participants included members of the young men's student division, the high school, junior high and elementary school divisions, the young men's division, the men's division, the culture bureau, the young women's division, the women's division and international members. During that period, Shin'ichi stayed at the head temple to oversee the training course, as well as to wholeheartedly encourage the members.

As the training course approached, he said to the leaders in charge: "Let us foster one hundred thousand capable people who will shoulder responsibility for the coming decade. I will pour all my energy into this effort with the determination to carry on a life-to-life dialogue with each of the one hundred thousand participants!

"For the members, each training session is a brief three days and two nights, but if, in that short time, they can transform their inner determination and their life-condition, they will develop into wonderful leaders and reveal their vast potential. An airplane's direction can be changed to go either to the east or the west by a slight movement of the control stick. In the same way, the direction of history can change in a single moment.

"How, then, can you enable the members on this course to transform their determination and how can you create a tide of the great victory of Buddhism? It is up to your inner resolve as leaders. One person's strong resolve inspires another's. Toward that end, all of you must be determined to waste not a minute in meeting with and sincerely encouraging the members, possessing the attitude that now is the last moment of your life."

Shin'ichi also proposed, "Let's have all the participants sign their names in an album. I'd like to observe their progress during the next three to five years." True to his words, Shin'ichi spared no effort in talking with the participants, striving to plant the seed of fresh determination in the lives of all one hundred thousand of them.

Attending an outdoor gathering held for the young men's division, he did his utmost to encourage the members, whom he deeply respected and regarded as his younger brothers. When the meeting was finished, he stood atop a small hill to see them off, waving until every last one had disappeared from sight. Microphone in hand, his voice grew hoarse as he called out to them with all his might: "Stay well! I'll be sending you my prayers!" His sincerity touched the young men deeply.

CULTURE BUREAU MEMBERS and two thousand overseas members from thirty-seven countries and territories around the world participated in the eighth session of the training course, held from August 16 through 18. Shin'ichi wanted to do whatever he could to encourage the overseas members, who had traveled to Japan with a burning desire to deepen their faith. He therefore set time aside to join them in commemorative photographs, and on another occasion, he personally served them slices of watermelon.

He also attended a mini culture festival at the temple's open field that was put on by members from Japan and abroad to celebrate the training course. The weather had been unsettled, and in the midst of the event, it began to rain. Unfazed, Shin'ichi continued to watch the overseas members' song and dance performances. He then picked up the towel that was on the table in front of him and handed it to a member sitting nearby, saying: "You're getting wet. Please use this."

Some members had umbrellas, while others didn't. After instructing the young men's division event staff to gather all the umbrellas from the lodging temples and bring them to the field, he grabbed the microphone and called out, "Everyone, please open your umbrellas!" He himself was soaked to the skin as he said this.

A member shouted: "Sensei! Please open one, too!"

"Don't worry about me," Shin'ichi responded. "I'm OK!" The members were surprised and deeply moved by his consideration.

A person's behavior eloquently reveals what is in his or her heart.

Gradually, the rain began to fall harder, and rivulets of water started streaming down the participants' faces. Representatives from thirty-seven countries and territories were on the stage. A leader sitting nearby remarked to Shin'ichi, "There are still many performances to go, but perhaps we should cancel at this point."

"If we do that," Shin'ichi replied, "the members who

have worked so hard to prepare for this day will be terribly disappointed. Let's think of another solution."

He then stood up and began making his way through the crowd toward the stage, members cheering and crowding around in order to shake his hand. Smiling warmly, Shin'ichi thanked them and offered them words of encouragement as he went.

SHIN'ICHI CLIMBED onto the stage and said to the performers, "Your performances have been wonderful, your singing and dancing truly uplifting and inspiring." He shook their hands as he praised their efforts.

Amid the pouring rain, he then picked up the microphone and addressed the entire gathering, "I don't want you to catch colds, so I'd like to propose that we halt the culture festival at this point."

A cloud of disappointment passed over the faces of those who had not yet performed, but with Shin'ichi's next words, their mood immediately changed.

"Let's move to the Grand Lecture Hall and finish the festival there instead. How about it?" At this, the members cheered and applauded.

Shin'ichi continued: "I know how hard you've all rehearsed for this day, and I really want to see the entire show. But the rain is too heavy now, so let's return to the lodging temples first, dry ourselves off, take a break and then we'll resume the festival later."

Shin'ichi's suggestion was full of consideration for the members. It is by always thinking about what will bring the members joy and contribute to their well-being that a leader is able to take the most appropriate action in any given situation.

The culture festival resumed in the Grand Lecture Hall with a folk dance by the Okinawa arts division, a ninety-eight-piece koto concert, and other performances. It became a memorable festival of friendship and peace.

Shin'ichi did his utmost to encourage all the members attending the various sessions during that summer's training course at the head temple. For example, he went with student division representatives to the nearby Shiraito Falls and took a boat ride with them. He also spent time conversing with women's division members under the trees on the temple grounds, listening to them talk about family matters or their children's education and sharing his thoughts with them.

The summer training course offered a wonderful opportunity to foster capable people. Shin'ichi knew that if he failed to make the most of it, it would be a setback to the carefully thought-out vision of kosen-rufu. That's why each day was absolutely crucial. He did everything he could possibly think of to encourage the members.

Shin'ichi believed that to waste even a moment and neglect what needed to be done was to make a cause for future regret, and he felt that to have regret was a disgrace to life.

O N THE MORNING of August 17, the second day of the culture bureau training session, which was the eighth session to take place during this summer course, the inaugural ceremony for the writers division was held. It was another landmark event in the effort to realize the creation of a humanistic culture.

The writers division was composed of authors, journalists and others who were engaged in literary activities. The establishment of the division had been announced at the Headquarters leaders meeting in December of the previous year (1968), with Akira Usuda appointed as division leader. The twenty-nine-year-old Usuda was a magazine editor with a deep appreciation for literature. While a student in the University of Tokyo's Faculty of Law, he participated in Shin'ichi's lectures on *The Record of the Orally Transmitted Teachings*, which solidified his resolve to devote his life to writing for the sake of kosen-rufu.

Usuda was in charge of the preparations for the writers division's establishment, and division members were selected from among Soka Gakkai members who were authors, journalists and poets. Student division members who showed promise as future writers were also chosen. In total, more than fifty people were selected as the division's first class.

At eleven in the morning on the second day of the culture bureau training session, the writers division members assembled in front of the Sessen-bo lodging temple, from where Shin'ichi was overseeing training course activities.

Wearing an open-necked white shirt, Shin'ichi stepped out of the building and said, "Thank you for coming!"

The members greeted him cheerfully in response.

"I've been looking forward to seeing you!" Shin'ichi added. "Well, then, let's begin the inaugural ceremony."

He picked up the flag that had been prepared for the occasion. The banner displayed a lion's profile in red on a white background, with the Latin word *littera,* from which the word *literature* derived, beneath it. The graphic was encircled by a laurel wreath in navy blue.

Presenting the flag to Usuda, he then said with expectation ringing in his voice, "Please become a division of the most capable writers!"

"We will!" the members replied with determination.

Shin'ichi imagined a towering mountain range of brilliant writers stretching into the future. He was certain that if the writers division members were firmly resolved and strove each day to overcome their own limitations while continuously advancing, there was nothing they could not accomplish.

NEXT, THE MEMBERS of the new writers division were introduced. Each person energetically replied, "Present!" when their name was called. After several members were announced, Shin'ichi reprimanded the leader reading out the list, saying: "All of the writers division members are literary figures, so they should be addressed with the honorific title *sensei*. Please start again from the beginning and announce their names using *sensei*."

The members were both surprised and embarrassed to hear Shin'ichi say this. Among them were a few famous authors of children's books and historical novels, but the majority of them were still completely unknown. Some did part-time jobs to support themselves as they pursued their writing, while others were university students who hoped to be writers someday in the future.

Shin'ichi's insistence that they all be called *sensei* revealed the incredibly high expectations he held for them. It was his fervent wish that many outstanding writers who would bring about a renaissance of humanistic literature would emerge from the new division.

The appointments were read again, this time with the honorific *sensei* following each name. While some of the appointees responded proudly, others blushed as they bashfully answered to the call. Shin'ichi shook each individual's hand with deep respect.

"I will forever keep each of your names and faces etched on my heart," he said. "Now, it's hot out here, so let's go inside."

A guidance meeting ensued inside the Sessen-bo lodging temple.

"I hope that all of you, the members of the writers division, will truly become accomplished in your respective field," Shin'ichi began. "If you do, the pace of kosen-rufu will speed up dramatically. I would like to see many of you receive illustrious literary prizes. At the same time, however, there is no need to be overly concerned with winning prizes. The important thing is how many people are moved and inspired by your work. If your writings gain the support and praise of the public, it will also be wonderful proof of the greatness of Buddhism.

"To achieve this, you need to challenge yourselves. Each day is crucial. Without making diligent and continuous effort to break out of your shell and forge open a vast state of life, you cannot triumph in society. This is because your competitors are giving their all to their work as well."

SHIN'ICHI YAMAMOTO spoke with great conviction: "I, too, am always writing—not only my serialized novel, but also articles and manuscripts requested by different publishers. There have been times when I was running a fever of nearly 102 degrees Fahrenheit, but even then I picked up my pen and pressed on, knowing that I couldn't stop. Things that I wrote amid such circumstances received a particularly powerful response from readers.

"It is said that writing reveals a person's character. In other words, it reflects one's heart, one's spirit, one's state of being. Indeed, the entire inner reality of one's life is manifested in one's writing. That is why writing that is born of pain and struggle, and that overflows with burning passion, touches people's lives.

"The same is true of our interactions with others—they are moved by our sincerity and earnestness, by our honest and enthusiastic appeals. It is important to win people's hearts. I hope that, with the determination to significantly contribute to the happiness of others, you will open your eyes to the world of thought and philosophy and become active in your respective fields of endeavor."

Lastly, Shin'ichi added: "I am very happy about the establishment of the writers division. I'd like to celebrate by having dinner together with you sometime in the near future."

The inaugural meeting for the new division thus came to an end. Shin'ichi regarded this as the start of a great stream of writers dedicated to upholding the spirit of Soka. The next step was how to broaden this flow. Shin'ichi keenly felt there was a need for a fresh flourishing of literary art based on Nichiren Buddhism.

The European Renaissance, considered the birth of the modern world, liberated humanity from the chains of Church authority and a worldview centered on God. With its call for a return to classical values and an emphasis on the human being, it was an age that celebrated freedom and established the victory of humanity. From that liberated spirit, an unprecedented new literary culture was born.

With the writings of such fourteenth-century Italian figures as Dante, Petrarch and Boccaccio, a great literary revival spread through Western Europe, giving rise to a number of prominent authors, including Erasmus in the Netherlands, Rabelais in France and Thomas More in England.

WHILE THE RENAISSANCE, which sought the liberation of humankind, did give people spiritual freedom, ironically, it did not bring them happiness and peace. The freedom initiated by the Renaissance brought about the dawn of the modern age and the rapid development of science and technology. But progress in these spheres was powerfully driven by human greed, ever-growing and unquenchable. This led to people being controlled by machines, to the creation of nuclear weapons and environmental pollution, and to the inhumanity and alienation of industrial society.

The Swiss historian Jacob Burckhardt described the Renaissance as the discovery of the world and the "whole nature of man."[8] The Renaissance did indeed bring to light the greatness of human beings, the protagonists of society, but it did not illuminate the profound inner reality of human life itself. As a result, it was not yet a complete discovery of humanity. It also failed to adequately elucidate life's complex interconnections—such as between love and hate, right and wrong, devotion and domination, self-sacrifice and ambition—that cause people to commit evil acts in spite of wishing to do good. And it did not restore true independence to the human being.

Now, however, the supreme teaching of Nichiren Daishonin's Buddhism, with its full explanation of human existence, was spreading widely throughout the world. It was therefore time to bring about a new Renaissance, a revival of literature and the arts, based on Buddhism. Japanese literature had long been in a state of stagnation and decline, with a dearth of great works displaying a high level of thought or philosophy. The decline of literature signals a decline in thought and a loss of interest in the written word, and leads to a deterioration of the human spirit.

The French philosopher Jean-Paul Sartre[9] once asked how literature could help starving children. Shin'ichi was deeply concerned about the future of Japanese literature in that it was losing its power to influence even the children of Japan, which was, at the time, enjoying a period of prosperity due to high economic growth.

Kosen-rufu is a struggle to revitalize all spheres of life—including literature, education and government—for the sake of human happiness.

THE DINNER that Shin'ichi promised to have with the members of the writers division took place the following month, on September 27, at a sukiyaki restaurant in Aoyama, Tokyo. When the meal began, one of the members—a middle-aged man wearing black-rimmed glasses—approached Shin'ichi holding a book. It was the children's author Wakaba Osada.

"This is a book I recently published," Osada said, presenting the volume to Shin'ichi. It was titled *The Future of Children's Literature.*

"Thank you," Shin'ichi replied as he accepted it. "I'll read it right away. I've heard much about you, Mr. Osada."

Osada was a well-known children's author who was a permanent board member of the Japan Juvenile Writer's Association, and a member of such prominent Japanese literary organizations as the Japanese Association of Writers for Children and the Japan P.E.N. Club.

Born in Osaka, Osada decided to become a writer out of his profound admiration for two alumni of the old-system junior high school he attended—Soichi Oya,[10] a renowned social commentator, and Yasunari Kawabata,[11] winner of the Nobel Prize in literature. After working as a teacher at a girls' high school, he set out to fulfill his dream. His career as a children's author began when the editor of a boys' magazine asked him to write a story for the publication.

At that time, most children's writing in Japan consisted of fairy tales and nursery rhymes, as well as works that were simply shallow and frivolous. Concerned about the lack of rich literary nourishment available to children, Osada felt that a new kind of children's literature needed to be created—something in the spirit of a novel that respects the character of young readers and explores human themes in a pure and wholesome fashion.

He thus concluded that he must assemble like-minded authors and form an association. He worked hard to realize this goal, meeting with writers and children's authors and passionately making his case for the development of a new genre in children's literature. He was extremely tenacious as he threw his entire being into the effort. Believing that nothing was more shameful than to abandon a goal without giving it his all and that doing so would be an insult to his convictions, Osada urged himself on to the best of his ability.

His earnest endeavors drew others to his cause and in 1939 he founded the Children's Literature Symposium.

MANY NOTED JAPANESE writers and poets joined the Children's Literature Symposium, among them Yasunari Kawabata, Soichi Oya, Masuji Ibuse, Koji Uno, Mimei Ogawa, Joji Tsubota, Yoshio Toyoshima and Shiro Murano. With Wakaba Osada as the symposium chairperson, the group published a journal titled *Juvenile Literature,* and the momentum for creating a new field of literature increased.

Wishing to blaze the trail in the endeavor, Osada wrote a long children's novel, which he titled *The Boy from the Land of Cherry Trees*. In the foreword, Yasunari Kawabata praised Osada's energetic commitment and efforts to revitalize children's literature.

At that time, Japan was being assailed by the harsh winds of militarism, and children's literature was strictly censored and used to promote national prestige. During this dark period, Osada compiled books for children in an effort to leave behind fine children's literature. Because of wartime shortages, it was difficult to secure paper for printing, but one publishing company took on the job of publishing Osada's books. It was the company run by Josei Toda, then general director of the Soka Gakkai.

World War II finally came to an end and freedom returned to Japan. But Osada suffered from tuberculosis and was forced to spend several years recuperating. Still, he fought valiantly against his illness, steadily producing a stream of fine works and gaining distinction as a children's writer.

Then fate dealt him another blow. In his late fifties, he had a heart attack. Fortunately, he survived, and after two years of convalescence he was once again able to write. At just that time, he was paid a visit by a young editor, who requested that he contribute a series of stories based on Japanese folklore to a children's monthly magazine.

Having still not fully regained his strength, Osada was reluctant to accept, but the young woman pleaded with him, her eyes shining with enthusiasm. "Children are losing their dreams," she said. "I would very much like you to write stories that give them hope, courage and vision for the future, and that cultivate rich spirituality in their lives." Her voice rang with firm conviction.

The young woman's pure spirit reminded Osada of himself in earlier days, and he felt inspired. He agreed to write the stories she requested.

The editor was a member of the Soka Gakkai young women's division.

EACH TIME Wakaba Osada went to the publisher to discuss the stories he would write for the magazine, he would leave a hired car and driver waiting outside for him. Because of his poor health, he wanted to be able to return home immediately after concluding his business. Learning of this, the young editor started to chant for his health. She felt terribly sorry for this man who, despite enjoying fame and status as a well-known children's writer, suffered from illness.

One day, she decided to talk to him about Nichiren Buddhism. "Mr. Osada," she began, "Buddhism is the law of life that enables us to tap our strongest life force. It is also a philosophy that gives us the power to change our karma and establish indestructible happiness. You have made numerous wonderful accomplishments in your life until now, but even more important, I believe, is the kind of life you lead from this moment on. I really want you to be healthy and strong, and to write many books that will be spiritual treasures for the children who will shoulder the twenty-first century."

The editor was young enough to be Osada's daughter, but her sincerity touched him deeply. Having also heard from a friend that Josei Toda, who had helped him publish a book during World War II, had become the second Soka Gakkai president, he decided to give Nichiren Buddhism a try. After joining the Soka Gakkai and beginning to chant, he felt incredible energy well forth from within, and gradually his health improved.

As he studied Buddhism's profound philosophy of life, Osada developed a strong desire to create humanistic literature based on Buddhist teachings. He was thus thrilled when he heard about the establishment of the Soka Gakkai writers division and joyfully attended its inauguration.

In addition to Osada, several other renowned children's writers, including the author of the famous children's novel *Child of War,* and the author of such children's stories as *Mister Three O'Clock* and *The Lost Donut*, became members of the new division.

At the dinner celebrating the group's establishment, Shin'ichi spoke about the importance of children's literature, saying: "As Japanese society's obsession with economic growth increases, I am concerned that the environment for fostering children's sound development is being polluted and eroded. This makes the role of children's literature all the more important in terms of creating a bright future."

SHIN'ICHI CONTINUED speaking with greater force: "Fostering the next generation means cultivating human character and nurturing the youth. The key to doing this is to nourish the hearts of young people, to teach them the best way to live as human beings. This is the fundamental mission of education, and should be made a top priority by both the nation and society.

"Should we fail to do this, though we may enjoy economic prosperity for a time, we are certain to reach an impasse in the future. If our children's hearts become impoverished, it will lead to society's collapse. And if Japan forgets about the spiritual development of its people, it is sure to end up as a third-rate nation. Together with all of you, I will do my utmost to support the development of our country's children, the protagonists of the future. We are laying the foundation for Japan four or five decades hence. In every age, Soka Gakkai leaders must pour their energies into raising successors. I say this to you in the hope that you will carry on this legacy."

Wakaba Osada and the other writers at the dinner nodded in agreement as they listened to Shin'ichi speak. Looking closely at each of them, he added: "The family plays the most important role in raising children, and children's literature is a very important tool for parents. It could be described as a child's first teacher in life. In my case, given that my wife spends the most time with our children, I have asked her to read many books to them. If parents take such action during their child's early developmental stages, the experience will stay with the child throughout his or her life.

"I hope that, as children's authors, you will live long and write many more fine books. I, too, will try my hand at children's literature. Let's work together."

Shin'ichi went on to do just that. Five years later he wrote his first children's story, *The Cherry Tree.* After that he published *The Snow Country Prince, The Princess and the Moon, Over the Deep Blue Sea* and many others. He also wrote a number of novels, such as *Journey to Hiroshima* for junior high school students and *Alexander's Decision* for high school students.

SHIN'ICHI CONTINUED to do everything he could to support and encourage the writers division members. For example, at the group's summer training course in 1970, he spent time talking with them under the shade of some trees on the head temple grounds. He also kept track of the members' personal situations and wrote poems to celebrate their gatherings, such as:

> *Benefits blossom*
> *as the lotus flower*
> *blooms from the mud.*

★

*If you act with firm resolve
the result will follow.
This is Buddhist practice.*

When several members had published new titles, Shin'-ichi held a reception for them and other division representatives at a prestigious hotel in Tokyo. He also took commemorative photographs with the members. In 1971, the group appointed its first secretary, and leaders were also designated in four different regions, including Kansai and Tohoku, further expanding the organization.

Hideki Isomura, who was made writers division leader of the Chugoku Region, was a teacher at a prefectural high school in Yamaguchi Prefecture and also a dedicated writer. While a student at Tokyo Imperial University (forerunner of present-day University of Tokyo) during World War II, he was mobilized and sent to the front in Southeast Asia. Narrowly escaping death, he made his way back to Japan. It was then that he determined to devote his life to the art of poetry.

He founded a poetry journal entitled *The Camel,* and in 1951 won the first Yamaguchi Prefecture Art and Culture Promotion Award for his poetry collection, *The Floating Lighthouse.* He also wrote numerous verse dramas, plays and children's stories.

Then, in the spring of 1965, Isomura was cast into the depths of despair when his second son suddenly contracted acute myelocytic leukemia. One day when Isomura returned home he heard voices chanting. Desperate to save their son, his wife had joined the Soka Gakkai. The thirteen-year-old boy had a high fever and was physically very weak, but together with his mother he sat in front of the Buddhist altar and chanted earnestly, his clear eyes steadily focused on the Gohonzon. Observing the sincerity with which his son prayed, Isomura felt he was seeing genuine human strength. He decided to chant with them, and in January of the next year, 1966, he also took faith.

When the doctors first diagnosed the boy, they said he might not survive another month. He lived, however, until the following March, when he passed away with a peaceful smile on his face.

ISOMURA FELT as if he had glimpsed life's mystery in his son's battle against illness and his death. He thus began to earnestly study the Buddhist philosophy of life. Struck by the profundity of such concepts as the eternity of life spanning the three existences, the mutual possession of the Ten Worlds, the oneness of body and mind, and the oneness of life and its environment, he set out to break new ground in the field of literature, making Buddhism the basis of his thought.

Gisuke Ikenaka, the Kansai Region writers division leader, once ran a produce store. When business was slow, he wrote novels, and later submitted them to literary contests. After winning several awards, he eventually became a full-time writer. When a new radio station opened in Kobe, he wrote a radio drama that ended up airing for eight years. He also created scripts for TV dramas and published serialized novels in sports newspapers, spending every waking hour at his craft.

Ikenaka often had the sense that something was missing from his work, but he didn't have the time to give it much thought. He was continuously plagued by the worry that he would be forgotten if he didn't keep writing.

Then in his mid–forties, at the peak of his productive years, he was afflicted with acute tuberculous pleurisy. That led to his joining the Soka Gakkai in January 1962. He eventually recovered from his illness, but at the same time, his contact with other Soka Gakkai members started him questioning his way of life until that point.

"Why are Soka Gakkai members so devoted to helping others?" he wondered. "Whenever they encounter people who are suffering, they listen to their troubles and encourage them, and when those people have overcome their problems, they rejoice with them wholeheartedly. They are unselfish and uncalculating.

"They're not just all talk; they actually strive with utter

sincerity. I feel that I am witnessing real and genuine goodness in their behavior. Compared to them, what have I done with my life so far? For what purpose have I been working? In the end, I've been solely motivated by a desire for fame and wealth. And to top it off, I became ill. I really must change my life."

He felt he had lost his true self in his pursuit of celebrity.

WHAT SURPRISED IKENAKA even more was the abounding joy with which members participated in Soka Gakkai activities while struggling with financial or health problems. This shook the very foundations of his personal values and worldview. He realized that his own ideas of happiness and unhappiness, of fortune and misfortune, were altogether superficial and abstract, and that he had been ignorant of the essential nature of human existence. If that was the case, he thought, how could he possibly write stories that would truly inspire others?

After coming to this realization, the popular writer found it hard to pick up his pen—or rather, he consciously resolved not to write for a time. He decided to make a fresh start in his life as a Soka Gakkai member and strive to polish and elevate his life-condition. He wanted to develop the wisdom to see the reality of human existence.

Having stopped writing, Ikenaka suffered financially. He was forced to sell his precious book collection and cash in his insurance policy in order to make ends meet. But he was excited about this new beginning. He chanted earnestly and shelved his writing to participate in Soka

Gakkai activities. He spoke with many members who had overcome bankruptcy or severe illness and were enjoying lives of happiness. He talked with women who worked full time while raising their children and with young factory workers who aspired to go abroad.

Through his participation in Soka Gakkai activities, Ikenaka learned about true human brilliance and strength and came to appreciate the incredible potential of all people. His inner realm was transformed and he began to feel fresh creativity stir in the depths of his being.

It was about this time that the writers division was formed and he was selected as one of its founding members. He resolved to pick up his pen again, and went on to write many historical novels that demonstrated a superb insight into the human condition. His comeback was a perfect example of the passage from Nichiren Daishonin's writings, "*Myo* [of Nam-myoho-renge-kyo] means to revive, that is, to return to life" (WND-I, 149).

With leaders such as Ikenaka and Isomura dedicated to fostering young writers, the division went on to produce many great Japanese authors and literary award winners, as well as journalists dedicated to truth and justice.

The creation of a magnificent culture based on humanism—this is the noble mission of the Soka Gakkai.

Notes

1. See Florence Nightingale, *To the Probationer-Nurses of the Nightingale Fund School, at St. Thomas's Hospital* (London: Blades, East and Blades, 1886), p. 6.

2. One of the ten mystic principles set forth by T'ien-t'ai (538–597) in *The Profound Meaning of the Lotus Sutra* interpreting the word *myo* of *Myoho-renge-kyo*, the title of the Lotus Sutra. The mystic principle of responsive communion means that the Buddha appears in order to respond to the peopole's desire to seek him is mystic. (See *The Soka Gakkai Dictionary of Buddhism*, pp. 674–75.)

3. Florence Nightingale, *Notes on Nursing: What It Is and What It Is Not* (London: Harrison, 1860), p. 3.

4. Rabindranath Tagore (1861–1941).

5. See *The English Writings of Rabindranath Tagore* (New Delhi: Sahitya Akademi, 1996), vol. 2, p. 328.

6. Akita Prefecture: Located in northern Honshu, Japan's main island, approximately 410 miles away from Tokyo.

7. Translated from French. Romain Rolland, *La Vie de Beethoven* (Paris: Librairie Hachette, 1927), p. 119.

8. Jacob Burckhardt, *The Civilization of the Renaissance of Italy* (London: Penguin Books, 1990), p. 198.

9. Jean-Paul Sartre (1905–80).

10. Soichi Oya (1900–70).

11. Yasunari Kawabata (1899–1972).

Fierce Winds

THE GREAT French writer Victor Hugo declared: "We must continue fighting day and night. We must fight in the mountains, on the plains and in the forests. Arise! Arise! Never rest!"[1]

Shin'ichi gave every ounce of his strength to carrying out his struggle. At the May 1969 Soka Gakkai Headquarters General Meeting, he announced a new goal of achieving 7.5 million member-households by May 3 of the following year, which would mark his tenth anniversary as Soka Gakkai president. This was ten times the membership that his mentor, second Soka Gakkai president Josei Toda, had sought to accomplish during his lifetime.

It would be no easy feat to realize this target while at the same time working to solidify the organization's foundation and to widely spread the ideal of Buddhist humanism throughout society. But doing so was critical to actualizing the great vision of kosen-rufu. This was why Shin'ichi was resolved to throw his entire being into the endeavor. He believed that victory hinged on fostering as many exceptional leaders as possible who would advance with the same spirit and awareness as he, and that the way to do this was to meet with and wholeheartedly encourage members in every corner of Japan.

On September 2, after completing the annual August summer training course at the head temple, Shin'ichi attended a Kansai leaders meeting in Kyoto, and then traveled to Osaka, Nara and Aichi prefectures. In mid-September he flew to Hokkaido, and in early October returned to the Kansai Region before moving on to Shikoku and then the Tohoku Region in the latter half of the month. In November he went to the Chubu, Kansai and Kyushu regions, and in early December he went once again to the Kansai, Chugoku and Chubu regions. At this time, he also visited the island of Awajishima. In between these long-distant guidance trips, he also made efforts to encourage members living in Tokyo and the nearby prefectures of Shizuoka, Kanagawa, Yamanashi and Ibaraki.

His schedule was extremely full, but everywhere he went he poured his entire being into inspiring each person he encountered. While in transit, he read members' letters to him, looked over documents that required his approval and each day wrote messages in the flyleaves of hundreds of books to send to members.

The strain of this intense struggle wore Shin'ichi out, and in mid-December he came down with a high fever. This, however, did not impede his incredible momentum.

ON DECEMBER 20, 1969, Shin'ichi sat slumped in his seat on the bullet train as he headed for Shin-Osaka Station. It was his seventh guidance tour to Kansai that year. He wore a large surgical mask so as not to infect others. His fever refused to abate, his throat was rough and irritated, and he could not stop coughing. Yet in spite of all this, he was filled with a fighting spirit.

Shin'ichi had fallen ill several times while traveling overseas, but he had never had such a high fever or severe cough. He was in bad shape. Observing his condition, one of the leaders traveling with him said in a worried tone: "President Yamamoto, you seem to be very ill. I think we should contact your wife and ask her to come and look after you, just in case." Shin'ichi nodded and replied, "Yes, that might be a good idea, just to be on the safe side."

Shin'ichi was determined to give his all to this Kansai visit in order to secure the future advancement of kosen-rufu. If the Kansai organization could take the lead of the entire Soka Gakkai by winning in every campaign it initiated, a fresh flow of kosen-rufu would be opened. This was because it would mark the beginning of a new era of development in which local regions played a central role. For that reason, it was crucial that this particular visit to Kansai be a great success.

Two days earlier, Shin'ichi had called his family together and said resolutely: "I'm going to Kansai despite my terrible physical condition. I may collapse or have to be hospitalized during the trip." At the time, Shin'ichi's oldest son Masahiro was sixteen, his second son Hisahiro was fourteen and his youngest son Hirotaka was eleven. They all looked at their father intently, earnestly trying to grasp his thoughts.

Shin'ichi continued: "But I'm going anyway. Kansai is engaged in a tough battle right now, and it must achieve victory for the sake of the future of kosen-rufu. The members there are waiting for me. I cannot disregard their feelings.

"Before his death, Mr. Toda also insisted on making a guidance trip to Hiroshima even though his health was extremely weak. As his disciple, I cannot allow the advance of kosen-rufu to be halted or delayed."

SHIN'ICHI GAZED at the faces of Mineko and each of his sons. He then remarked, wanting to make sure they were ready for anything, "What I'm saying is that, no matter what happens, no matter how things turn out, you mustn't be alarmed or dismayed." Mineko and the boys nodded in resolute acknowledgment.

Shin'ichi also made thorough preparations in case he should collapse during the trip or be unable to speak at a meeting because of a high fever. For example, he prepared a recording of a speech he had given at a local leaders meeting on December 9 in Suginami, Tokyo, in which he had emphasized that strong faith and unity are the driving force for victory. If worse came to worse, he thought, the tape could be played instead. His firm determination to encourage the Kansai members under any circumstances was manifested in his careful preparation.

Being careless or making oversights indicates a lack of earnest commitment to standing up and taking full responsibility. If we are serious and have the strong resolve not to allow a single failure, we will naturally be meticulous. It was with such awareness that Shin'ichi agreed to ask Mineko to join him on the trip.

The itinerary for this Kansai tour included visits to Osaka, Wakayama and Nara prefectures in the three days from December 20 through 22, followed by a visit to Mie Prefecture on December 23.

It was just after half past three in the afternoon on Saturday the 20th, and the train would soon be arriving at Shin-Osaka Station. The Kansai leaders meeting was scheduled to be held at the Higashi-Osaka Municipal Central Gymnasium at five, which meant that Shin'ichi had to go directly to the venue without taking a rest.

Noticing that Shin'ichi had a fever and an awful cough, Hisao Seki, who was accompanying him from Tokyo, said in a serious tone, "President Yamamoto, we will take care of today's Kansai leaders meeting so you can rest and recuperate."

Standing next to Seki, Kazumasa Morikawa added, "Yes, please get some rest."

But Shin'ichi was adamant. "No, I'm going," he said. "My beloved Kansai members, with whom I have shared sufferings and joys, are waiting for me. I must attend. That's why I came."

THERE WAS NOTHING more the leaders could say to convince Shin'ichi otherwise. At 3:40 PM, the train pulled in to Shin-Osaka Station. The Kansai leaders waiting at the station could not hide their surprise when they saw Shin'ichi with his coat collar turned up and his face covered with a large surgical mask. "Thank you for coming!" Shin'ichi said. "I seem to have come down with a bad cold." He tried to appear cheerful, but his eyes were bloodshot.

Normally, Shin'ichi would have started asking the local leaders detailed questions about their activities, but today he headed silently toward the car. At that moment Kansai leader Seiichiro Haruki, who knew Shin'ichi well, apprehended that he was seriously ill. He felt terrible that President Yamamoto had made this trip to Kansai in such a condition.

In the car, Shin'ichi fought the chills. Though the car was heated, his body shook uncontrollably. After about an hour's drive, Shin'ichi and the others arrived at the Higashi-Osaka Municipal Gymnasium for the Kansai leaders meeting, which was about to begin.

One of the leaders in the car said: "Sensei, we will open the meeting and oversee things until it's time for your speech. Until then, please rest in the waiting room."

"All right," Shin'ichi replied. "I'll take you up on that suggestion." He wanted some time to get his symptoms under control.

As the meeting began, Shin'ichi lay on a sofa in the waiting room. Several Kansai leaders, watching Shin'ichi's labored breathing, realized the gravity of the situation and were afraid he would not be able to participate in the meeting. But all of a sudden his wheezing stopped and he stood up. "OK, let's go!" he said, and strode out of the room.

When Shin'ichi appeared on the stage, a storm of cheers and applause erupted from the audience. He bowed to the participants and walked briskly to his seat as if nothing were the matter. Everyone was happy to see him looking well.

It was Shin'ichi's determination that if he were going to engage in a struggle, he would not give the members any cause for concern.

A BANNER BEHIND the podium read, "Victorious Departure into the Next 10 Years!" Soon after Shin'ichi made his entrance, General Administrator Hisao Seki concluded his remarks. It was Shin'ichi's turn to speak.

As he mounted the podium, Shin'ichi said, "Let's begin with a cheer to express our determination at this point of victorious departure!" The members all rose from their seats.

"Great victory for Kansai!" Shin'ichi cried out energetically. The members then echoed his call. Shin'ichi's flushed face, caused by his fever, appeared to them to be a sign of his health and vigor.

Shin'ichi then delivered his speech, drawing from such writings of Nichiren Daishonin as "A Sage Perceives the Three Existences of Life" and "The Unity of Husband and Wife." He said: "We are the ones who will shoulder Japan's destiny and create a people's movement for world peace. Firmly believing this fact, let us advance together with the spirit and courage of the lion king! Nichiren Daishonin's statement, 'If a commanding general is faint-hearted, his soldiers will become cowards' (WND-1, 464), can be taken as a guideline for leadership. If leaders are timid and lack courage and passion, no one will follow them. Victory depends on the leaders' resolve.

"Nichiren also states: 'If a bow is weak, the bowstring will be slack. If the wind is gentle, the waves will never rise high. This all accords with the principles of nature' (WND-1, 464). I hope that all of you, the great generals of kosen-rufu, will stir up a fresh wave of advancement with the powerful winds of prayer. I am strongly convinced that the time has come for Kansai to create a golden record of achievement that will lead the way for the entire Soka Gakkai."

Shin'ichi's words were filled with firm resolve and the members responded with a thunderous round of applause that conveyed their own determination.

As the meeting came to a close, everyone sang Soka Gakkai songs led by youth division leaders, the general administrator and other leaders from Tokyo. When the emcee prepared to announce the end of the meeting, members shouted, "Sensei!" They wanted Shin'ichi to lead them in a Soka Gakkai song.

Shin'ichi smiled and said, "All right, then, let's sing the Osaka favorite, 'Ah, the Dawn Approaches.'"

WITH A JAPANESE FAN in hand, Shin'ichi stood up once again to lead the song. The members applauded vigorously, and the song's stirring melody began. The leaders from Tokyo who were aware of Shin'-ichi's condition wanted to jump up and stop him, but Shin'ichi proceeded resolutely. Watching him anxiously, they chanted in their hearts that he would be all right.

Shin'ichi led the song with the power and grace of a magnificent eagle soaring through the skies. Deeply moved, the Kansai members sang and clapped in time to the music with all their might, silently vowing to realize great advancement and victory. Their fighting spirit burned brightly, and their enthusiasm was irrepressible. They all felt refreshed, as if President Yamamoto was giving them his life force. For Shin'ichi, it was indeed a life-or-death struggle.

When he returned to the waiting room, Shin'ichi collapsed on the couch, completely exhausted. The leaders accompanying him knew they had to get him to bed as soon as possible. They waited until Shin'ichi could sit up, then rushed him to the Soka Gakkai Kansai Culture Center. Severe chills continued to rack Shin'ichi's body. When the group finally reached the center, Shin'ichi's bed was not yet made up. Once it was ready, he removed his suit jacket and slid under the covers with his shirt and trousers still on.

"I'm so cold. I feel like I'm in Siberia," he said.

A hot water bottle was prepared for him, but it did not help. Sick as he was, however, Shin'ichi's thoughts remained with the Kansai members, and he asked the leaders with him about them.

"I hope everyone returned home from the meeting in high spirits," he remarked. "Tomorrow we go to Wakayama. That's important, too." Shin'ichi's mind was already on his next destination.

After a short while, just before seven, his wife, Mineko, arrived. When she saw Shin'ichi's condition, she said to Fumiko Haruki, Seiichiro Haruki's wife and also a Kansai women's division leader, "I wonder if you could call a doctor."

Fumiko at first didn't know who to call, but eventually decided on a Soka Gakkai member who had a private medical practice in neighboring Moriguchi City.

THE DOCTOR COULDN'T come straightaway, but he said he would get there as quickly as possible. After thirty or forty minutes, Mineko, who had been taking care of Shin'ichi, came out of his room. Mineko always had a smile on her face, but now her expression was tense as she asked Fumiko Haruki, "Is the doctor here yet?" Mineko's behavior told Fumiko that Shin'ichi was in a bad condition.

The doctor finally arrived shortly before eight that evening and immediately began examining Shin'ichi, who told him of his cough and the tightness in his chest. The doctor took his temperature. It was a very high 104.9 degrees Fahrenheit, and the inside of Shin'ichi's mouth was white as a result. The doctor placed his stethoscope against Shin'ichi's chest and listened to his rasping breath. Discerning that Shin'ichi's lungs were seriously inflamed, the doctor diagnosed him with acute bronchial pneumonia. He decided to give the patient an injection of antibiotics as well as some oral medicine, and then observe his condition for a while.

Mineko scrutinized each medication the doctor prescribed, rejecting ones whose side effects she felt were too strong for her husband. The doctor was surprised at Mineko's knowledge of medication and her understanding of Shin'ichi's physical constitution. He realized that she must constantly be thinking about her husband's health and devotedly supporting him.

When the doctor returned to check on Shin'ichi, the latter announced determinedly: "Tomorrow I'm scheduled to go to Wakayama. I really must go. The members there are waiting for me. It's OK, isn't it?"

Shin'ichi was supposed to attend a local leaders meeting at the Wakayama Prefectural Gymnasium on the evening of the following day, December 21.

The doctor didn't know how to respond. Of course Shin'ichi was in no condition to travel. In fact, it would be wrong to let him do so. But overcome by Shin'ichi's firm resolve, the doctor couldn't refuse him. Then it occurred to him that the fresh air in Wakayama might actually do Shin'ichi good.

HESITANTLY, THE DOCTOR replied, "In order to make the trip tomorrow, your fever has to drop below one hundred degrees Fahrenheit," thinking that would be impossible. When Shin'ichi heard this, however, his eyes lit up and he said, "I see. Under one hundred degrees, right?"

An hour later, the doctor took Shin'ichi's temperature again. It had fallen slightly to 103.6 degrees Fahrenheit, and Shin'ichi had stopped coughing.

"Thank you," Shin'ichi said to him. "I feel better. I'll be fine tonight, so please go home and come back again tomorrow if you can. I'm sorry for the trouble I caused you."

The doctor was touched that Shin'ichi could be so thoughtful even though he was in such poor condition. "All right, then," he replied. "I'll be back in the morning. Please stay in bed and rest well tonight."

When the doctor had gone, Shin'ichi said to Mineko, "I really must go to Wakayama tomorrow, no matter what!"

He continued to perspire profusely through the night, changing his underclothes so frequently that he ran out of fresh ones. Though he remained in bed, he could not sleep soundly, drifting in and out of slumber all night long. Mineko sat in the next room, quietly chanting and listening closely for any sounds from Shin'ichi's room. Hearing him wheezing through the thin walls, she was beside herself with worry. In the end, unable to sleep a wink herself, she stayed up chanting until morning.

The next day, Shin'ichi tried to sit up in bed. His fever seemed to have dropped, but he remained very weak, perhaps because he hadn't eaten since the day before. Still, he had no appetite. He wanted to fortify himself by having something nutritious, but all he could manage to swallow was a few mouthfuls of broth. After he had finished what he could, Mineko said to him, "Earlier, General Administrator Morikawa stopped by with some of the other leaders to say that they would go to Wakayama in your place and ask that you please take some more time to get well."

SHIN'ICHI QUIETLY lay down again and closed his eyes. Mineko thought this meant he had abandoned his plan to go to Wakayama. Inwardly, she was relieved, feeling this was for the best in the long term. But Shin'-ichi had by no means given up. Chanting silently to be able to go to Wakayama, he continued to battle his illness. Nichiren Daishonin's words, "Nam-myoho-renge-kyo is like the roar of a lion. What sickness can therefore be an obstacle?" (WND-I, 412), echoed through his mind. "I won't be defeated by this illness!" he cried out in his heart, praying earnestly. He felt himself perspiring again.

At about eleven in the morning, Shin'ichi opened his eyes and asked what time it was. He then got up to change his underclothes once more.

Seeing that Shin'ichi had awakened, the doctor, who had arrived earlier, came into the room to examine him. First, he took Shin'ichi's pulse, then his temperature. He looked surprised.

"What's my temperature?" Shin'ichi asked.

"It's dropped to one hundred degrees Fahrenheit," the doctor replied.

Shin'ichi's face lit up. "I can go to Wakayama then."

"Mmm . . . ," the doctor said doubtfully as he placed his stethoscope against Shin'ichi's chest. His face clouded over. He could still hear abnormal sounds coming from the patient's lungs. Lifting his head, he continued, "I cannot prevent you from going . . . ."

A broad smile spread across Shin'ichi's face, "That's great!"

But the doctor added hastily, "Keep in mind, however, that your minor improvement is barely being sustained by the antibiotic injections, and really you should be having complete bed rest."

"I understand," Shin'ichi replied. "I'll be very careful."

His trip to Wakayama was thus decided, the news being quickly relayed to the leaders in his party.

When his lunch was brought to him, he could eat very little. He put aside his chopsticks and lay down again. Hearing updates of Shin'ichi's condition, the leaders were deeply concerned.

KAZUMASA MORIKAWA said to Hisao Seki, "Is Sensei really up to going to Wakayama?"

With a serious expression, Seki replied: "He said he's going, so you can bet he will. No doubt he's pushing himself beyond his limits, though."

"Yes, I'm sure he is," Morikawa agreed. "Mr. Seki, why don't we ask him one more time to cancel his trip? As disciples, we cannot stand by and do nothing while Sensei sacrifices his own well-being. I think we should say something, even if he scolds us for it."

Seki voiced his agreement and remarked: "The unfortunate reality is that we're unable to encourage the members the way he does. At the Kansai leaders meeting yesterday, his guidance and powerful leading of the song touched the members deeply and inspired them to make a fresh determination. It's sad to admit, but even if we go in his place, we won't have the same impact. That's why I'm in such a quandary, to tell you the truth."

Nodding, Morikawa said: "I know what you mean. No matter how much we might try to encourage the Wakayama members on Sensei's behalf, they're going be disappointed if he doesn't show up. On the other hand, if we are honest and convey Sensei's feelings to them, along with explaining the severity of his condition, they're bound to understand. If we tell them that Sensei will visit them once he's recovered and then earnestly encourage them to work hard aiming for that day, I'm sure they'll rise to the challenge. At any rate, I think the most important thing right now is for Sensei to rest and recuperate."

"You're right," Seki replied.

The two men decided that Morikawa would go and see Shin'ichi. When Morikawa arrived, he said to Shin'ichi, who was still resting: "Sensei, I need to speak with you. Let me come right to the point. I entreat you to please stay in bed, at least for today."

SHIN'ICHI SAT UP and fixed a steady gaze on Morikawa. In the next moment, his determined voice rang out. "Isn't it the greatest honor as a Buddhist to die while in the midst of the struggle for kosen-rufu? I intend to keep going until I've used every last ounce of my strength. So let's go to Wakayama!"

At 2:40 PM, Shin'ichi and his party departed from the Kansai Culture Center. Shin'ichi wore a heavy overcoat with the collar turned up, a scarf around his neck, a wool hat pulled down to his eyes and a surgical mask. The group drove to Japan National Railways (now Japan Railways) Tennoji Station and boarded an express train for Waka-yama. The doctor accompanied Shin'ichi on the train, keeping an anxious watch on his patient.

As Shin'ichi sat slumped in his seat, images of the faces of his beloved Wakayama members filled his mind. It was only fifty minutes by express train to their destination, but to him the journey seemed to last forever.

The news that President Yamamoto was on his way to Wakayama was immediately conveyed to Wakayama Joint Headquarters Leader Kasuke Nagayama. Excitedly, he headed for the station to meet President Yamamoto and the others in his party.

Nagayama had long been waiting for this visit to be realized, but early that morning he had received several telephone calls from Kansai leaders explaining that President Yamamoto had fallen ill and might not be able to make it. He had been told similar news the day before, but then also heard that Shin'ichi had given powerful guidance at the Kansai leaders meeting and even led a Soka Gakkai song. He therefore didn't think that President Yamamoto's condition was so serious.

The members in Wakayama had been chanting earnestly for some time to be able to welcome President Yamamoto to their area. That is why, unaware of Shin'ichi's true state, whenever Nagayama received a call from Kansai leaders, he replied: "The members here are eagerly awaiting the arrival of President Yamamoto. Please just tell him that." The Kansai leaders didn't know how to respond.

WHENEVER THEY HAD met in the past, Nagayama had invited Shin'ichi to Wakayama. He had also written numerous letters to Shin'ichi asking him to visit, and Shin'ichi had promised that he would. That is why Nagayama was so certain, no matter what the Kansai leaders told him, that President Yamamoto would make the trip. Filled with excitement, he waited on the platform for the train to arrive from Osaka.

The train pulled in and Shin'ichi and his party disembarked. Shin'ichi wore a large surgical mask, and instead of his usual brisk, resolute gait, he was moving very slowly. Nagayama was overcome with emotion, thinking: "President Yamamoto is obviously unwell, yet he has come to Wakayama anyway. My persistence put him in this position!"

He was both deeply touched and stricken with guilt. "Oh, Sensei! I am so sorry!" he said, but was then at a loss for words.

Shin'ichi, however, with a warm twinkle in his eyes, nodded and replied, "I came because I promised you I would."

Before going to the Wakayama Prefectural Gymnasium, where the leaders meeting would be held, Shin'ichi and his party stopped by the Soka Gakkai Wakayama Community Center to rest for a little while. Climbing the stairs to the center's second floor, Shin'ichi had to stop several times to catch his breath, leaning on the rail for support. Perhaps because his fever was starting to go down, he no longer had the chills, but he was perspiring profusely and his throat was congested, causing him to cough incessantly.

Mineko wanted her husband to eat something to restore

his strength. Kansai women's division leaders, learning that Shin'ichi liked curry and rice, had prepared that dish along with rice balls for him at the center. But Shin'ichi didn't quite have the appetite for curry yet, which he felt bad about considering the members' kindness. Though he said he wasn't hungry, Mineko wanted him to at least eat a rice ball. She therefore remade them into smaller portions so they would be easier for him to eat, and Shin'ichi was able to swallow one or two. He smiled at her and said, "I'll be fine now."

THE DOCTOR EXAMINED Shin'ichi once more. Taking his temperature, he found it had dropped to 98.9 degrees Fahrenheit, but this did not mean that the pneumonia was cured. The injections and medications were merely controlling the fever and cough. Moving around was sure to aggravate Shin'ichi's symptoms.

When the doctor was finished, Shin'ichi said in a determined voice, "All right, let's go to the leaders meeting." His voice resonated with the force of a lion's roar.

Shin'ichi and the others arrived at the gymnasium at a quarter past five. Though there was still plenty of time before the meeting was scheduled to start, the venue was already packed. A local leader reported that the members, excited to be seeing President Yamamoto, had begun arriving from early in the day and that the gymnasium had filled to capacity an hour before starting time. Hearing that everyone who was expected to attend had assembled, Shin'ichi suggested that they begin the meeting right away.

The leaders accompanying Shin'ichi strictly urged him

to rest in the waiting room until it was time for his speech. Shin'ichi complied, but after drinking a cup of tea, he immediately got up and went to the auditorium. The start of the meeting had just been announced when Shin'ichi appeared on the stage. Thunderous applause erupted as members rose to their feet, some shouting out to him and others waving handkerchiefs.

In this joyous atmosphere, general administrators Seiichiro Haruki and Kazumasa Morikawa delivered remarks. Hisao Seki also spoke, telling members that President Yamamoto had decided to come to Wakayama in spite of a high fever and the protests of the other leaders. But seeing President Yamamoto seated calmly before them with a big smile on his face, no one took Seki's comments seriously. They all thought he must be fully recovered.

The time came for Shin'ichi's speech. Shin'ichi tried to stand up, but at that moment, he was seized by a coughing fit. He wanted to take a few moments to catch his breath before starting to speak.

TRYING TO SUPPRESS his coughing, Shin'ichi said, "Let's play the tape!" The tape he had brought with him from Tokyo should have been ready to go just in case he was unable to speak, but it didn't start on cue. While it was being set up, therefore, the young men's division Brass Band performed.

When the tape was ready, Shin'ichi's strong voice began to ring throughout the gymnasium over the public address system. In his guidance, he called on members to abandon illusory views of happiness caught up in the pursuit of fame or prestige, and to focus on achieving their human revolution and leading a glorious life of contribution to society. He then recited his poem, "Courageous Advance into the 1970s," which had appeared in the recently published January 1970 issue of *The Daibyakurenge* study journal:

> *Resolutely and unflinchingly,*
> *with indomitable courage,*
> *I will leap into the dirty rain*
> *resembling Dante's Purgatory.*
> *Follow me, my comrades in a shared mission!*
> *Amidst the chaos and destruction,*
> *let us open the way to joyous creativity.*

Both the words of the poem and Shin'ichi's booming voice overflowed with his fierce determination to boldly triumph in the cause of humanism during the 1970s, a new decade for the Soka Gakkai beginning on the tenth anniversary of his presidency.

The members were jubilant when they thought about the fact that the vigorous speaker on the tape was the very individual standing before them. The tape came to an end. Shin'ichi's coughing had also subsided, and he stood up energetically. Excited applause broke out.

"My friends from Wakayama—it's been a long time! Are you well?"

"Yes!" roared the members in reply.

"It looks like I'm the only one not feeling so good," Shin'ichi said humorously. "I seem to have caught a cold."

"Sensei! Hang in there!" came a voice from the audience.

"That's right!" Shin'ichi said. "I have to do my best! OK, let's do a cheer together!"

The gymnasium was enveloped in an exuberant atmosphere. Raising his fist in the air, Shin'ichi shouted, "Wakayama will fight!" The joyous voices of the members reverberated throughout the gymnasium as they repeated the cheer.

"WAKAYAMA WILL ABSOLUTELY triumph!" "Watch Wakayama!" Their faces flushed with enthusiasm, the members continued repeating Shin'ichi's cheers. Shin'ichi next offered words of appreciation and encouragement to the members of the various groups present, including the Fife and Drum Corps, the Brass Band and the high school division, which put the participants at ease and made them feel united.

Drawing from Nichiren Daishonin's writing "On Rebuking Slander of the Law and Eradicating Sins" (see WND-1, 435), Shin'ichi pointed out that, in accord with the teachings of Buddhism, it was only to be expected that baseless slander and persecution should arise in response to the ascendance of a new people's power movement based on the Mystic Law. He told them that facing and struggling against such difficulties was the direct path to accumulating great good fortune and benefit, transforming one's karma, and attaining Buddhahood in this lifetime.

"Authority," he said, "has the potential to become a destructive, negative force that seeks to control and enslave the people. It therefore uses every means to obstruct the emergence of a people's movement. That is why it is crucial that the people become strong and wise. Kosen-rufu is a struggle to create an age of true democracy in which the people are sovereign, and all of you are the leaders of that endeavor!"

Shin'ichi then quoted the passage from "The Actions of the Votary of the Lotus Sutra" that states: "The destiny of Japan depends solely upon Nichiren. A house without pillars collapses, and a person without a soul is dead" (WND-1, 772). Touching on the relationship between religion and society, he then remarked: "Our philosophy and way of thinking is reflected in such things as education and government, and religion is the underlying basis of that thought. As such, religion determines the direction of the age and of society.

"What teaching, then, has the power to positively transform society, characterized by a growing sense of alienation, degradation of the natural environment and social disorder? The answer is the unsurpassed tenets of Nichiren Buddhism. The Soka Gakkai, which upholds the banner of humanism while striving to rebuild society based on that teaching, is indeed the golden pillar supporting the nation and society. Let us all be absolutely confident that no religious movement, no people's movement other than ours has the power to truly revitalize the human spirit and invigorate society and the times. Uniting our efforts, let us stir up an even greater tide of kosen-rufu that will spread far and wide."

SHIN'ICHI POURED his entire life into delivering his speech. Ten, fifteen, twenty minutes passed. Mineko, his doctor and the leaders accompanying him watched him anxiously, certain he had reached the limits

of his strength. The doctor wished earnestly that Shin'-
ichi would finish quickly. But the latter continued speaking for twenty-four minutes.

When he ended, the emcee announced that it was time
for Soka Gakkai songs. Nagayama led "Song of
Indomitable Dignity," followed by "Ah, the Dawn
Approaches," led by Seki, Morikawa and two other general administrators. While everyone was singing, Shin'ichi
invited some elderly members he had noticed sitting in the
audience to the edge of the stage and presented them with
sets of prayer beads and shook their hands to encourage
them.

When the songs were finished, cries of "Sensei!" rose
from throughout the gymnasium. Then one member
shouted, "Please lead a song!" Shin'ichi smiled and nodded
his assent. But at just that moment, he began to cough vio-
lently. He covered his mouth and coughed five, then six
times, his back shuddering as he did so. He took a deep
breath, but that didn't help, and more than a dozen painful
coughs racked his body. The microphone on stage picked
up the sound.

After his coughing stopped, the members could hear his
labored breathing, and they all gazed at him with concern.
But as soon as he regained his composure, Shin'ichi stood
up briskly and said: "I'm fine. All right, I'll lead a song!"

The members cheered joyously.

"I'll do anything if it will make you happy. I'm your
president, after all."

Everyone applauded.

"What shall we sing?" he asked.

"'Takeda Bushi!'"[2]

"OK! Let's begin!"

The Brass Band started to play the powerful melody.

"Please, stop!" shouted the doctor from the side of the stage, but his voice was drowned out by the members' loud clapping to the music.

> *The mountains of the province of Kai*
> *glow in the light of the sun.*
> *I feel no regret*
> *as I depart to the front . . . .*

WITH A JAPANESE FAN in hand, Shin'ichi began to lead the song. His movements were dignified and graceful, as if he were soaring through the vast skies. In his heart, Shin'ichi resolutely called out to the devilish forces of the universe: "Devils of illness, come forth! No matter what happens, I will continue to fight!"

With her eyes fixed on her husband, Mineko chanted fervently under her breath, praying that he would not collapse. Mineko had always felt that, if she could, she would bear any sickness in place of Shin'ichi, whose life was crucial to kosen-rufu. In fact, she had actually prayed for illness to come to her instead. When Shin'ichi realized what she was doing, however, he had gently corrected her, saying: "You mustn't do that. Praying for the health of oneself and others alike is the correct way of practicing Nichiren Buddhism." Since then, Mineko had changed her way of praying, but her wish to take on her husband's sufferings so that he could devote himself energetically to kosen-rufu remained unchanged.

The Wakayama members were deeply moved by Shin'-

ichi's powerful leading of the song, and many had tears in their eyes. At the same time, some of the women's division members, worried about Shin'ichi's condition, suppressed the urge to cry out for him to stop. Everyone present engraved the scene in their hearts, vowing: "I'll do my best, too! I will win!" They clapped with all their might and sang along at the top of their voices.

The emotion-filled chorus came to an end, and the close of the meeting was announced amidst high-spirited applause. Shin'ichi picked up his jacket and, waving his right arm in the air, called out: "See you all again! Please stay well!"

The members cheered in response. Shin'ichi strode off the stage as if everything was fine, but as he began to walk down the stairs at the side of the stage, he nearly stumbled.

SHIN'ICHI HAD EXPENDED all his energy. Not wanting to worry anyone, though, he steadied himself and said lightheartedly: "I'm beat! You know me, I just cannot say no!"

Without stopping to rest in the waiting room, Shin'ichi went straight to the car and headed for the hotel where he was staying that night. As he sunk into the backseat, he thought: "I won! I'm sure Wakayama is going to achieve great victory toward the coming decade. I will never forget today as long as I live."

He was utterly exhausted, and his body was so heavy that he felt as if he were being pulled into some other realm. But it was a pleasant, satisfied tiredness that came from having put everything he had into an important effort. That evening, he sent the doctor who had been attending him back to Osaka. He didn't want to cause the physician, who had a private medical practice, any further inconvenience.

The following day, December 22, Shin'ichi attended a guidance meeting for Nara Joint Headquarters at the Soka Gakkai's Nara headquarters building in Kashihara City, Nara Prefecture. Beset by chills once again, he wrapped a towel around his waist and inserted two body warmers. Despite his condition, at the meeting he lectured on various passages from such writings of Nichiren Daishonin as "The Selection of the Time," speaking energetically for thirty minutes on the importance of unity and other topics.

He said: "Though you are firmly determined, you may find that the thick wall of established local customs makes you feel that it's impossible to realize kosen-rufu. But it's that feeling of impotence itself that is our greatest enemy. In order to overcome such sentiments, conquer our inner weakness, rid ourselves of negligence and apathy, and move forward, we must forge solid unity with our fellow members."

Seeing Shin'ichi speak so passionately for the sake of Nara's development, no one suspected that he was battling illness. When he returned to Osaka that evening, he was once again examined by the doctor. His fever was still a high one hundred degrees Fahrenheit, but Shin'ichi said with a smile: "I really appreciate what you've been doing for me. Thanks to your treatment, I'm feeling much better. I can keep going now. Tomorrow we travel to Mie Prefecture."

EVERY DAY WAS a continuing, uninterrupted struggle for Shin'ichi. He could not afford to ease off on his efforts for a single day, not even a single moment.

The unprecedented work of kosen-rufu—the task of bringing flowers of happiness to bloom in the earth of the people and of building a peaceful society—is by no means easy. It is only made possible through ceaseless advancement and tireless, wholehearted exertion.

Learning from Shin'ichi's example of utterly selfless devotion, the top leaders of Kansai engraved his spirit in their hearts.

On December 23, Shin'ichi departed Osaka and arrived at the Soka Gakkai Matsusaka Community Center in Matsusaka City, Mie Prefecture, just before two in the afternoon. Approximately four hundred members were waiting there for him.

At the meeting, Shin'ichi cited the passage from "The Opening of the Eyes" that states: "Although I and my disciples may encounter various difficulties, if we do not harbor doubts in our hearts, we will as a matter of course attain Buddhahood. Do not have doubts simply because heaven does not lend you protection. Do not be discouraged because you do not enjoy an easy and secure existence in this life. This is what I have taught my disciples morning and evening, and yet they begin to harbor doubts and abandon their faith" (WND-1, 283). Some members were hearing this passage for the first time, but even if they didn't grasp its entire meaning, they all understood its implication that persecutions would arise.

Shin'ichi's voice rang with firm conviction as he continued, "Foolish men are likely to forget the promises they have made when the crucial moment comes" (WND-1, 283). He then said with great force: "If you can truly read this passage with your life, you are practicing the essence of Buddhism. I would like you to make these words of Nichiren Daishonin the guiding principles you uphold from now on throughout your lives. Those who do so are genuine disciples of Nichiren Daishonin."

He then began to lecture specifically on the passage, saying: "The words *I and my disciples* express the profound spirit of the oneness of mentor and disciple. A true disciple is one who works for kosen-rufu with the same spirit as Nichiren Daishonin, with the same conviction as one's mentor. Faith has nothing to do with titles or status; it is all about the heart. And the path to attaining Buddhahood in this lifetime is found by advancing in unity with one's mentor."

HAVING SOME TROUBLE breathing, Shin'ichi inhaled deeply. He then said: "'Various difficulties' refers to the persecutions, setbacks and obstacles we face in life. There may be times when your neighbors criticize you or when the Soka Gakkai is attacked by the mass media. And it may also happen that the authorities and other forces become intent on crushing our organization and engage in all sorts of plots and schemes to do so. But whatever happens, whatever events occur, you must never doubt the Gohonzon. It's important that you chant abundantly and advance resolutely with the Soka Gakkai, the organization that is carrying out kosen-rufu.

"As long as you remain doubt-free, as long as you maintain a sincere commitment to faith, you will 'as a matter of course attain Buddhahood,' just as Nichiren Daishonin promises. In the end, you will accumulate great good fortune and benefit and experience a state of supreme happiness. Even if the protective functions of the universe seem to be failing to do their job, and you are experiencing hardship and difficulty, you must not waver. Even if you are criticized or persecuted, and you are not enjoying peace and security in your present existence, you mustn't complain—this is what Nichiren is saying."

Shin'ichi looked intently at the members, who were all listening carefully. He then remarked: "Nichiren Daishonin laments, however, that although he has continually instructed his disciples in this way, when confronted with difficulties, they abandon their faith. As is often the case with the weak-willed and foolish, he says, at the crucial moment, they forget their promises.

"What will we do at the crucial moment? That is when our daily efforts in faith become manifested. A person who is always lax and lazy cannot suddenly bring forth strong faith when the time comes. The same is true of such martial arts as judo or kendo, isn't it? A person who never trains and always loses in practice matches isn't going to all of a sudden become a champion in a real match.

"That's why our daily practice of Nichiren Buddhism is so critical. It's important to carry out faith that flows like water, continuing with perseverance and quiet determination. We need to polish and fortify our lives and cultivate absolute conviction in faith. When we can do that, we will be able to rouse tremendous strength at the crucial moment."

SEEKING TO AROUSE the determination of each person present, Shin'ichi continued: "On the individual level, 'the crucial moment' is a time when you or someone you love is struck by a serious illness or has some unforeseen accident, or you lose your job or your business. Such events are the manifestation of your karma from the infinite past and serve as an opportunity for you to change your destiny.

"Having your faith challenged or opposed is another example of a 'crucial moment,' as are times when the Soka Gakkai is persecuted or faced with some difficulties. The only way to attain happiness is to establish a diamond-like, indestructible state of life and enable it to shine. Obstacles and adversity are the best tools for polishing and forging your life.

"Times of great persecution are therefore the perfect chance for us to change our karma and transform our life-condition. That's why we need the courage to bravely confront such onslaughts. We must not be cowardly. In the last ten years, the Soka Gakkai has sailed along smoothly, realizing tremendous growth and development. But this cannot continue forever. Doesn't Nichiren Daishonin tell us: 'If you propagate it [the Mystic Law], devils will arise without fail. If they did not, there would be no way of knowing that this is the correct teaching' (WND-1, 501), and 'not to expect good times, but take the bad times for granted' (WND-1, 998)? If we do not experience great persecution, Nichiren's words will be false.

"I hope that when the crucial moment arrives, you will all stand up with me and fight together with the Soka Gakkai, creating a record of proud achievement as champions of kosen-rufu."

"We will!" shouted the members, their faces glowing with determination.

After he finished speaking, Shin'ichi shook hands with several of the men's division members. Though many of them noticed that Shin'ichi's hand was unusually warm, none of them attributed it to illness.

After leaving the Matsusaka Community Center, Shin'ichi visited the Ise Community Center, also in Mie Prefecture, speaking again with all his might for another thirty-five minutes. This guidance trip, spanning Osaka and Mie prefectures, was an intense struggle in which Shin'ichi pushed himself beyond his limits.

THE YEAR 1969 was brought to a close with the dissolution of the Lower House of the Japanese Diet on December 2, followed by general elections later in the month. With the start of the campaigning officially announced on December 7, and the election itself held on the 27th, it was a very rushed year-end campaign. The main points of contention this time were Okinawa's reversion to Japan and the renewal of the US-Japan Security Treaty.

In November, Japanese Prime Minister Eisaku Sato had visited the United States and met with President Richard Nixon, which resulted in the signing of a joint communiqué that addressed the return of Okinawa. With this, Japan's ruling Liberal Democratic Party announced that the issue of Okinawa's administrative control had been resolved and that Okinawa would be returned to Japan in 1972 "without nuclear weapons and under the same conditions as the mainland" on the premise of the long-term extension of the US-Japan Security Treaty.

The opposition parties, however, expressed concern about the communiqué, saying that it opened the way for the emergency reintroduction of nuclear weapons into Okinawa and was therefore an attempt to deceive the Japanese people, who sought the permanent removal of such weapons from their land. The various political parties also held widely differing positions on what to do about Japan's security after the fixed term of the current US-Japan Security Treaty expired in June of the following year, 1970. In that sense, the upcoming election was one in which the fundamental direction of future national policy would be determined.

It was the Clean Government Party's second Lower House election. The party's view was that, in the context of the Cold War, the US-Japan Security Treaty was a source of growing discord between Japan and the nations of the socialist bloc, and that while it did on the one hand provide security to Japan, it also had the potential to embroil the country in conflict. Believing that the future mutual abrogation of the treaty by Japan and the United States was the ideal outcome, the Clean Government Party advocated a gradual move in that direction.

The party felt that the treaty's immediate abrogation would spark tension and friction in US-Japan relations, as well as contribute to destabilizing Japan's position in the world. It therefore proposed resolving various security issues before the treaty was abrogated, such as the removal of US military bases from Japan and Okinawa's immediate and unconditional return. With regard to the bases, the Clean Government Party had already conducted a general inspection and was quite active in the movement for their withdrawal.

Concerning the larger issue of Japan's security, the Clean Government Party called for adopting a policy of equidistance and nonalignment whereby the country would take a completely neutral position unbound by ideology and promote peaceful and friendly relations with all nations. This policy was born as an attempt to realize the vision of global citizenship as articulated by second Soka Gakkai president Josei Toda.

AT THE TIME of the Lower House's dissolution, the Liberal Democratic Party had 272 seats, the Japan Socialist Party, 134, the Democratic Socialist Party, 31, the Clean Government Party, 25 and the Japan Communist Party, 4. There were also 3 independent as well as 17 vacant seats. The Clean Government Party fielded 76 candidates in the election, and a fierce campaign got under way in constituencies throughout Japan.

With the understanding that this election was likely to decide the country's fate for the decade of the 1970s, Soka Gakkai members worked harder than ever to support the Clean Government Party candidates. Upholding the spirit of "establishing the correct teaching for the peace of the land," they burned with the mission to build a peaceful society based on Buddhist ideals. As a result, they had a strong interest in seeing how prosperous their country could become and how much it could move in the direction of lasting peace, both of which were significant indicators of the advancement of kosen-rufu. They therefore threw themselves into the election campaign, believing that the reform of government was indispensable to the achievement of those aims.

With voting day fixed for December 27, the members set out to gain support for the party amidst their busy holiday preparations. Determined to win no matter what, they were filled with enthusiasm.

In December, before visiting the Kansai region and Mie Prefecture, Shin'ichi Yamamoto had traveled to Kyoto, Okayama, Aichi, Saitama, Kanagawa and Shizuoka prefectures, as well as the island of Awajishima, where he wholeheartedly encouraged the members so that they would be able to make a fresh start toward the 1970s. His tireless fighting spirit and words of encouragement inspired the members, tapping an explosive energy that fueled their various activities, including the election campaign. In particular, the efforts of the members in Wakayama and other places Shin'ichi had visited while he was suffering from a high fever were especially remarkable. Through Shin'ichi's encouragement, the flame of faith in the heart of each member became a tremendous force for social change.

The results of the election were announced the day after voting, on the evening of December 28. The Clean Government Party achieved a great victory by securing forty-seven seats, almost double its previous number, thus becoming the third largest political party in the Lower House. In Tokyo, Kansai and Kyushu, every single Clean Government Party candidate who ran was elected.

The LDP increased its number of seats by 16, for a total of 288, while the JSP experienced a dramatic drop from 134 to 90. The DSP, meanwhile, came in with 31, the JCP with 14 and independents garnered 16 seats. Newspaper headlines blared the Clean Government Party's triumphant rise to the third most powerful party. It was a historic victory that would change the course of Japanese government thereafter.

SOKA GAKKAI MEMBERS, who had given their all to supporting the Clean Government Party candidates in the election, were overjoyed at this incredible win. The fact that it had been such an unexpectedly hard fight made victory all the sweeter. The campaign had taken place amidst severe attacks against the Soka Gakkai and the Clean Government Party, which were being accused of interfering with the publication of a book written by political commentator Tatsuzo Fujisawa that was highly critical of the Soka Gakkai.

Four months before the election, Fujisawa published the first book in a series that was to address important issues facing Japanese society. It was on the subject of education. At the end of August, posters advertising the book's release were hung in trains, announcing additionally that the second volume in the series would be a critique of the Soka Gakkai. This infuriated members, who had suffered two-and-a-half years earlier when Fujisawa had written a defamatory article about the Clean Government Party and the Soka Gakkai for a monthly magazine that was full of conjecture and bias. Known for his sharp tongue, Fujisawa frequently appeared as a commentator on television and radio, where he denounced the Soka Gakkai as an organization of religious fanatics. He had also publicly made disparaging remarks about women's division members.

Fujisawa's latest attack on the organization fueled the anger of the Soka Gakkai members, who had been subjected to his abuse for some time. They couldn't understand why he was so bent on harassing them.

Shin'ichi was also filled with indignation at the writer's speech and actions. He could take personal criticism, but he could not forgive defamation of the women's division members, who were selflessly devoted to working for the sake of the Law and society.

Shin'ichi, however, was extremely busy at this time. Beginning with his guidance tour to Kansai from September 2, his schedule was booked solid through to the end of the year with trips around the country to encourage members and ceremonies related to the construction of the Grand Main Temple. It was crucial that he concentrate his energies on this period leading to the tenth anniversary of his presidency the following May, an occasion that would mark the start of a fresh era of growth for the Soka

Gakkai. He was constantly on the move, taking not a moment to rest.

SHIN'ICHI WAS TRAVELING around Japan non-stop, but at the same time he was making preparations for a major project that he was determined to initiate the next year. It was to be a fundamental restructuring of the Soka Gakkai that would begin with the tenth anniversary of his presidency and was designed to enable the organization to realize great advancement in the coming decade. His vision was to modernize the organization so that it could sink its roots deeper into society and that members could demonstrate their fullest potential.

At the time of second president Josei Toda's death, the Soka Gakkai had a membership of about eight hundred thousand member-households. Now it was virtually the largest religious organization in Japan, with nearly 7.5 million member-households. It had begun to make earnest efforts aimed at transforming society, and the Clean Government Party, which the organization had given birth to, was emerging as a new force in Japanese politics. Amid these developments, there were growing expectations for the Soka Gakkai and its potential contributions to local communities and society at large.

Kosen-rufu is a movement to improve the times and society through Buddhist humanism. In order to carry out that mission, the Soka Gakkai's structure and organization needed to adapt to the changing world, making it open, trusted and better able to make positive contributions to society. Until this point, the basic framework of the Soka Gakkai had remained unchanged since the pioneering days. Having grown so big, however, there was an urgent need to streamline and reform the organization so that it could respond to the times. Doing so, Shin'ichi felt, was the key to fresh advances in kosen-rufu.

One important step was to completely change the vertical line structure—whereby new members automatically joined the same local organization as the person who introduced them to the practice, regardless of where they lived. The goal was to introduce a horizontal block structure centered on geographical areas. At the time, this new structure was already operative on the prefectural level, which meant, for example, that people residing in the Hokkaido or Kyushu regions no longer belonged to chapters in Tokyo. In Tokyo, however, members in a given chapter lived throughout the metropolitan area as well as in the adjacent prefectures. The switch to a geographically based block system was indispensable to enabling Soka Gakkai members to develop relationships with people in their local communities and to contribute more actively on that level.

AIMING TO CREATE a more efficiently run organization, Shin'ichi planned to introduce a new position of vice president so that he could delegate some of the duties and responsibilities now overly concentrated in the post of president. In addition, with regard to the relationship between the Soka Gakkai and the Clean Government Party, he sought to draw a clear distinction between the two groups, both in terms of operation and structure, in order to avoid public misunderstanding. Realizing these goals one by one and making preparations for the Soka

Gakkai's entry into a new age was his top priority.

Shin'ichi considered the coming year to be the time to institute these changes, rejuvenate members' awareness and make a fresh, hope-filled departure. At the September Headquarters leaders meeting, he therefore announced that 1970 would be called the Year of Innovation and also the Year of Revitalization.

The appearance of the advertisements for Tatsuzo Fujisawa's book criticizing the Soka Gakkai concerned leaders of both the Soka Gakkai and the Clean Government Party. Rumors of an approaching Lower House election had been spreading since the beginning of the year, and all of the political parties were gearing up for that eventuality. Soka Gakkai leaders were particularly worried that the publication of a book filled with malicious, unfounded criticism of the Soka Gakkai and the Clean Government Party just prior to the election would unfairly sway the outcome.

In mid-September, Eisuke Akizuki, general administrator of the Soka Gakkai and executive director of the *Seikyo Shimbun* newspaper, together with a Soka Gakkai leader who was also a Clean Government Party representative on the Tokyo Metropolitan Assembly, went to visit Fujisawa at his home. The assemblyperson knew Fujisawa and had visited him on his own just two weeks earlier. Akizuki hoped to meet with the commentator on a personal level and communicate his honest feelings to him.

During the encounter, the Soka Gakkai leaders said that if Fujisawa wanted to write about the organization, they hoped he would forgo extreme statements based on conjecture and carefully research the subject, writing according to the facts. They also offered to provide Fuji-sawa with materials and information and to take him to the head temple. Additionally, the two men conveyed their belief that publishing a book critical of the Soka Gakkai and the Clean Government Party just before the election was, from the party's perspective, an attempt to obstruct election activities.

AKIZUKI AND THE Tokyo assemblyperson politely expressed their wishes to Tatsuzo Fujisawa. And with Fujisawa's consent, they also paid a visit to his publisher a few days later to convey their concerns. But neither Fujisawa nor the publisher paid them any heed and the book was released as scheduled at the beginning of November.

Just before the book's release, a young men's division member who worked in publishing was shown a sample copy of the volume while visiting a publisher's distributor. Sitting down to read it, the youth found himself going pale and trembling with rage as he turned the pages. The contents represented nothing more than a smear campaign against the Soka Gakkai and the Clean Government Party prior to the Lower House election.

The book said, for example, that the Soka Gakkai planned to use the Clean Government Party to gain control of Japan, change the constitution and make Nichiren Shoshu the national religion. This had become a standard attack against the Soka Gakkai, and Shin'ichi had clearly denied it in public on many occasions. Besides, from a logical point of view, why would the Soka Gakkai, whose essential aim was to spread the teachings and philosophy of Nichiren Daishonin around the world, need to establish a national religion in Japan?

At the Headquarters general meeting on May 3, 1967, Shin'ichi had once again addressed the issue, saying: "Claims such as that we aim to make Nichiren Shoshu the state religion and build a national sanctuary are completely emotionally charged and off the mark. They are all preposterous conjectures based on an utter ignorance of Buddhism."

Fujisawa, however, refusing to listen to such declarations, had no qualms about asserting that the Soka Gakkai sought to establish a national religion. Furthermore, without ever visiting the Soka Gakkai Headquarters to interview leaders or gather information, he based his book entirely on other publications that were critical of the Soka Gakkai. He also claimed that, in regard to election activities, the organization made no attempt to raise members' political awareness, but rather kept members in the dark and simply mobilized them to collect votes. His statements were an affront to the intelligence and integrity of the Soka Gakkai members; they made a mockery of the dedication of these individuals who were filled with a sense of mission to improve society and restore government to the hands of the people.

FUJISAWA WROTE that the Soka Gakkai enforced blind obedience to the organization and required members to move en masse to a certain electoral district in order to increase votes for a given candidate. On what grounds could he have made this claim? Moreover, based on these unfounded accusations, he declared that the Soka

Gakkai and the Clean Government Party were enemies of democracy and demanded that the party be disbanded.

He also shamelessly charged that the Soka Gakkai's propagation activities were taking advantage of the misfortune of others. But had he ever observed Soka Gakkai members' sincere efforts to engage others in dialogue out of an earnest wish for their happiness? In addition, he dismissed members' endeavors to give hope, courage and a new lease on life to the suffering as merely helping the dregs of society. His writing was also full of factual errors, including his calling Shin'ichi a former Soka Gakkai youth division leader, a post that the latter had never filled.

The young man reading the sample copy of the book was enraged. He felt that the freedom of speech had been exploited to produce a pack of lies and abuse aimed at slandering and defaming the Soka Gakkai. It was vicious libel in the guise of free speech. Other Soka Gakkai members working in publishing and advertising had also seen Fujisawa's book at the distributor. They told their colleagues who were members, as well as their young men's division leaders, just how inexcusable and outrageous the book was.

Everyone who heard about it was incensed. In a discussion on the matter among young men's division members, one said: "I thought the book might be something like that. And because this political commentator is also a university professor, it's likely that many people will believe his lies."

"The publication of this book is sure to hurt the Soka Gakkai," remarked another.

"Protecting the freedom of speech does not mean sitting idly by while someone peddles falsehoods and slander. We simply mustn't take this abuse lying down," said another.

The young men decided to speak to everyone they knew about what a slanderous book it was, and some even went to talk to bookstore owners about how this publication was actually an underhand attempt to influence the upcoming elections.

FUJISAWA'S BOOK was published in early November and immediately picked up by a commentator who introduced it on television, criticizing the Soka Gakkai and praising Fujisawa for his bold actions against the organization.

The Lower House was dissolved on December 2, with the official campaign period kicking off on December 7. A few days earlier, Fujisawa had appeared at a symposium sponsored by a political philosophy research group affiliated with the Democratic Socialist Party. There he spoke of how the Soka Gakkai and the Clean Government Party had harassed and pressured him to block the publication of his book. A weekly tabloid magazine then featured Fujisawa's allegations in an issue that went on sale around the time that campaigning started.

Fujisawa also gave an interview to the Japan Communist Party newspaper, *Akahata* (Red Flag). Despite the fact that he was widely known as anti-communist, he appeared in the JCP publication with no apparent compunctions. The front-page headlines of *Akahata's* December 17 issue blared: "Clean Government Party Obstructs Freedom of Speech and Press," and the paper continued to carry articles on the subject for several days. The Japan Socialist Party organ *Shakai Shimpo* (Socialist News) also ran a similar article on December 21. As if timed to coincide with the elections, the subject of the Soka Gakkai and Clean Government Party's alleged interference with the freedom of speech and press had suddenly surfaced.

Eisuke Akizuki, who had met directly with Fujisawa, could not understand how their conversation could be so grossly misconstrued. Fujisawa himself knew better than anyone that Akizuki had conveyed his concerns in a most reasonable manner, but now the writer was claiming to have had his rights infringed upon. *Perhaps*, Akizuki thought, *all along Fujisawa had planned to announce his publication of an attack on us and then, after we had responded, make it look like we had tried to suppress it.*

It also came out that Fujisawa had secretly taped his conversation with Akizuki and the Clean Government assemblyperson, which he loudly proclaimed to be conclusive evidence of his assertions. Fujisawa further spoke to the mass media, maintaining that he had received numerous threatening phone calls, and that distributors and advertisers were rejecting his book because of pressure from the Soka Gakkai.

WHEN TATSUZO FUJISAWA began to complain that he was being persecuted, several other authors who had written books critical of the Soka Gakkai or the Clean Government Party in the past joined in the clamor. Lower House election activities took place amid this frenzied attack on the two organizations, making it a tough battle. Brandishing tabloid articles, people accused the Soka Gakkai and the Clean Government Party of being like the military government during World War II in their efforts to suppress free speech.

This, however, did not faze Soka Gakkai members in the slightest, for they were utterly committed to improving society. The fierce winds of adversity only fanned the flames of their fighting spirit. "What are you saying?" they responded to such attacks. "The first two Soka Gakkai presidents risked their lives standing up to the military government for the sake of religious freedom. And isn't it the Soka Gakkai that's been continually persecuted and had its name dragged through the mud with lies and groundless accusations?"

Transforming their frustration and anger into determination, the members resolutely continued campaigning for the Clean Government candidates, eventually helping the party win an unprecedented forty-seven Lower House seats. They were overjoyed. Their achievement was a vibrant song of triumph reserved for those who have overcome every obstacle and trial through their own efforts.

While the joy of the members' victory was still fresh, 1970, the Year of Innovation, also known as the Year of Revitalization, began. Shin'ichi contributed a poem titled "Sounds of Innovation" to the January 1 edition of the *Seikyo Shimbun*. Engraving the poem in their hearts, members set forth into the new year vowing to make great advancements in the second decade of Shin'ichi's presidency.

Shin'ichi attended a New Year's meeting at the Soka Gakkai Headquarters in Tokyo on January 1, and then traveled to the head temple in Shizuoka Prefecture the following day. At this time, he still wasn't feeling well. In fact, he greeted 1970 in the worst of health.

His fever had persisted after his year-end trip to Kansai, and he continued to suffer from a respiratory condition. It was a battle against the devil of illness, the likes of which he had not encountered since before his inauguration ten years earlier. Nevertheless, he steadily proceeded with his endeavor to reform the Soka Gakkai's organizational structure and policies, aiming to raise the curtain on a new age.

JANUARY 2 was Shin'ichi's forty-second birthday. Nichiren Daishonin was forty-two when he encountered the Komatsubara Persecution. Not only did he sustain a cut on the forehead, but two of his followers were killed in an ambush by a group of armed men led by Tojo Kagenobu.[3] As a disciple of Nichiren Daishonin, Shin'ichi was determined to demonstrate strong, unshakable faith in the face of all obstacles. He was also firmly resolved to advance with every ounce of strength he possessed to realize Nichiren's wish of kosen-rufu. He sensed that more raging storms lay ahead.

At a leaders meeting held at the head temple that evening with representatives from throughout Japan, Shin'ichi gave guidance based on the following passage from "The Actions of the Votary of the Lotus Sutra": "A priest who incurs the enmity of the ruler and others [because of the Lotus Sutra] is surely practicing the correct teaching. Devadatta was the foremost good friend to the Thus Come One Shakyamuni. In this age as well, it is not one's allies but one's powerful enemies who assist one's progress" (WND-I, 770).

Putting everything he had into his words, he said: "No matter how just one's cause is—in fact, the more just it is, the more certain it is to provoke groundless attacks and accusations. This passage explains the significance of obstacles based on this principle. First of all, Nichiren Daishonin declares, persecution by the nation's leaders is proof that one is practicing the correct teaching. Great difficulties and hardships are what make a person strong. In that respect, Devadatta was the 'foremost good friend' of Shakyamuni, he says.

"A 'good friend' is a person who assists us in attaining Buddhahood. In the sense that Devadatta opposed Shakyamuni he was an 'evil friend,' but because Shakyamuni struggled against and defeated him, Shakyamuni was able to demonstrate his greatness and his religious order developed enormously. That is why Devadatta, despite his relentless persecution of Shakyamuni, is considered to be his 'foremost good friend.'

"The same applies to the modern world, Nichiren Daishonin says. It is our strong opponents rather than our friends who contribute the most to our personal growth and development. He likewise states that it was because of the persecutions by Tojo Kagenobu and Ryokan of Gokuraku-ji[4] temple that he was able to reveal himself as the votary of the Lotus Sutra."

SHIN'ICHI CALLED out to the assembled leaders from around Japan: "Just as Nichiren Daishonin states in his writings, we, too, can forge our lives and carry out our human revolution by confronting hardships and struggling against and defeating negative forces. This is how we will attain Buddhahood in this existence. The Soka Gakkai will also develop tremendously through overcoming such challenges.

"Let us be determined that the more fiercely the storms of abuse and criticism rage, the more we will, in accord with Nichiren's teachings, advance powerfully, strengthen our unity, deepen our faith and rouse our courage."

Unfortunately, most of the top leaders failed to grasp the urgency of Shin'ichi's words on this occasion.

On January 5, 1970, the first general administrators meeting of the year was held at the Soka Gakkai Headquarters. Here it was decided that the new post of vice president would be inaugurated, with Kiyoshi Jujo, Kazumasa Morikawa and Eisuke Akizuki appointed in that capacity. The reorganization and revitalization of the Soka Gakkai that Shin'ichi had envisioned was finally under way.

The eldest of the new vice presidents, Kiyoshi Jujo, was just forty-six, while Eisuke Akizuki, the youngest, was thirty-nine. These youthful leaders would now share Shin'ichi's responsibilities in leading the Soka Gakkai's nearly 7.5 million member-households.

At the same time, former general director Takeo Konishi, and others who had served under second president Josei Toda, such as Katsu Kiyohara and Chuhei Yamadaira, were appointed as Headquarters senior counselors. A clear generational shift had been implemented.

As long as there is a continuous emergence of youthful power that has the support of others, a fresh path of advancement will always open.

At this general administrators meeting, it was additionally decided that the Clean Government Party chairperson and secretary would resign from their leadership positions in the Soka Gakkai in order to concentrate on their party and government duties. This was part of a plan to eliminate the concurrent holding of posts in the Soka Gakkai and the Clean Government Party by elected officials in both the national Diet and local assemblies.

After giving the matter serious consideration, Shin'ichi had reached the conclusion that it was important to make a distinct demarcation between the Soka Gakkai and the Clean Government Party in terms of both finances and personnel, and that the party operates in a fully independent manner. The other Soka Gakkai leaders, thinking of the organization's future, agreed with Shin'ichi, as did the Clean Government Party.

THE RIGHT of the Soka Gakkai to support the Clean Government Party and of Clean Government representatives to practice their religious faith was guaranteed by the Japanese Constitution. Article 20 of the constitution stipulates the separation of religion and politics, the latter referring to the government of the nation. In other words, the article declares that the state shall remain neutral and may not interfere in matters of religion. It does not by any means prohibit religious organizations from engaging in political activities.

This article was adopted primarily to guarantee the religious freedom of Japanese citizens, given the errors of the Japanese state prior to and during World War II in establishing State Shinto as the national religion and persecuting all other faiths. Accordingly, the relationship between the Soka Gakkai and the Clean Government Party was in no way in violation of the separation of religion and politics outlined in Article 20. Given that understanding, to avoid causing unnecessary misconceptions or alarm, the two organizations voluntarily decided to restructure, drawing a clear line between them by separating their personnel.

Important steps for securing the future advancement of the Soka Gakkai were steadily being taken, and the wheels of a new age were starting to turn. Members were excited to think that they would be able to celebrate the tenth anniversary of Shin'ichi's presidency amid a great momentum of continuous victories. But the astonishing rise of the Clean Government Party, dedicated as it was to the welfare of the people, was on the verge of changing the course of Japanese history. As such, it was a threat to the established powers, who could not sit by silently and watch the party's growth.

On January 14, the Sixty-third Special Diet Session began. During this session, each of the opposition parties adopted an adversarial stance toward the Clean Government Party, calling for a thorough investigation of the alleged violation of freedom of speech and press by the party and the Soka Gakkai. In addition, a discussion group to address the issue was also convened on this day. The group consisted of academics, religious leaders and cultural figures who had been gathered in December of the previous year at the urging of scholars affiliated with the Japan Communist Party and priests of established Buddhist schools. The participants—one hundred ten in all, including people from the publishing world—decided to call for an investigation into the matter in the current Diet session.

The group treated the allegations of the freedom's obstruction by the two organizations as an incontrovertible fact, and in no time the issue became a major political scandal.

THE FIERCE WINDS buffeting the Soka Gakkai continued to blow with increased intensity. But the members, burning with a strong desire to make a positive contribution to society, set out joyously from the beginning of the year to share Buddhism with others. A fresh wave of propagation was rippling across Japan as members aimed to achieve the goal of 7.5 million member-households by the May 3 Headquarters leaders meeting, which would mark the start of President Yamamoto's second decade of leadership.

Though the media frenzy regarding the alleged infractions of the Soka Gakkai and Clean Government Party persisted, members kept up their efforts to spread Nichiren Daishonin's teaching in the highest of spirits.

Discussing the problem with fellow members, one member remarked, "Some of the opposition parties are calling for an investigation in the Diet, but if the Soka Gakkai really had infringed on someone's rights or engaged in intimidation, why aren't they taking the matter to the courts?"

"They're just upset because the Clean Government Party did so well in the recent elections," replied another.

"It seems like a conspiracy to me," chimed another. "But whatever happens, we mustn't allow this to hinder our advance. Now is the time for propagation. We need to talk to as many people as possible about the greatness of our cause and Nichiren Buddhism."

On January 28, another general administrators meeting was held at the Soka Gakkai Headquarters. At this time, the statistics bureau announced the latest membership figures. The leader making the announcement stood before the microphone and declared in a booming voice, his face flushed with excitement: "First of all, I am proud to say that at present our membership is 7,557,777 member-households. We have attained our long-awaited goal of 7.5 million!"

At that moment, the expressions of all the participants lit up as they broke into cheers and applause. They had achieved their goal three months ahead of schedule. Members had brilliantly turned the winds of adversity in their favor. Nichiren Daishonin states, "When great evil occurs, great good follows" (WND-1, 1119). This does not mean that great good automatically comes after great evil; it means that, by regarding difficulties as opportunities and possessing the firm resolve to use them as springboards for growth, we can realize great good.

The spirit to stand tall in the fiercest of winds, to face the harshest of blizzards—it is in this fearless spirit of continuous advance that the true strength of the Soka Gakkai is found.

IN FEBRUARY, the attacks on the Soka Gakkai reached new heights of ferocity. On February 3, the discussion group for the freedom of speech and press issue assembled approximately three thousand people at the Bunkyo Public Auditorium in Tokyo for a forum protesting the obstruction of those rights by the Soka Gakkai and the Clean Government Party. The speakers at the meeting included Tatsuzo Fujisawa and two other writers who had authored books critical of the two organizations, as well as various religious leaders and officers of the Japan Socialist Party and the Japan Communist Party.

On February 9, seven writers announced that they would no longer contribute articles to Soka Gakkai–affiliated publications. Then, at the Lower House plenary session of the Sixty-third Special Diet Session held on February 17, a JSP representative questioned the prime minister about the freedom of speech and press. At the subsequent full sessions of the Lower and Upper Houses on February 18 and 19, respectively, a JCP member asked the prime minister if he intended to conduct an investigation into the charges against the Clean Government Party in the Diet.

On February 23, the stage shifted to the Lower House Budget Committee, where a JSP politician requested that Fujisawa and the other writers be summoned to appear as witnesses in the matter. On the same day, the discussion group on free speech held a press conference, at which it played a secretly recorded tape of some remarks that Clean Government Party Diet Affairs Committee Chairperson Goro Watari had made at a Soka Gakkai student division leaders meeting in January.

On that occasion, Watari had humorously shared his personal thoughts about how wildly exaggerated the accusations being made against the Soka Gakkai and Clean Government Party were. Because he was speaking not only at an internal Soka Gakkai meeting but also before the student division, of which he had formerly been the leader, Watari had been very relaxed. His remarks were therefore extremely informal, as if he were bantering with roommates at their dormitory. Obviously fed up with the harassment of the Soka Gakkai and Clean Government Party over the issue, Watari blatantly ridiculed and made fun of the authors of books critical of the two organizations. He spoke quite harshly about the other political parties as well.

HAVING ENDURED the one-sided attacks against the Soka Gakkai by the opposition parties and the mass media, the student division members were delighted by Watari's rebuttals. The meeting venue was filled with laughter and applause. Watari was an eloquent speaker.

Feeling at ease in the company of fellow members, he gave his talent full play, even to the point of going overboard.

People are more apt to make mistakes in the areas where they excel. They get carried away and lose their discretion and prudence.

Watari's speech was surreptitiously recorded and then made public by the discussion group on free speech and press. It was subsequently picked up by some tabloid magazines and aired on TV and radio programs. Since the broadcasts exclusively featured Watari's ridicule and harsh criticism of the other opposition parties, they gave the impression that he had delivered an extremely offensive and inflammatory speech.

The parties who were the targets of Watari's jibes were outraged when they heard the tape. On February 25, Watari held a press conference and made a public apology, saying, "My remarks were personal statements delivered to a private audience, but I apologize for their lack of moderation, as well as for any trouble I have caused others." This did not placate the offended parties, however; they were intent on pursuing the matter. No longer able to successfully carry out the interparty negotiations required of him as chairperson of the Clean Government Party Diet Affairs Committee, Watari resigned his position on February 27.

This encouraged the opposition parties to step up their attacks. Also on February 27, during a meeting of the Lower House Budget Committee, a JCP representative once again requested that witnesses be summoned to the Diet, this time calling for them to include authors of critical books, people from the publishing industry, and Clean

Government Party representatives. The next day, a DSP member, who had himself written a book criticizing the Clean Government Party, spoke up at the budget committee meeting, suggesting that the real culprit in the obstruction of free speech matter was not the Clean Government Party, but the religious organization behind it, the Soka Gakkai.

His conclusion was based on the biased viewpoint that the Soka Gakkai had systematically violated election laws and that Soka Gakkai members were also the perpetrators of an increasing number of crimes. He vehemently demanded an investigation and for Soka Gakkai President Yamamoto to be summoned to appear before the committee as a witness. His accusations were utterly unfounded and lacking in any validity.

THE JAPAN SOCIALIST PARTY also called for President Yamamoto's summons to the Diet. The focus of the attack had at once shifted from the Clean Government Party to the Soka Gakkai and, more specifically, Shin'ichi. When Soka Gakkai members learned of this, they were outraged.

Members in one area addressed the matter during a discussion meeting. A young men's division member said, "Some representatives are demanding that President Yamamoto testify before the Diet, but what does he have to do with the issue?"

Another young man spoke up: "Absolutely nothing! This has no doubt been their aim from the beginning. I'm sure they just want to call Sensei before the Diet and force him to apologize for suppressing free speech. They want to paint the Soka Gakkai as an antisocial organization and make him take responsibility. It's a despicable ploy."

A women's division member then remarked indignantly: "I've never heard anything so absurd as that the Soka Gakkai should be investigated because crimes caused by its members are on the rise! If they're going to do that, they should first investigate the religious affiliations of every person who breaks the law. Then we'd see just how ridiculous their charges are!"

Expressing his agreement, a men's division member said: "I joined the Soka Gakkai at a time when my business had failed and I was considering committing suicide together with my family. My leaders and fellow members encouraged me wholeheartedly every day, but it was still a year before I was able to cope mentally. During that period I thought about killing myself several times, and it wouldn't have been surprising if I had. I was really up against a brick wall.

"When you think about it, the Soka Gakkai has always, out of its commitment to eliminating unhappiness from the world, been the first to reach out to those suffering from illness, poverty, family discord or problems with human relations. This is because it upholds a religion whose mission is to enable all people to become happy. The Soka Gakkai has continued to advance together with people who are faced with various hardships, taking on the challenges of its individual members. And it has given numerous people who were in the depths of despair a new lease on life. This is something not even the government could do. By rights, political parties and the mass media should be recognizing and praising the Soka Gakkai's achievements."

SOON, ISSUES completely unrelated to the charges of the obstruction of free speech were being brought before the Diet, such as whether the relationship between the Soka Gakkai and the Clean Government Party violated the separation of religion and politics outlined in Article 20 of the Japanese constitution. Some Diet representatives who were pursuing the matter held press conferences in which they claimed that they had received threatening phone calls, insinuating, without the slightest proof that the calls came from Soka Gakkai members. Such statements were then picked up by television and radio programs as well as newspapers, creating the image that the Soka Gakkai was an extremely antisocial organization.

Newspapers and tabloid magazines were filled with accusations that the Soka Gakkai and the Clean Government Party had violated the freedom of speech and press. Advertisement posters for magazines displaying provocative headlines were also hung throughout the nation's trains and subways.

As the attacks against the Soka Gakkai intensified in January 1970, Shin'ichi Yamamoto wished to travel even more extensively around the country and wholeheartedly encourage the members. He wanted to fan the flames of courage in each person's heart. But his health wouldn't permit him to do so.

Feeling terrible that the members had to endure such hardship, his heart ached. His health, however, had shown no signs of improvement since the arrival of the New Year. According to his doctor, his respiratory system was already weakened by the tuberculosis he had contracted in his youth, and the accumulated exhaustion of his punishing efforts had further taken its toll on him. Shin'ichi wanted to go out and encourage the members anyway, but his doctor told him: "If your condition grows any worse, you will cause irreparable harm to your health. Please rest until you have recuperated completely, no matter how long it takes."

Shin'ichi had no choice but to try to rest while at the same time staying on top of his work, of which he had an incredible amount to accomplish. Unfortunately, though the vice president position had been established in order to delegate some of his burden, it would still be some time before the new system was fully operational.

Having completed volume five of his serialized novel *The Human Revolution* in August of the previous year, he was also now receiving earnest requests from both the *Seikyo Shimbun* and individual members for him to resume writing. Because he found it difficult to refuse such appeals, Shin'ichi promised to start writing installments of volume six in early February.

WHILE SHIN'ICHI WAS determined to begin writing, his fever persisted and he was extremely weak. Most likely from extended stress and worry, his shoulders and neck were so cramped that it was difficult for him to even hold a pen. He therefore dictated the novel into a tape recorder, which he would then have someone transcribe onto paper. Utterly exhausted, when he began speaking into the recorder, he immediately experienced trouble breathing. His throat became congested and he would often have coughing fits, breaking into a clammy sweat. But still, he continued.

Volume six opened with the celebration at the head temple of the seven hundredth anniversary of the establishment of Nichiren Daishonin's teaching. On that occasion, some young men's division members confronted the priest Jiko Kasahara, who had advocated the fallacious doctrine that Buddhism was subordinate to Shinto and triggered the persecution of the Soka Gakkai during World War II. They forced Kasahara to admit his error and apologize before the grave of first president Tsunesaburo Makiguchi, who had died in prison for his beliefs during the war. Consequently, the Nichiren Shoshu Council, deeming that the fault for this incident lay with the Soka Gakkai, issued a three-point disciplinary action against President Josei Toda, demanding that he submit a written apology, be dismissed from his position as Nichiren Shoshu senior lay representative and be suspended from visiting the head temple.

Because the Soka Gakkai had struggled to protect the correct teaching of Nichiren Buddhism and had sought to rectify error, Josei Toda had been exposed to fierce winds of adversity. When Shin'ichi thought of his mentor's valiant struggle, he felt courage welling up in his own heart. Now, while suffering from illness, Shin'ichi bore the brunt of all attacks against the Soka Gakkai. It was a vicious onslaught.

From the time the Clean Government Party decided to field candidates for the Lower House (in 1966), Shin'ichi had been prepared for the day when the Soka Gakkai, the party's main supporter, would come under concentrated fire. This was because the Soka Gakkai had been the target of constant attack from the time it had risen up to change society for the better.

It was in 1955 that the Soka Gakkai first had members run as candidates in local assembly elections, with the goal of restoring government to the people. In that year, the Japan Socialist Party, which had been split into left- and right-wing factions, reunited, and two conservative parties, the Liberal Party and the Japan Democratic Party, had merged to form the Liberal Democratic Party. This was the start of the political system that would rule Japan for decades after the postwar period. Known as the 1955 Status Quo, it was a system in which the government was split between conservative and progressive parties.

IN THE FOLLOWING YEAR, 1956, the Soka Gakkai backed six candidates for the Upper House elections, of which three were elected. Then in 1957, it fielded a candidate for an Upper House by-election in Osaka. Though the candidate in this latter election lost by a narrow margin, the emergence of a new popular force in the Upper House had begun to stir a major reaction in society at large.

A first sign of this was seen in Yubari, Hokkaido. In the summer of 1957, the Yubari Coal Miners Union, which had always backed Japan Socialist Party candidates, tried to bar Soka Gakkai members from its ranks [because Soka Gakkai members supported their own candidate in the previous Upper House election]. This was later known as the Yubari Coal Miners Union incident.

Right after that, authorities in Osaka used the excuse of election law violations by a small number of overzealous Soka Gakkai members in that year's Upper House by-election to launch an all-out attack on the Soka Gakkai. They unjustly arrested Shin'ichi Yamamoto, who was in charge of the campaign, in what would come to be known as the Osaka Incident. At the end of the court case that dragged on for four-and-a-half years, he was fully exonerated of all charges in January 1962.

In the same month, the Soka Gakkai formed the Clean Government Political Federation, which became the Clean Government Party in November 1964. During that time, the number of Clean Government representatives in the Upper House increased steadily, with the party winning eleven seats in the Upper House elections of July 1965. Together with the nine previously elected members, this brought their total to twenty.[5]

In this summer election, a number of candidates were either affiliated with religious organizations or being endorsed by various Buddhist schools, earning it the nickname "the religious war." Political parties aligned themselves with religious organizations and relied on them for votes, and the religious groups in turn sought the help of political parties to destroy the Soka Gakkai.

For example, at a nationwide conference of the Japan Buddhist Federation held in August of this year (1965), an anti-Soka Gakkai measure was discussed, based on the consensus that the organization's establishment of the Clean Government Party would have a major impact on the future of Buddhism in Japan. Conference participants decided to strengthen their unity and change their strategy against the Soka Gakkai from defensive to offensive.

According to reports in the religious newspaper *Chugai Nippo* (from the September 1, 1965, edition), federation members would implement the following measures: (1) The head of each religious group and of regional Buddhist associations will issue strict orders to crush the heretical religion, (2) In order to counter the Soka Gakkai's incredible publicity, we will gain control of the mass media using popular weekly magazines published by the Japan Buddhist Federation and (3) Seizing the right opportunity, we will petition the Diet and the government to take action against the Soka Gakkai.

D URING THE JAPAN Buddhist Federation conference, it was also suggested that the group's petition to the Japanese government claim that the doctrine upheld by the Soka Gakkai contained immoral and illegal elements that needed to be verified and exposed. It was a completely biased proposal based on prejudice and conjecture. An attorney who attended the conference advised, as reported in the *Chugai Nippo,* that "The elimination [of the Soka Gakkai] must be carried out carefully and in accord with the law in order to be effective" (September 1, 1965 edition). In other words, discussions toward actualizing the federation's aim of bringing down the Soka Gakkai had begun in earnest.

At the same time, a group of the so-called new religions,[6] the Federation of New Religious Organizations of Japan, held a board of directors meeting at the beginning of September 1965, and decided to mobilize the approximately seven million members of its more than ninety affiliated organizations in opposition to the Soka Gakkai and the Clean Government Party. They would launch a campaign to disassociate members from the Soka Gakkai. The group also discussed a strategy toward the mass media, stating that it was "prepared to take a hard stand against any newspaper or other media that appeared to curry favor with the Soka Gakkai and Clean Government Party, and to initiate a boycott movement countering such media if need be" (September 8, 1965, *Chugai Nippo*).

What the various religious groups feared most was the Clean Government Party gaining seats in the Lower House. But their apprehensions were based on profound error. They were obsessed with the notion that if the Clean Government Party were to someday come to power, it would make Nichiren Shoshu the national religion of Japan, build a national sanctuary and prohibit the practice of any other religion. They firmly believed this in spite of the Soka Gakkai's consistent denials of such ideas. It was fear driven by this misunderstanding that was at the root of the harsh attacks on the Clean Government Party and the Soka Gakkai.

In December 1965, another group called the Conference of Believers to Deal with the Current Situation, comprised of approximately one hundred followers of Shinto, Buddhism, Christianity and the new religions, was formed in opposition to the Soka Gakkai.

Not a single religious organization or political party was supportive of either the Soka Gakkai or the Clean Government Party. Their only ally was the people.

This was the atmosphere amid which, in January 1967, the Clean Government Party fielded its first candidates for the Lower House and gained a stunning victory of twenty-five seats.

NUMEROUS CANDIDATES Backed by religious organizations ran in the January 1967 Lower House elections. The Japan Buddhist Federation and the Federation of New Religious Organizations of Japan each officially sponsored more than one hundred. The latter, in particular, established a political association immediately prior to the election called the New Religious Organizations Political Alliance, which endorsed candidates throughout Japan and consolidated its influence over the political arena.

These religious organizations backed candidates across the political spectrum, with the most coming from the ruling LDP, and including the DSP, the JSP and others. While criticizing the Soka Gakkai and the Clean Government Party for obscuring the distinction between religion and politics, these religious groups and political parties were actually strengthening their ties with each other.

In February, after the elections, the Conference of Believers to Deal with the Current Situation held a general meeting at which it was decided to submit a request to the LDP and DSP asking them not to become aligned with the Clean Government Party. The various religious organizations had thus joined forces and were calling on the political parties to work with them to bring down the Soka Gakkai and the Clean Government Party. Nevertheless, the Clean Government Party was moving forward with incredible momentum, and in the Upper House elections of the following year, 1968, it won thirteen seats for a total of twenty-four in the Upper House.

During the period of a few years around that time, Shin'ichi Yamamoto had made a number of peace proposals. At the November 1966 youth division general meeting, he called for the immediate cessation of hostilities in

Vietnam. At the student division general meeting in August 1967, he discussed the problem of Okinawa and urged its immediate return to Japanese sovereignty as well as the removal of all nuclear facilities. At the Headquarters general meeting of May 1968, he spoke of the nuclear problem and called on all nuclear powers to meet together in one room to earnestly explore the issue of eliminating present nuclear arsenals and prohibiting their future production, testing or deployment. Then, at the September student division general meeting that same year, he proposed the normalization of diplomatic relations between Japan and China as well as the admission of the People's Republic of China to the United Nations.

All of Shin'ichi's proposals were the inevitable result of his serious contemplation of how to achieve world peace based on the Buddhist principles of respect for the dignity of life and human equality. Soka Gakkai members strongly supported his proposals and, with a deepened awareness of their social mission as practitioners of Nichiren Buddhism, further expanded their popular movement for peace.

JAPAN'S POLITICAL and business circles, which in the context of the Cold War had maintained the country's prosperity by toeing the US line, were alarmed by Shin'ichi's proposal for the normalization of relations between Japan and China. In fact, at the US-Japan Security Treaty conference that took place immediately following Shin'ichi's 1968 proposal, a high-ranking official of the Japanese Ministry of Foreign Affairs openly criticized it in front of the US ambassador, the commander of US forces stationed in Japan and other US officials, calling it detrimental to Japan's foreign policy.

The powers controlling the Japanese government seemed to genuinely regard both Shin'ichi and the Soka Gakkai as an impediment. Other religious groups and political parties as well appeared to strongly oppose, resent and fear the rapidly growing Clean Government Party and the Soka Gakkai, eagerly awaiting the perfect opportunity to launch an offensive against them.

It was largely believed that the Lower House would be dissolved and a general election held in the following year, 1969. This was also the year that a Democratic Socialist Party Diet member wrote a book criticizing the Clean Government Party. Several others, including Kuniya Kudo, a journalist for a national newspaper, and Senzo Kumada, an editorial writer for a regional newspaper who used the pen name Yasuyuki Fukuyama, also published books attacking the Clean Government Party and the Soka Gakkai at about the same time.

Kumada was a graduate of the Nakano School, an institution formed by the Imperial Army of Japan for the purpose of training intelligence agents for the military. He was also a leader in a religious organization and had strong ties to right-wing forces. He had previously authored a critical book under another pen name, and in later years became the editor of a rightist magazine that published many scandalous articles about the Soka Gakkai. These writings were so outrageously fabricated that the Soka Gakkai filed a lawsuit against him, and he was convicted of libel.

In other words, several sensationalist books criticizing

the two organizations were published along with Tatsuzo Fujisawa's prior to the Lower House elections.

The citadel of truth and justice was beset by a storm of malice. In addition, poisoned arrows of slander aimed at bringing down Shin'ichi had also been launched. It was amidst these crashing waves of adversity that Soka Gakkai members carried out their election campaign activities.

THE CLEAN GOVERNMENT PARTY won. They overcame all obstacles to achieve a remarkable victory of forty-seven seats in the 1969 Lower House election. Shin'ichi knew that the various forces that had been seeking to bring down the Soka Gakkai and the Clean Government Party would not stand silently by in the face of this tremendous advance. And in fact, with the start of the new year, 1970, a barrage of criticism regarding the freedom of speech and press issue was launched in full force.

It was true that certain members had conveyed their objections to the authors of the highly biased books and had even asked them to correct their statements. Shin'ichi was prepared, as Soka Gakkai president, to acknowledge any wrongdoing and apologize if the members had gone too far. That was his honest feeling.

The problem was that the Soka Gakkai's opponents were blowing such incidents all out of proportion as a means to attack the organization. While on the surface the opposition parties were leading the onslaught, some factions of the governing party also appeared to be plotting against the Soka Gakkai and the Clean Government Party. In fact, Tatsuzo Fujisawa himself said that he had received advice from a vice chief cabinet secretary on how to have the free speech and press issue brought before the Committee on Judicial Affairs.

Realizing that most of the political parties had close ties with and the support of religious organizations that detested the Soka Gakkai, Shin'ichi perceived a formidable dark power in the form of an alliance of government authority and religion behind the turbulent waves buffeting the Soka Gakkai. Nichiren Daishonin states, "When an evil ruler in consort with priests of erroneous teachings tries to destroy the correct teaching and do away with a man of wisdom, those with the heart of a lion king are sure to attain Buddhahood" (WND-1, 302).

Shin'ichi thought: *This collusion of opposing political parties and religious groups for the purpose of attacking the Soka Gakkai is exactly what Nichiren Daishonin predicts. He also declares, however, that if we stand up with the heart of a lion king amid such circumstances, we will definitely attain Buddhahood. Such times as these, when the Soka Gakkai is assailed by storms of criticism, provide us with a perfect opportunity to carry out our human revolution and to elevate our life-condition.* In his heart, Shin'ichi called out: "My fellow members, do not be defeated! Rise up like courageous lions!"

WHEN THE MASS MEDIA began trumpeting the Soka Gakkai and Clean Government Party's so-called obstruction of the freedom of speech and press, the Soka Gakkai Headquarters started to receive anonymous menacing letters and phone calls. Some of the telephone calls were quite intimidating, with callers cursing and shouting over the line and threatening physical violence.

Precautions needed to be taken at Shin'ichi's home as well. Shin'ichi was terribly worried about his wife, Mineko, and their children, but Mineko took it all in stride. She began performing *ushitora gongyo*, an early morning sutra recitation conducted between the hour of the ox (*ushi*) and the tiger (*tora*)—that is, between around two and four in the morning—to pray for the realization for world peace, which she would continue for the next two years, praying for the Soka Gakkai to overcome the unprecedented tempests seeking to destroy it. She also diligently read Nichiren Daishonin's writings whenever she had a spare moment. When she viewed the current situation in light of the clear, all-illuminating mirror of Nichiren's writings, she felt her eyes of faith opening and courage and conviction welling forth within her.

One day when reading the "The Great Battle," she encountered the following passage: "The devil of the sixth heaven has roused the ten kinds of troops and, in the midst of the sea of the sufferings of birth and death, is at war with the votary of the Lotus Sutra to stop him from taking possession of and to wrest away from him this impure land where both ordinary people and sages dwell" (WND-2, 465). Mineko knew better than anyone how, since becoming president, Shin'ichi had devoted himself earnestly to kosen-rufu, thinking of nothing but world peace and the happiness of humanity. It had truly been a battle to which he had given his whole life just as Nichiren Daishonin taught.

Now the Soka Gakkai had become the largest people's movement in Japan, with a membership of 7.5 million member-households. Mineko was certain that since the

Soka Gakkai, in accord with the Buddha's intent, had achieved such remarkable progress and was taking the offensive against the devil king of the sixth heaven, the organization had stirred up the wrath of various opposing forces, which were now attacking it on all sides. Persecution, she concluded, served as testimony to the correctness of one's cause, and as such, it was a badge of honor. She felt this in the depths of her being.

ONE DAY in February, Shin'ichi said to Mineko: "You never lose your smile, no matter what happens. You are so strong. When I see how confident and serene you are, it gives me courage and energy."

Smiling gently, Mineko replied: "What we're facing now is nothing. Persecutions are only to be expected if you live in accord with Nichiren Daishonin's teachings. It's like watching an exciting drama unfold day after day."

"You're right," Shin'ichi agreed. "I know the day will come when we look back fondly on these exciting times."

They both nodded. Such were the couple's conversations during that time when the Soka Gakkai was under constant attack.

Shin'ichi was also concerned about their children. The freedom of speech and press issue was constantly in the papers and on the television and radio. In addition, there were growing calls for Shin'ichi to testify before the Japanese parliament. It was conceivable that the subject would come up at his children's schools, and that they would be taunted about it in some form or another. Shin'-ichi felt sorry for his sons, but at the same time he believed that this was an important learning experience for them.

One day when Shin'ichi arrived home, he sat his three children down and said: "I know you are aware of the situation the Soka Gakkai is facing right now. Criticism of me is also intensifying." The boys nodded in understanding.

"But you mustn't let it upset you, and you mustn't be afraid. I've done nothing wrong. The Soka Gakkai's aim is kosen-rufu, which is happiness and peace for people everywhere, without exception. That's what I'm fighting for.

"Still, there are people who, out of ignorance or jealousy, want to harm the Soka Gakkai, and they say nasty things and attack us. It's just something we have to live with."

SHIN'ICHI HOPED THAT, through this experience, his children would learn what it meant to lead a life dedicated to truth and justice. "In every age," he continued, "people who try to make the world a better place are persecuted. Many individuals who have worked for peace and the happiness of the people have been unfairly incarcerated. The first president of the Soka Gakkai, Mr. Makiguchi, was arrested during World War II for challenging the oppressive militarist government and he died in prison. President Toda was imprisoned, too.

"The most important thing is to lead a just life and never compromise your principles. That's how I've lived my life, and I will continue to do so. I'm a lion, so you, as my children, are lion cubs. That means you mustn't allow yourselves to be defeated by anything. I hope you will laugh off all obstacles and advance proudly and with confidence."

"We will!" the three boys replied in unison.

The eldest, Masahiro, said in a spirited voice: "Don't worry about us. We won't be beaten. We think it's an honor for our family to face difficulties for the sake of kosen-rufu."

"Me, too!" piped in the youngest boy, Hirotaka, who would soon enter the sixth grade.

"That's great!" Shin'ichi replied. "You're all my strong lion cubs, then!" This made him happy.

Many Soka Gakkai members were also being assailed by the fierce winds of persecution.

Trials reveal a person's true nature and sift out those not genuinely committed to kosen-rufu. They show who is brave and who is cowardly, who has principles and who is a hypocrite, who has integrity and who is a traitor.

During this time, dozens of craven, self-serving individuals left the Soka Gakkai, spewing harsh words as they betrayed their fellow members. Many of them had been high-handed and arrogant leaders. Witnessing this desertion, Shin'ichi's sincere disciples, thoughtful and passionate individuals dedicated to the cause of good, were outraged. *At last they've shown their true colors!* they thought. *We will resolutely protect the Soka Gakkai and our mentor! We will continue to challenge such cowardly people throughout our lives and come out triumphant in the end!*

With this spirit, Shin'ichi's disciples stood up valiantly.

MANY JAPANESE PUNDITS, seeing the Soka Gakkai come under intense fire from multiple quarters, anticipated the organization's collapse. In February, a group of writers announced that they would no longer contribute articles to Soka Gakkai–affiliated publications. Eventually, a large number of writers, thinkers and other cultural figures would also decide to distance themselves from the Soka Gakkai or sever relations with the organization altogether.

In later years, however, those people would be astounded by the Soka Gakkai's tremendous development. In spite of the unprecedented criticism and abuse that had been heaped upon it, the Soka Gakkai's membership continued to burn with increasing joy and energy, realizing great progress as it set in motion ripples of peace throughout society. Moreover, in 2003, the humanistic network of the Soka Gakkai International, would expand to 186 countries and territories, and be recognized and lauded globally as an organization dedicated to the actualization of genuine peace and culture, and the promotion of democracy and human rights. The Soka Gakkai would become a bright sun of happiness illuminating the world as it rose in the skies of the twenty-first century.

But pseudo-intellectuals and cultural figures, swayed by the vagaries of public opinion at the time, failed to grasp the significance of the Soka Gakkai and its movement, as well as Shin'ichi Yamamoto's true intent. Amazed by the organization's remarkable growth after overcoming such incredible odds, one scholar would even call it a miracle of the twentieth century.

The cowardly former members who had abandoned the Soka Gakkai were also thunderstruck to see the organization surmount every obstacle and go on to achieve such brilliant success. Some of them apologized deeply and, showing sincere regret for their actions, returned repentantly to the Soka Gakkai. It was pitiful to behold. While those disciples who had stayed and fought alongside Shin'-ichi welcomed them back and even forgave them, they would never forget their actions.

Another sad sight was those who, lacking a solid understanding of Nichiren Buddhism, were unable to withstand the fierce winds of criticism and left the Soka Gakkai, thinking, *This isn't what I bargained for.* They, too, came to regret their actions, realizing that they had veered from the path to true happiness.

The Buddhist law of cause and effect is strict; it is a stern judge of life.

THE MEMBERS of the student division, the young lions who would carry on the Soka Gakkai's legacy, were the first to stand up in the struggle to protect the organization. They were outraged when they learned that an unauthorized recording of Goro Watari's remarks at their student division leaders meeting had been made public at the February 23 press conference held by the discussion group for the freedom of speech and press issue.

Speaking to his fellow members, one young man remarked: "That was a meeting sponsored by the Soka Gakkai student division exclusively for its members. As far as I know, the only requests to report on the meeting were from our in-house publications. That means the tape was surreptitiously recorded and acquired by some underhanded means."

"Someone is taking advantage of our right to assemble! It's totally unacceptable!" replied another.

"What about copyright? It must be a violation of copyright law to publicize or reproduce remarks that have been secretly taped without the speaker's permission," said another.

"These people consider themselves a gathering of scholars and cultural figures dedicated to upholding democracy and protecting freedom of speech, press and expression, yet they have no compunctions about violating the basic human rights of others. It's outrageous. We must do something about this," concluded another.

Students from Waseda University were especially angry because the coordinator of the discussion group, a scholar of Russian literature, was a graduate of their school. They thus decided to select several representatives to go and speak with him. On the morning of February 28, the day after Watari resigned as Clean Government Party Diet Affairs Committee chairperson, the students headed for the scholar's home, which was listed as the discussion group's contact. Among the visitors were Masaaki Kato, a third-year student majoring in political science and economics who was a leader of the Waseda University student division group, and Kikuji Nakayama, a fourth-year student of commerce.

They were tense. They had no idea how the scholar would respond. He might refuse to talk with them, or they might have a heated argument. He could also be out. The man lived in a public apartment building in a Tokyo suburb. After confirming the nameplate on the door, Kato, who was wearing his student uniform, rang the bell.

A middle-aged man opened the door halfway and peered out at them.

THE CONFIDENT-LOOKING Masaaki Kato introduced himself and said, "I'm a Waseda University student and a member of the Soka Gakkai student division." Standing behind him, the taller Kikuji Nakayama introduced himself as well. The man gazed at the students in surprise.

Kato immediately announced the reason for their visit: "The other day your group made public a tape of our student division meeting without our authorization. We have come to express our objections to that action."

So saying, he handed the man a statement of their objections in an envelope. The statement described the students' concern that the discussion group had violated copyright law by using possibly illegal means to obtain a recording of comments made during a private meeting and then publicizing them in the press. It also expressed the students' feelings that such actions were an abuse of their right to assemble and speak freely. In addition, it demanded within three days an apology as well as an explanation of how the group had acquired the tape.

Keeping the door half open, the coordinator said simply, "I see," and took the envelope.

Kato summed up the students' objections, and when he had finished speaking, the man shut the door. The young men left in high spirits, satisfied that they had achieved what they had set out to do.

Three days passed without any response from the freedom of speech and press discussion group. The actions of the students, however, were reported in the *Seikyo Shimbun*. This energized Soka Gakkai members in general, who had begun to consider what practical steps they could take to defend the organization. Inspired by the students, many members rose into action, thinking: *Now is the time to speak to as many people as possible about the Soka Gakkai's cause and true intent. I, too, can convey how wonderful this organization and Nichiren Buddhism are by sharing my personal experience. I'll do my best!*

On March 11, 1970, a certain weekly tabloid magazine published a transcript of the discussion that had taken place between Eisuke Akizuki and Tatsuzo Fujisawa in September of the previous year. The headline of the article blared, "Clean Government Party's Obstruction of Freedom of Speech—Full Transcript of the Secret Tape!"

THE SECRET TAPE referred to the recording that Fujisawa had surreptitiously made of his discussion with Akizuki—which the magazine had transcribed and printed. This was the tape that Fujisawa had claimed to be decisive proof that the Soka Gakkai had obstructed his freedom of speech. But though he had been constantly threatening to make it public, it took a very long time to get out. It was now finally being published.

No doubt the public was thinking, *At last we will see the incontrovertible evidence that the Soka Gakkai interfered with the freedom of speech and press!* But many who read the transcript were not convinced that the conversation contained pressures and threats as had been maintained.

At this time, representatives of the Japan Socialist Party, the Democratic Socialist Party and the Japan Communist Party were making a great fuss over the issue in the Lower House Budget Committee, demanding that a special committee be established to investigate the problem and call witnesses. The budget committee then held a directors meeting at which it was decided that the matter would be left to talks between the Diet Affairs Committee chairs of the respective parties.

On March 11, the LDP, JSP, DSP and Clean Government Party chairs held a meeting. The JCP was excluded at this time because it was engaged in a vociferous dispute with the DSP over a recent Kyoto Prefecture gubernatorial election. The parties involved felt that the JCP's inclusion would hinder the discussion. The JSP, DSP and JCP alliance to attack the Soka Gakkai and Clean Government Party was starting to show signs of dissolution.

At the meeting of Diet Affairs Committee chairs, it was decided to halt discussion of the freedom of speech issue at Lower House Budget Committee sessions and transfer it to a more suitable venue. The question of calling witnesses to testify before the Diet was also discussed.

The Clean Government Party adamantly opposed the suggestion, which it said was being made solely for partisan purposes. The LDP also concluded that this was not an issue to be dealt with in the Diet.

Faced with the opposition of the Clean Government Party and the LDP, the JSP and DSP decided there was no point in any further discussion, and the talks between the Diet Affairs Committee chairs ended in a stalemate.

O N MARCH 17, representatives of the JSP, DSP and JCP invited Fujisawa and six other writers and publishers who claimed to have had their rights trampled on by the Soka Gakkai and the Clean Government Party to speak at a special Diet members conference held to investigate the issue. Though the DSP and JCP were still at odds with each other, they had no qualms about casting aside their differences in order to attack the two organizations.

Seventy to eighty representatives of the three parties from both houses assembled in the Lower House Number One Diet Members Office Building. Following the procedure of testimony before the Diet, the conference proceeded with the guests responding to the representatives' questions. From start to finish, their remarks were filled with criticism of the Soka Gakkai and Clean Government Party. Finally, a joint statement was made announcing that each party would work to investigate the truth of the matter.

On March 19, two days after the conference, the DSP submitted a summary of questions to the government inquiring whether the relationship between the Soka

Gakkai and the Clean Government Party was in violation of the Japanese Constitution. The government replied that the separation of politics and religion did not prohibit religious organizations from engaging in political activities. On April 2, the DSP again pressed the government on this issue. The JSP, meanwhile, raised the freedom of speech question before the Upper House Budget Committee.

The opposition parties were clearly determined to persist in their attacks using every means at their disposal. They were obsessed with causing major damage to the Soka Gakkai and the Clean Government Party and were taking advantage of the current situation to do so.

During this time, no matter how ill Shin'ichi Yamamoto was, he attended each monthly Headquarters leaders meeting. He could not help pouring his all into encouraging the participants and leading Soka Gakkai songs if the members asked him. Naturally, this only aggravated his poor physical condition. Even while resting in bed, he would continue to think about the future of the Soka Gakkai as well as that of Japan and the world.

In March 1970, Shin'ichi's health finally began to improve. The first thing he did at that point was to meet with Kenzo Matsumura, the pioneering advocate of Japan-China friendship. They spoke of realizing the normalization of relations between the two nations and opening the way for lasting friendship and mutual trust.

THE SEASON OF cherry blossoms was drawing near. On April 2, 1970, a solemn service commemorating the thirteenth memorial of second Soka Gakkai president Josei Toda's death was carried out at the head temple's Grand Reception Hall. Shin'ichi had not yet fully recovered from his illness, but he was brimming with vitality as he attended the ceremony. The participants from throughout Japan were relieved to see him there looking so energetic. Aside from the monthly Headquarters leaders meetings, he had attended almost no gatherings in February and only a few in March, leading members to worry about his health.

After the burning of incense and the completion of the sutra recitation, Shin'ichi spoke. As if talking directly to his mentor, he said, "In memory of our revered and respected mentor, Toda Sensei." His voice was powerful. After reminiscing about President Toda's life and praising his virtues, Shin'ichi reported to Mr. Toda about the struggles his disciples had engaged in since his passing: "Sensei! Lacking in ability though we are, we exerted ourselves bravely and vigorously, and somehow, under my leadership, have advanced our movement of kosen-rufu to embrace a membership of 7.5 million. Ten years have passed since I inherited the presidency as your heir. Though I am inexperienced, through the tremendous power of the Gohonzon and the support of many other members, I have been able to achieve the goals you entrusted me with."

Shin'ichi was overjoyed to be able to proudly tell his mentor of kosen-rufu's valiant advance. He continued: "At this very moment, the Grand Main Temple, the symbol of the realization of kosen-rufu, is beginning to take magnificent shape. Moreover, the Gohonzon's brilliant power has spread across the seas and is shining brightly in places as distant as North and South America, Southeast Asia,

Europe and Africa, where countless numbers of your disciples are actively promoting the noble cause of kosen-rufu. In a splendid manifestation of your dream of one global family, representatives of these Bodhisattvas of the Earth from around the world will assemble for the ceremony marking the Grand Main Temple's completion."

The familiar image of President Toda's smiling face filled Shin'ichi's mind.

SHIN'ICHI'S VOICE resounded throughout the Grand Reception Hall: "Sensei! The flow of kosen-rufu has at last grown from a rushing stream into a mighty river. I'm certain that the day when it will pour into the vast ocean is on its way. Shimmering waves of hope dance in the dawning light of the Mystic Law, and a joyous song of life can be heard from beyond the horizon.

"I firmly believe that the boundless compassion of Nichiren Daishonin and the vision cherished by you, our beloved mentor Josei Toda, the leader of kosen-rufu in the Latter Day of the Law, will shower all living beings in the Latter Day with the wonderful benefit of the great pure Law. As a result, all people will be able to realize lives of supreme happiness, and a peaceful society of Eternally Tranquil Light will be achieved.

"No matter how the storms may rage, no matter how the angry breakers may crash, as children of the Buddha, as cubs of the lion king, and with pride as your disciples, we pledge to erect monuments of victory in the places of our respective missions. Engraving deeply in our hearts your final injunction never to retreat a single step and never to slacken in our efforts, we, as your disciples, are determined to fight together against all obstacles in unity and high spirits."

Shin'ichi's words were imbued with a passionate vow. The forces that feared the Soka Gakkai's efforts to improve society had set their sights on Shin'ichi and were bombarding him with relentless attacks. But he was not swayed in the least. Rather, he solidified his resolve to advance straight ahead on the path of mentor and disciple, the path of kosen-rufu.

May 3, 1970, the start of Shin'ichi's second decade as president of the Soka Gakkai, was fast approaching. Day by day, Shin'ichi was regaining his strength. As he had announced at the memorial service for Josei Toda, the flow of kosen-rufu was expanding from a rushing stream into a mighty river. It was at this juncture that the freedom of speech and press issue had occurred.

Nichiren Daishonin writes: "There is definitely something extraordinary in the ebb and flow of the tide, the rising and setting of the moon, and the way in which summer, autumn, winter, and spring give way to each other. Something uncommon also occurs when an ordinary person attains Buddhahood. At such a time, the three obstacles and four devils will invariably appear, and the wise will rejoice while the foolish will retreat" (WND-1, 637). In light of this passage, it was clear that the attacks against the Soka Gakkai about the free speech issue were fierce winds arising at a turning point in history, when ripples of kosen-rufu were spreading far and wide and a fresh movement spearheaded by people awakened to humanistic ideals was emerging.

IN ORDER TO take flight into a new age, the Soka Gakkai was steadily implementing its organizational reform. It may well have been that the criticism surrounding the issue of the separation of religion and politics stemmed from the opposing forces' awareness of the Soka Gakkai's move to restructure; they deliberately chose to focus on an area—the relationship between the Soka Gakkai and the Clean Government Party—that the Soka Gakkai was preparing to address.

Shin'ichi was reminded of a line from "The Opening of the Eyes," which Nichiren Daishonin wrote while he was in exile on Sado Island, "subjected to persecution under a false charge of having committed worldly offenses" (WND-I, 279). Persecution occurs on the pretext of worldly offenses that are dug up or even fabricated by opponents. It was therefore crucial, Shin'ichi thought, to eliminate any unclarity that could lead to public misunderstanding, and to do away with any negligence or arrogance that would disrespect society's rules. Such conduct would only provide opponents and other negative forces with an advantage.

This meant that the Soka Gakkai and its individual members needed to be vigilant about their public image, exhibiting model behavior that could not be faulted. Though the Soka Gakkai's opponents may have intentionally devised the present controversy, Shin'ichi still felt a responsibility as Soka Gakkai president for the stir it had raised. He thus calmly analyzed the Soka Gakkai's response to the problem from the public's point of view.

First of all, he looked at where the root of the problem lay when Akizuki and the other leader had contacted Fujisawa and his publisher in order to present their concerns about the critical book prior to its publication. Hoping to avoid any problems by taking preemptive action, the two men had politely expressed their thoughts and requests, without specifically intending to interfere with the book's publication. But the fact that they had contacted the author and publisher at all before publication had become a key point in the ensuing controversy. The harsh reality was that if someone wrote an intentionally defamatory book with the purpose of spreading falsehood, nothing could be done about it. The leaders' advance contact thus became fodder for the organization's opponents, giving the false impression that the organization tried to obstruct the freedom of speech. From a societal perspective, it would perhaps have been better to approach the situation more cautiously from the outset.

A T THIS TIME, it was widely reported that the Soka Gakkai had attempted to apply organized pressure on distributors and bookstores to dissuade them from handling Fujisawa's book. Apparently, some members who worked in the publishing business told distributors and bookstores what an unfair book it was and asked them to consider not carrying it. Ultimately, however, it was the autonomous decision of those companies whether or not they would do so based on the content of the book and the record of the publisher. It seems only natural for a distributor to weigh carefully whether or not to handle a book that harshly criticizes a particular religious organization or political party or that is by an unknown publisher.

In addition, the actions of a small group of members, driven by righteous indignation against the attacks on the Soka Gakkai, were touted in the media as an organized effort to stop the book's publication. Shin'ichi understood the feelings of those members but, without question, their individual acts had lacked prudence and had been made without considering objectively the possible repercussions.

In regard to the charges that key advertisers such as newspapers and commuter trains had turned down advertisements for the book because of pressure from the Soka Gakkai, was, in fact, a conclusion reached by the advertisers themselves, due to their own business ethics practices. It is unlikely that major newspapers, which are supposed to be fair and impartial, would carry advertisements for a book that attacked the Soka Gakkai and Clean Government Party and thus threatened to interfere with the upcoming Lower House election.

What about the accusation that the Soka Gakkai tried to halt publication through a campaign of intimidating phone calls and letters of protest? It is true that Soka Gakkai members were outraged at having their organization insulted as a band of fanatics, fascists and fools; anyone would be angered by such derision. And it is understandable that some would take action, going as far as to respond with irate and possibly incoherent phone calls and letters.

The Soka Gakkai had more than 7.5 million member-households. If even one in a thousand or ten thousand wrote a protest letter, it would have seemed like a flood to the recipient, making the person feel pressured and annoyed. What Shin'ichi found strange, however, was the claim that the menacing letters and phone calls had continued in an uninterrupted stream.

SOKA GAKKAI MEMBERS knew that by making threats they would be exposing the organization to increased criticism. Shin'ichi couldn't believe they would risk demeaning the Soka Gakkai in that way. Therefore, if there really were threatening calls and letters, they may well have been part of a plot to intensify the opposition and hostility toward the Soka Gakkai. Unfortunately, there was no way to prove this.

At any rate, it was because of the Soka Gakkai's size that incidents that would have been inconsequential had it been a small organization were perceived as a threat by its opponents. For its part, because the Soka Gakkai was still so young, it may have been too sensitive about criticism. Shin'ichi keenly felt that, having now grown into Japan's largest religious organization, it needed to foster the maturity and tolerance to embrace society.

As Soka Gakkai president, Shin'ichi was inclined to apologize for the ultimate trouble that the present controversy had caused to concerned parties and society at large. On the other hand, everyone has the right to stand up to false accusations and it is important never to lose the pure spirit to fight for justice, rejecting all corruption and iniquity. The challenge for the Soka Gakkai from now on would be to strike a balance between such pure-heartedness and tolerance, Shin'ichi thought. If a genuine commitment to truth and justice was lost, the age of the flourishing of kosen-rufu would become a polluted age.

In April, the opposition parties continued to harp on with the alleged obstruction of the freedom of speech and press issue in the Lower House Committee on Judicial Affairs and the Upper House Budget Committee, persisting in their attack on the Soka Gakkai. The darkness remained thick, and fierce winds continued to blow.

This was the first great trial Shin'ichi had faced since becoming president of the Soka Gakkai. But it only strengthened his determination to create a model organization. In the end, this obstacle became a springboard for the Soka Gakkai's future development.

In Shin'ichi's heart, a brilliant sun of revitalization was making its ascent. At the May 3 Headquarters General Meeting, he issued an apology for the free speech controversy and expressed his determination for a new beginning based on a magnificent vision of worldwide kosen-rufu.

NOTES

1. Translated from French. Victor Hugo, *Depuis l'exil: 1870–1885,* in *Actes et Paroles,* vol. 3. (Paris: Albin Michel, 1940), p. 44.

2. Takeda Bushi: An old Japanese folk song by Aishi Yoneyama recounting the story of Takeda Shingen (1521–73), a skilled military leader of the sixteenth century.

3. Tojo Kagenobu: A steward of Tojo Village in Nagasa District of Awa Province (present-day Chiba Prefecture) and a devout follower of the Pure Land (Nembutsu) teachings.

4. Ryokan of Gokuraku-ji temple (1217–1303): A priest of the True Word Precepts School who was widely revered by influential figures in the Kamakura government and others. He resented Nichiren Daishonin, who had pointed out his fraudulence, and was behind various schemes to persecute Nichiren and his followers.

5. The Upper House has a complex election system. Its members are elected for six-year terms and seats are divided into nationwide and prefectural districts. Elections for the Upper House are staggered so that half of the representatives in each district are up for reelection alternately every three years.

6. New religions: Term commonly used in reference to religious movements outside organized Shinto and Buddhism that have emerged in Japan since the nineteenth century.

Mighty River

A FRESH BREEZE BLEW beneath the clear blue skies. The current of Soka was at last expanding from a rushing stream into a mighty river, making its way for the ocean of happiness and peace for all humanity.

On May 3, 1970, the Thirty-third Soka Gakkai Headquarters General Meeting, marking Shin'ichi's tenth anniversary as president, was held at the Nihon University Auditorium in Ryogoku, Tokyo. A giant backdrop hung behind the stage emblazoned with the number ten in gold—indicating the ten-year milestone—and the Chinese characters for revitalization in red.

The start of the meeting was announced at 10:50 AM.

The majestic sounds of an orchestra reverberated throughout the auditorium as it played a vigorous overture to celebrate the occasion. A chorus performed next, followed by the Fife and Drum Corps and Brass Band, all delighting the audience.

The second part of the meeting proceeded with opening remarks and progress reports, and then a speech by President Yamamoto. Many broadcast and print journalists were on hand, and when Shin'ichi stood up to speak, he was met with a flurry of flashing cameras and bright video lights.

Shin'ichi bowed deeply to the audience and began speaking in resonant tones: "Due to your earnest and diligent efforts during the past ten years, we have succeeded in building a shining age of kosen-rufu. Words cannot convey the gratitude I feel for the tireless endeavors made by all of you who have supported me in spite of my youth and inexperience. Though these are all too common words, it is with the profoundest appreciation that I say to each and every one of you, 'Thank you so much!' "

These were Shin'ichi's heartfelt sentiments. He knew that it was because of these dedicated and sincere members that the Soka Gakkai had been able to overcome storms of obstacles and realize tremendous advancement. It was because of their courage and conviction that the organization had not wavered in the slightest. Shin'ichi wanted to embrace each of them. He wanted to praise and encourage them with his entire being.

That morning, he had composed the following poem:

Surmounting
fierce storms of
relentless persecution,
capable people of splendid ability
have emerged.

As he celebrated a decade of leadership, Shin'ichi was prepared to give his very life for the sake of his fellow members.

SPEAKING OF the significance of this landmark, Shin'ichi said that the age of pioneering and construction had just finished and they were now entering the age of completing the foundation, in which the individual contributions to society of each member were of utmost importance.

He then went on to discuss kosen-rufu. The Soka Gakkai was currently working hard to realize a number of goals with its sights set on the completion of the Grand Main Temple in October 1972, two years hence. Many members believed that once those goals were achieved, the times and society would undergo some sudden and dramatic transformation. Shin'ichi therefore wanted to specifically address this point.

He said: "Kosen-rufu is not a finite goal. Based on the fundamental principle of Buddhism, I don't think we can regard it as some sort of terminus. The Buddhism of Nichiren Daishonin is the Buddhism of True Cause—of moving ever forward from the present moment. It is the correct teaching that extends forever into the future. The fact that Nichiren referred to "the ten thousand and more years of the Latter Day of the Law" means that kosen-rufu flows on eternally without ever ceasing. Kosen-rufu is not a destination; it is the journey itself, a process of bringing Buddhism to life within society."

Hearing this, many members felt as if they understood something for the first time. If kosen-rufu was the journey itself, then it was a continuous endeavor. That meant that to devote oneself to kosen-rufu was to engage in the struggle forever, and that true happiness and the joy and dynamism of life was to be found therein.

Stating that religion is the foundation of culture and the basis of our humanity, Shin'ichi defined kosen-rufu as a great cultural movement unfolding in the realm of the Mystic Law.

He then declared: "The Soka Gakkai is an organization that seeks to embrace all people while actually carrying out the mission to promote the creation of a magnificent culture for the sake of the people's happiness and victory. Let us set forth once again with perseverance and fresh resolve, aiming to win society's trust and understanding. How about it?"

The members expressed their agreement with thunderous applause, feeling a deeper sense of awareness of their proud mission to contribute to society.

SHIN'ICHI NEXT TURNED to the subject of the recent freedom of speech controversy, saying: "The problem, I believe, arose from the simple and pure-hearted desire of Soka Gakkai members to have our organization correctly understood and the passionate endeavors of individuals in that direction. While I'm certain that no one ever intended to obstruct free speech, the reality is that the actions of some came to be interpreted in precisely that manner. I truly regret that the other parties felt that their freedom of expression was being compromised, and that this incident caused such distress to the general public."

Shin'ichi then noted that during the controversy, various newspapers and magazines had quoted the famous remark attributed to the French writer Voltaire, "I disapprove of what you say, but I will defend to the death your right to say it."[1] Observing that this statement represented the essence of the freedom of speech, he continued: "While our actions may have been in defense of our reputation, we need to recognize that until now, we have been oversensitive to criticism and intolerant of other views, and have consequently alienated ourselves from society. I would like to take this opportunity to apologize to all parties involved as well as the citizens of Japan for all the trouble this controversy has caused." So saying, Shin'ichi bowed deeply in apology.

The audience members were completely taken aback. They couldn't comprehend why President Yamamoto was apologizing when the Soka Gakkai hadn't broken any laws. Some gazed at the podium in bewilderment, while others shed bitter tears on his behalf. Others, seeing Shin'ichi take all blame upon himself as Soka Gakkai president and sincerely apologize for the incident, were at once profoundly moved and chagrined. They vowed in their hearts never to do anything that would cause problems in society, because that would mean causing problems to the Soka Gakkai.

Still others contemplated the new goal of winning the public's trust and understanding that Shin'ichi had just articulated. They saw Shin'ichi's actions as an example of how to reach out with open-mindedness and show respect for society.

AFTER SPEAKING of the importance of freedom of speech, Shin'ichi Yamamoto earnestly called on the members to reaffirm with him their shared commitment to protecting that right. Everyone responded with hearty applause.

Shin'ichi then addressed the mistaken viewpoint held by some sectors of society that the Soka Gakkai intended to make the Grand Main Temple, which was currently under construction, a national sanctuary, and that this was the organization's reason for sending members into politics. He reiterated the Soka Gakkai position that the "sanctuary of the essential teaching" referred in no way to some sort of national shrine, and forthrightly denied the allegation that the Soka Gakkai had such designs.

He also explained the relationship between the Soka Gakkai and the Clean Government Party. While the Soka Gakkai would support the Clean Government Party as its main backer, he said, a clear distinction would be made between them structurally and organizationally. Shin'ichi had always regarded the two organizations as separate institutions, which was one reason why he did not attend the political party's inaugural meeting in 1964. He thus announced five guidelines to differentiate the two groups in reality as well as in the public perception:

(1) The institutional separation of the Soka Gakkai and the Clean Government Party will be further solidified.

(2) Clean Government representatives who concurrently hold leadership positions in the Soka Gakkai will relinquish their Soka Gakkai posts and concentrate their energies on their party responsibilities.

(3) While the Soka Gakkai as an organization will be the main backer of the Clean Government Party, Soka Gakkai members as individuals are free to support the political party and candidates of their choice.

(4) As the Clean Government Party's main supporting body, the Soka Gakkai will naturally engage in election campaign activities, but the party should establish the necessary organizational structures to conduct such activities under its own auspices.

(5) The Clean Government Party should build a strong foundation by recruiting party members both from within and without the Soka Gakkai.

Shin'ichi then said to the audience: "I would like to make these five points the guidelines for ensuring the separation of the Soka Gakkai and the Clean Government Party. Those of you who agree, please raise your hands."

Everyone's hand shot up. Thus, a new direction in the relationship between the two organizations was set.

"IT GOES WITHOUT saying that the party will remain autonomous in its personnel and policy decisions," Shin'ichi remarked. "As for my own intentions, I am determined to live out my life as a religious leader, and I would like to declare once again that I have no plans to enter the political arena."

At this time, there were widespread rumors that Shin'-ichi's true ambition was to enter politics, become prime minister and take control of Japan. These, however, were nothing more than malicious lies to give people the impression that the Soka Gakkai had founded the Clean Government Party for that very reason. The fact was that Shin'ichi had never entertained such ludicrous notions, and he had repeatedly asserted so during the years. Wishing to put an end to these spurious rumors, he therefore decided to clarify his stance once more.

Shin'ichi also wanted to reconfirm the meaning of Nichiren Daishonin's teaching of "establishing the correct teaching for the peace of the land" (*rissho ankoku*), because it was perhaps the most fundamental issue with regard to the relationship between the two organizations. He said: "Nichiren Daishonin stated that establishing the correct teaching (*rissho*) is the indispensable foundation for realizing the peace of the land (*ankoku*). Establishing the correct teaching means to carry out an unprecedented religious revolution based on the Buddhist philosophy of life that teaches respect for life's sanctity. This is the only means by which to achieve our human revolution, a fundamental transformation of our lives that takes place in the realm of faith.

"The peace of the land refers to social prosperity, the happiness of the people and world peace. While establishing the correct teaching belongs to the realm of faith, securing the peace of the land takes place on the level of society. The peace of the land depends directly on the principles of reverence for life, respect for humanity and peace. These are universal ideals sought by all people and stem from the very essence of human existence, transcending differences of religion, race, ethnicity or ideology. The philosophy of humanism aims to actualize these principles and is the starting point of all our endeavors."

SHIN'ICHI DECLARED that by rights, religion should pursue the ideals of reverence for life, respect for humanity and peace, adding that the members of the Soka Gakkai uphold Nichiren Daishonin's Buddhism, which gives these ideals practical substance.

He then said: "These ideals are the meeting point between establishing the correct teaching and securing the peace of the land. As a result, *rissho ankoku* does not mean imposing religion directly on government or any other social sphere. Rather, it is a goal realized by polishing one's character through faith, thereby bringing these principles to shine in one's own life and then in society through one's endeavors. This is fundamentally different from a unification of religion and government. It thus follows that to impose religion on social functions such as government in fact completely deviates from the idea of *rissho ankoku*."

Shin'ichi then remarked that it was the responsibility of government to come up with practical methods for implementing these universal principles. Stating that the Clean Government Party was founded for that reason, he further discussed the relationship between the party and *rissho ankoku*: "The Clean Government Party's role is to work for the peace of the land, or the nation. It is the right of each party representative to consider the issue of establishing the correct teaching while individually practicing their faith, but it is neither necessary nor appropriate for them to make this or any other religious goal the party's objective."

Asserting that the party should respect freedom of religious belief as defined in the Japanese constitution, Shin'ichi added: "I do, however, hope that the Clean Government Party will firmly uphold the ideals of reverence for life, respect for humanity and lasting peace. As long as it does so, and as long as it fields candidates who share the same ideals, whether they be members or nonmembers, the Soka Gakkai will have no objections to supporting its candidates in elections."

Shin'ichi then touched on the way the organization should conduct itself from now on, stressing the importance of strict guidelines for new members, such as attendance at discussion meetings.

"UNTIL NOW," Shin'ichi said, "the Soka Gakkai's foundation has been built on the relationships between new members and those who introduced them to the practice—what we have called, in other words, a vertical line organization. But now that the groundwork for kosen-rufu has been solidified, it is time to promote closer ties within our local communities and make great contributions to society at large. I'd therefore like to propose that we shift to a geographically based, block system—that is, a horizontal structure. Do you all agree to this change?"

The members expressed their agreement with vigorous applause.

A gradual move toward the new block system had already been under way from the previous year and most members were aware that a full-fledged changeover was coming. Now Shin'ichi was announcing its official implementation. The members felt as if a new phase of kosen-rufu had arrived. At the same time, however, some were concerned whether the close interpersonal relationships characteristic of the vertical framework could be recreated in a block structure.

The relationship between new members and those who had introduced them to the practice was naturally very strong. It is difficult to help others take faith without having an understanding of their personal circumstances, including their state of mind, their problems and their family situation, and without being able to speak with them openly and honestly. It was just such bonds that had made the vertical organization solid and fostered powerful solidarity.

In contrast, the relationships among members in the block structure were not yet so strong—particularly in large cities, where people tended to move far more frequently than in outlying areas. It was often the case that no sooner had members of a certain block become familiar with one another than someone would move away to another location. The challenge of deepening and maintaining friendships was indeed regarded as the biggest obstacle for the horizontal organization.

But this was precisely why Shin'ichi felt it was vital to make the structural transition and establish a strong heart-to-heart network between Soka Gakkai members and the other people living in the same local community. This, he believed, was the key to overcoming the growing sense of alienation among people and restoring human warmth to contemporary society.

He was counting on the shift to the block structure to have a positive and significant influence on both the Soka Gakkai and society at large.

SHIN'ICHI CONTINUED speaking vigorously. He still, however, had not fully recovered his health, and there were times during his speech that he had to sip water to suppress his cough. He said, "From now on, the Soka Gakkai must make even greater efforts to function in accord with the principles of democracy, respecting the opinions of each member and drawing on the wisdom of all as we advance.

"Nichiren Daishonin's teachings are undisputable and we strive to apply them to our lives just as they are. But when it comes to our activities, it's important to openly and freely exchange ideas regarding the best way to carry them out. Then, once a plan is decided on, everyone should work together to make it happen. This is the spirit of democracy as well as the Buddhist principle of many in body, one in mind.

"It's also crucial for everyone to have a firm awareness that they are shouldering the destiny of the Soka Gakkai and playing a significant role in advancing our cause. If members have even the slightest feeling that they are spectators and that kosen-rufu can be left to the Soka Gakkai president or leaders, then we cannot create a genuinely democratic organization.

"Though it may be presumptuous for me to say so, for

the past decade—and in fact, since the time of President Toda—there hasn't been a moment that I haven't thought about the Soka Gakkai. And I have given every last ounce of my energy and devoted my entire being to the struggle for kosen-rufu. I hope that all of you will work together with the same spirit to protect and support our organization.

"At this time when the Soka Gakkai is entering a new stage, the most important thing is for everyone to unite with a heightened consciousness and fresh awareness. I am convinced that this is the key to the Soka Gakkai's great future development."

Shin'ichi went on to say that the Headquarters would also take on a more modern structure with the aim of making the Soka Gakkai a truly democratic and pioneering religious organization. Hearing his words, the members sensed a new start for the Soka movement and were filled with excitement.

SHIN'ICHI NEXT SPOKE of his vision for the 1970s and the twenty-first century. He shared his belief that the 1970s would represent the first step in attempting to solve the problems of contemporary civilization that had fully come to the fore in the 1960s. Pointing to the fact that the advance of science and technology had brought about a spiritual vacuum in which people were being reduced to automatons with no self-identity, he suggested that the computerization of society would also lead to human rights abuses and that it would therefore be necessary to establish regulations in order to prevent such an eventuality.

He further spoke of how the Japanese government was tightening its control over its citizens, stating that the time had come for people to liberate themselves from the chains of national subjugation and take an active role in creating an age of respect for the sanctity of life. It was time for a shift, he said, from national interests to human interests. Emphasizing the importance of making the twenty-first century an age of humanity in which people utilized science and technology for their own benefit instead of being used by them, he insisted that a religion that elevated the human spirit was indispensable to that end.

"This age of scientific advancement must also be an age of religion," Shin'ichi declared, "otherwise, humanity and life on the planet as a whole cannot function as they should. That is why I'm convinced of the need for a new and unprecedented religious movement. The twenty-first century lies thirty years hence. I would like to propose that we make this year, 1970, the dawn of such a great movement. What do you say?"

Thunderous applause shook the auditorium.

Buddhism offers the wisdom and philosophy to overcome the various problems faced by every age and society, and it is the mission of Buddhist practitioners to illuminate society with that light.

In conclusion, Shin'ichi remarked: "The Soka Gakkai is giving rise to a culture of wisdom and creation born from the cultivation of human life—in other words, the culture of Soka. With such an awareness, let us strive to make wonderful contributions to society!" He thus clearly outlined the direction for the organization in the second decade of his leadership.

Shin'ichi spoke for close to ninety minutes. Inspired by his call, the members enthusiastically and courageously set forth into the hope-filled frontiers of a new era.

THE THIRTY-THIRD Headquarters General Meeting marking Shin'ichi's tenth anniversary as president of the Soka Gakkai came to an end. The organization had thus set forth into the "age of the mighty river," holding high the banner of culture in a fresh advance toward the hope-filled ocean of kosen-rufu.

Shin'ichi's main concern at the start of this new phase of development was whether the members—and leaders in particular—could fundamentally transform their outlook. No matter how much an organization or structure is modernized, real change cannot take place unless the people comprising them also completely alter their way of thinking. Such a transformation would only be realized when, as Shin'ichi had said at the Headquarters general meeting, each member stood up with the awareness that they were shouldering the destiny of the Soka Gakkai and playing a significant role in advancing kosen-rufu. In other words, each member needed to feel that they themselves were the Soka Gakkai and to have the same sense of responsibility as Shin'ichi.

Whether we have such awareness is the key to genuine unity and determines our success or failure, victory or defeat, in all our activities. If we lack that awareness and become passive, we are unable to view things from a broad perspective. Ultimately, we become selfish and self-centered, thinking only about what others can do for us, instead of what we can do for others. Such an attitude causes us to feel dissatisfied and discontent with our present situation and leads us to complain. Eventually, we start to criticize our leaders and fellow members, which disrupts our precious organization as a whole. Indeed, our inner attitude powerfully influences our perspective.

Therefore, one of the most important conditions as the Soka Gakkai moved toward operating in a truly democratic fashion was that all members take action as protagonists in the kosen-rufu movement.

Shin'ichi also hoped that after the Clean Government Party representatives who now held dual responsibilities in the party and the Soka Gakkai withdrew from their Soka Gakkai leadership positions, they would continue to vigorously pursue their faith as Nichiren Buddhists and ordinary Soka Gakkai members. Individuals are free to follow the faith of their choosing; this is a basic human right. If, after stepping down from their Soka Gakkai posts, the Clean Government Party officials ceased to carry out a daily Buddhist practice, they would end up cutting themselves off from the path of human revolution and attaining Buddhahood in this lifetime.

AFTER THE GENERAL meeting, several Clean Government Party leaders gathered in a reception room at the meeting venue to speak with Shin'ichi. Many of them appeared gloomy, unable to conceal their personal feelings regarding the separation of the two organizations. Speaking on behalf of the others, one of them addressed Shin'ichi, "Now that the Clean Government Party and the Soka Gakkai have been completely divided, how should we, as party representatives, approach our Buddhist practice from here on?"

Looking closely at each of them, Shin'ichi replied: "Though you are stepping down from your Soka Gakkai positions and concentrating on your Clean Government responsibilities, there should be no change in your commitment to working for the happiness of the people and world peace. This itself is the Soka Gakkai spirit, and it is on this point that both groups must always be united.

"Your mission is to put the ideals of Buddhist humanism into practice in the political sphere. For that reason, it is crucial that you polish and deepen your faith, which is the foundation of those ideals. Practicing within the Soka Gakkai organization as leaders, you are always surrounded by fellow members with whom you work together to develop your faith. You also have seniors who help you understand your weaknesses and encourage you. But given your party responsibilities, you may have few opportunities to participate in activities now.

"You may think this means you will have more freedom, but the reality is that in terms of pursuing your faith, you are going to experience various difficulties. That is why you must never stop challenging yourself. What matters most is how much, as an individual practitioner, you continue to have a seeking spirit toward the Mystic Law and what you do to carry out your Buddhist practice.

"Though you may be able to fool others, you can't deceive yourself. The law of cause and effect that governs all life is very strict. No one can escape it. I hope that all of you will maintain pure faith as individuals, never being defeated by your weaknesses. That is the only path to building indestructible happiness."

The Clean Government Party representatives nodded solemnly in understanding, their eyes shining with firm resolve.

FOR SOKA GAKKAI members, shifting from a vertical line organization to a horizontal, community-based structure was an enormous change. The previous year, 1969, there had been an extended period where the organization focused on block activities. This was repeated again in March of this year, which helped smooth the way for the full-fledged transition.

Until this time, the unit had been the smallest organizational level, followed in ascending order by the group, the district, the chapter, the joint chapter, the headquarters and the joint headquarters. With the new structure, the unit was eliminated and the rest became respectively the sub-block, the block, the greater block, the general block, the joint block and the joint headquarters. The district and chapter of the former organizational structure were now the block and greater block.

In addition, under the old system the names of the young women's and young men's divisions organizational components were somewhat different from those of the women's and men's divisions. The young men's division, for example, had long used the terms *unit*, *group*, *company* and *corps*. In January, however, these names were changed to ones that more appropriately reflected the times. It was also decided that in the new block system, the same sub-group names would be used for all four divisions.

The youth division's use of such military terms as *corps* and *company* invited unwarranted criticism of the Soka Gakkai as militaristic or fascist, labels that ignored the organization's true nature. Originally, the terms had been chosen not only as an expression of President Toda's hopes that youth would be "soldiers of peace" fighting for the happiness of all people, but also to convey the spirit of the youth division of the early days as they courageously strove to fulfill that mission.

The present youth division members spoke excitedly of the new changes, saying: "Though we are using different terms now, we mustn't lose our spirit to reform society. This is a new age, and we are pioneers!" "To create a fresh record of achievement, we need to act with even more courage than before. This transitional period is indeed a crucial time."

Proud to be the pioneers of a new age, the Soka Gakkai youth threw themselves enthusiastically into their activities.

BECAUSE THE NEW block system was based on the local community, it saved members a huge amount of time. Under the line organization, it might take members one or two hours to travel to a district meeting. But now, those living in cities could get to their activities in just five to ten minutes, saving in travel expenses as well as time. Large apartment complexes would have both blocks and greater blocks, and members rejoiced that they could make their way to meetings without even opening an umbrella on a rainy day. They now had more time to spend with their families and to make contributions to their local communities.

With the shift to the block structure, Shin'ichi keenly felt the importance of members becoming a central force in Japanese society and creating a community-based human network. Particularly in large cities and their environs, which were experiencing a tremendous population influx, there was a serious lack of community spirit. Though the cities were teeming with people, those living on their own felt lonely and isolated. Often, people in the same apartment complex didn't even know who their next-door neighbors were, and it was not rare for them to pass each other in the hallway without so much as a greeting.

With so many singles and nuclear families living in the cities, Shin'ichi believed that forming strong community ties through which fellow residents could assist one another was especially crucial to protect the fabric of society. Tragedies, such as the death of an elderly person living alone going unnoticed for days, could be averted if only neighbors interacted on a daily basis. And for parents who had to leave their children at home while they went to work, having a neighbor willing to keep an eye out for the children could give them peace of mind.

Living in a place without any human interaction creates a cold and unfriendly atmosphere—a sort of spiritual desert in which flowers of genuine happiness cannot bloom. Lively contact among people fosters happy and prosperous communities.

LOCAL COMMUNITIES comprise the foundation of all societies and nations. During World War II, militarist Japan was supported by a network of neighborhood groups formed across the country. Consisting of about ten member-households each, these groups worked together in mutual cooperation and were collectively responsible for such activities as rationing daily necessities. As such, they served as the smallest unit of authority for asserting government control over the people. It would not be an exaggeration to say that this nationwide system made the general execution of the war possible. Women in particular, aware of their responsibility to defend the home front, made especially significant contributions. The government exploited these dedicated, hardworking Japanese women for the purposes of war.

With the growing trend toward individualism after the war, people reacted against such interference at the community level and gradually came to distance themselves even from their neighbors. The increased mobility of people that accompanied urban development and the housing boom also contributed to the weakening community relations and the breakdown of local connections. This resulted in an increased sense of loneliness, isolation and alienation among citizens.

Observing such developments during recent years, Shin'ichi keenly felt the importance of building community networks that would enable people to support and encourage one another in the cause of promoting peace and happiness. He believed that women would play a major role in this endeavor as champions of peace, thereby raising the curtain on a century of women. This was the primary reason Shin'ichi had strongly called for the shift to the block system.

In this arrangement, the block discussion meeting was pivotal in launching new activities. On May 8, just five days after the official announcement of the change was made at the Headquarters general meeting, block discussion meetings were held nationwide. Each gathering brimmed with the members' resolve to personally take responsibility for constructing a Soka Gakkai that would be accepted and trusted by the public. Everyone renewed their determination to make the local discussion meeting a model of human harmony, and a fresh advance was initiated. The mighty river of Soka thus began to flow in the direction of community kosen-rufu.

A TIME OF REVITALIZATION is a time of fresh growth. The Soka Gakkai had surmounted numerous hardships, and now blue skies of hope stretched out before it. Shin'ichi Yamamoto had begun to take new and resolute steps toward that limitless future, his gaze directed thirty years hence, into the twenty-first century.

About two weeks after the May 3 Headquarters general meeting, Shin'ichi responded to requests from the media and held a press conference to field questions about the relationship between the Soka Gakkai and the Clean Government Party. Some of the journalists' questions merely ridiculed the Soka Gakkai, but Shin'ichi boldly declared: "Please watch the Soka Gakkai and see what it becomes in the twenty-first century. It will definitely produce numerous people of outstanding talent and ability who will contribute greatly to society. That will be the proof of my victory!"

Shin'ichi was determined to personally foster genuinely capable people so that the twenty-first century would be a century of peace and life. He wanted to raise true disciples. Since kosen-rufu was the Buddha's intent and decree, he was absolutely convinced that disciples would appear who would take his vision to heart, be deeply aware of their mission as successors and stand up to carry on the work of kosen-rufu in the twenty-first century. But he also knew that without effort, he could not make this happen. Fostering people meant inspiring them and enabling the seed of mission to germinate in their hearts. And the only way to do so was to devote himself patiently and earnestly for two or three decades to that task.

Until now, in order to ensure the steady flow of capable people into the future, he had founded various groups for young people, including the high school division, the junior high school division and the elementary school division. Within the high school division, he had established a core gathering called the Young Phoenix Group, which he strove to personally train and nurture through lectures on Nichiren Daishonin's writings and other activities. Regional branches of the Young Phoenix Group had been formed throughout Japan, and during the years they had produced many talented youth. After graduating from high school, the members went on to become leaders of their generation.

Now, looking toward the twenty-first century, Shin'ichi knew he needed to concentrate on raising the leaders of the next generation. After consulting with the central figures of the high school, junior high school and elementary school divisions, he decided to hold a training session for representatives from each of those groups.

O N JUNE 27, 1970, Shin'ichi awaited the arrival of the young representatives at the Soka Gakkai training center in Hakone, Kanagawa Prefecture. Having not yet fully recovered his health, he had refrained from attending most activities in May and June, save for the Headquarters leaders meetings and other important events, in order to rest. But whatever else he might postpone, he strongly felt the need to speak with these young people for the sake of later generations; in fact, being able to meet with these emissaries from the future was his greatest pleasure.

That evening, sixty members from the Tokyo metropolitan area arrived by bus for the training session. A dinner of curry and rice was served immediately in the center's cafeteria. Shin'ichi sat with the young people, who ranged from ten-year-old fourth graders to seventeen-year-old second-year high school students.

"I've been waiting for you," Shin'ichi said. "Let's eat."

Everyone started in on the meal with gusto. Shin'ichi had hoped to talk with his guests while they dined, but they were all completely focused on the task at hand. Shin'ichi and his wife, Mineko, watched with amusement as the young people devoured their food in no time.

After dinner, they all gathered in a Japanese-style meeting room. Addressing the group, Shin'ichi explained the significance of the Hakone Training Center in terms of the Soka Gakkai's history.

In July 1957, Shin'ichi had been arrested on trumped-up charges of election law violations in what became known as the Osaka Incident. Behind this underhanded scheme were powerful authorities who sought to bring an end to the rise of the Soka Gakkai as an alliance of ordinary people dedicated to reforming society. For about four-and-a-half years, Shin'ichi was engaged in an intensive legal battle until his complete exoneration by the court in January 1962.

Shin'ichi remarked: "It was a slyly contrived plot and even our attorneys said we had no chance of winning, but the youthful members of the Soka Gakkai were determined to triumph and prove the correctness of our cause. And it was in this building that they gathered to discuss how to achieve victory."

THOUGH SOME of the training session participants were elementary school students, Shin'ichi did not modify his words. He wished to convey the Soka Gakkai's true history to these young people, the future leaders of the kosen-rufu movement. He also wanted to impress upon them that kosen-rufu is a fierce struggle against the devilish nature of authority that aims to subjugate the people.

The younger students nodded in grave understanding as he spoke.

Changing the subject, Shin'ichi then began discussing in simple terms the origins of local place names. Everyone listened intently to his stories, their eyes sparkling. Because he spoke in such a way as to pique their curiosity, they were never bored.

Shin'ichi went on to emphasize the importance of having an inquiring mind and exerting oneself diligently in study. He said: "I hope you will all study hard so that you can stand on the side of the people and work for their happiness. I expect you to grow up to be great leaders in your respective fields, whether as writers, scientists, journalists or political leaders. I want all of you, in whatever path you choose to follow, to aim to be the very best.

"One lion is stronger than a thousand sheep! To become a lion takes effort. What is the secret to genius? It is working ten times, one hundred times harder than others.

"And at what age do you know whether you have been victorious in life? There are many ways of looking at this, but I think fifty is a good age at which to take stock. It is then that your true worth shines through.

"If you set a concrete goal, clearly visualize what you want to achieve, and then do your absolute best, you are certain to attain results that will satisfy you. The important thing is that you make daily, diligent efforts. No matter how difficult or challenging your circumstances, you need to keep striving with all your might without giving up. That is how you plant firm roots into the foundation of your life. All tall trees have deep roots.

"Though people may achieve fame or renown in their

twenties or thirties, often this doesn't give their life true meaning. In fact, it is frequently the case that such people lose sight of life's value, becoming caught up in delusions of grandeur."

Shin'ichi was talking to the students about how to live—a theme rarely touched upon in school, but in fact the most crucial subject of all.

LOOKING CLOSELY at the young people before him, Shin'ichi continued: "I will be watching to see what your lives are like when you are fifty. Please do your best!"

"We will!" the students replied energetically.

In a stricter tone of voice, Shin'ichi added: "Saying you will do your best is easy, but the real question is whether you actually do it or not. The key is to always diligently challenge yourself. People tend to be defeated by their own weakness. Those who win over themselves are the true champions."

The young members were deeply touched by Shin'ichi's words, and they felt a powerful determination surge forth within them.

Shin'ichi then invited them to ask any questions they might have. A junior high school student spoke up, saying, "What does it mean to be smart?"

Nodding with a smile, Shin'ichi replied: "That's an excellent question. I remember once when President Toda took out a piece of paper and drew a line across it. Pointing to the areas above and below the line, he said: 'The difference between someone who is smart and someone who isn't is the difference between being above and being below this line. As you can see, there's almost none.' Everyone has things they're good at and things they're not so good at. The fact is that each of you has the potential to excel in some area. Looking at it from a broad perspective, there is not much difference in people's ultimate ability.

"Today I bought some goldfish. I was impressed by the skill with which the pet shop owner scooped them up in his net. Later, we're all going to enjoy fireworks together. Some fireworks technicians are first rate in their field. At the same time, some people are skilled at raising plants and flowers. And while some may be naturally considerate, others may have a knack for making people laugh. Some are talented at drawing or writing, and some are great baseball players.

"Being smart doesn't just mean having a good memory or being able to understand things quickly. Some people have a strong desire to learn, and others have wonderful creativity.

"It's of course to your benefit to get good grades in school, but grades are far from the only measure of your ability. There is no need for those of you whose grades haven't been so good to put yourselves down or think you are incapable."

THE STUDENTS LISTENED eagerly as Shin'ichi continued: "Someone once said that being smart means always having an inquiring mind. I agree. Such people, instead of merely accepting what they are told, are always asking why, or whether things are true, or if there is a better way. This is certainly a trait shared by all the world's great inventors and discoverers.

"You may often find that you don't know the answer to some question or problem right away. That's when you should ask your teacher at school or read a book, and try to find out more on your own. The desire to learn more is very important.

"Everyone is different. Just as no two people look exactly alike, everyone has unique abilities. For that reason, I hope you will respect and support one another as young lions while striving to be the best in whatever path you choose to pursue."

To be a lion is not to be something special. It simply means to devote ourselves to our personal mission and make the most of our individual talents and abilities.

Shin'ichi went on: "You were born into this world because you have a significant mission. Everyone has a mission. When you awaken to your life's purpose and steadfastly make efforts in that direction, your talent will blossom rapidly. All of you have a great mission to shoulder kosen-rufu in the twenty-first century. If you are genuinely aware of this, you will not fail to develop your individual skills and you will demonstrate tremendous ability. Moreover, you have the Gohonzon, which enables you to tap boundless wisdom!"

The students' faces brightened with confidence.

Another junior high school student then asked: "In the future, I would like to contribute to world peace. How should I prepare for that?"

Overjoyed by her sincere attitude, Shin'ichi smiled and said: "The first thing to do is to decide that your purpose in life is to realize world peace and then exert yourself steadfastly in faith. Buddhism alone, which expounds the

sanctity of life, teaches the fundamental path for achieving peace for all humankind. I therefore hope that you will
study and practice Nichiren Buddhism in earnest and
deepen your conviction in the power of faith."

SHIN'ICHI POURED his entire being into reply-
ing to the student's question: "Health is also a crucial
factor in realizing your ideals, so get plenty of exercise and
build a strong body. I had a weak constitution when I was
young, so I understand more than anyone the importance
of good health.

"The next thing is to study. To actually contribute to
peace, you will need some sort of special knowledge or
skill. Now is the time to thoroughly study and build a solid
foundation. Language ability is especially important. This
is because peace begins with dialogue. Without a mastery
of other languages, you cannot communicate with people around the world.

"Finally, you need to polish your character. I hope you
will become the kind of person everyone can rely on,
someone who doesn't argue with her mother or her
friends. People who are always talking about peace but
cannot get along with others are hypocrites. Peace starts in
your immediate environment.

"In order to become such a person, you need to challenge your own self-centeredness as well as your prejudices
and discriminatory attitude toward others. At the same
time, you need to cultivate compassion—in other words,
a strong mind that desires the happiness of others and takes
action toward that end—and elevate your own humanity.

"It is people who start wars. Therefore, we need to

change people's hearts and build fortresses of peace therein. That is the process of human revolution, and chanting Nam-myoho-renge-kyo is the source that enables us to carry it out. Communicating the philosophy and practice of human revolution to the rest of the world is the basic path to creating peace. Do you understand what I'm saying?"

They all nodded, their eyes shining with clear determination.

Shin'ichi knew that one of the participants had lost her father, and he wanted to say something to comfort her. Encouraging those who are experiencing the greatest suffering is the Soka Gakkai spirit. He remarked: "Everyone has different family circumstances. Some of you might not have a mother or a father. Anyone with two parents is very lucky. But from the Buddhist perspective, those who have lost one or both parents can actually become the happiest of all. Why is that?"

SHIN'ICHI YAMAMOTO'S voice rang out vigorously: "If you have lost one or both of your parents, you may have endured financial hardship and emotional pain. But difficulties provide us with an opportunity to polish and forge ourselves. They also enable us to understand the sufferings of others and to encourage others based on our own experience. In short, hardships are an important requirement for making us stronger and shaping us into leaders of the people. We can therefore say that suffering is ultimately a source of happiness.

"In addition, some of you may have parents who don't practice Nichiren Daishonin's Buddhism. That also has a profound significance. In my case, when I took faith, I was the only one in my entire family to do so. As a result, I was determined to do my absolute best for the sake of my family's happiness and well-being. Such resolve enabled me to practice in earnest, never slackening in my efforts. I want you to know that adversity is the training ground for our personal growth and helps us solidify the foundation upon which to build happiness."

The students all nodded in understanding. One second-year high school student in particular, a tall young woman sitting near Shin'ichi, had tears in her eyes as she listened intently. Her name was Kyoko Komori and her father had died three years earlier from a stroke. At the time, she was in her second year in junior high school and her younger sister was in the fifth grade. Their mother had raised them on her own since then.

The Komori family had joined the Soka Gakkai when Kyoko was two. Soon after she was born, Kyoko had developed a hemangioma [commonly known as a strawberry mark], an abnormally dense collection of dilated blood vessels that created a red lesion on her face. Radiation therapy caused the exterior swelling to go down, but the mark remained. It was around this time that her mother heard about Nichiren Buddhism from a neighbor and decided to take faith.

Kyoko's strawberry mark soon disappeared, and her father, seeing this proof, also joined the Soka Gakkai. For years, she and her family had suffered financially due to the failure of her father's business, but through faith, they surmounted that hardship. A short while later, however, Kyoko's father suddenly died.

TO SUPPORT her two daughters, Mrs. Komori became a crossing guard, helping children get to and from school safely each day. Observing her mother standing on the street, whether in snow, rain or the hot summer sun, Kyoko decided that she, too, would get a job right after high school so that she could assist her mother in some way.

One day at a junior high school division meeting she was very moved to hear a leader talk about how she had worked her way through college. *I didn't know you could work while attending college,* Kyoko thought. *I'd like to try that.* In high school, she applied herself diligently to her studies while working part time at a ceramics store. She wanted to ease her mother's burden as much as possible. "I have to do my best," she would constantly tell herself.

Shin'ichi's guidance at this training session inspired her deeply. Tears filled her eyes as she vowed in her heart: "Hardships are the fuel for great accomplishments. No matter what happens, I will develop into a person who can help others become happy, and I will never be defeated!"

From that moment on, she was firmly determined to go to college. Given her family's straitened circumstances, she figured her only option was a national university, which had the lowest tuition. She studied very hard.

When Soka University opened in 1971, Kyoko decided she wanted to attend this school founded by President Yamamoto. Compared to other private universities, Soka University's tuition was less expensive, but it was still higher than a national institution. Kyoko prayed earnestly day after day to be able to go there.

In December of her third year in high school, as university entrance examinations approached, she made up her mind to share her thoughts with her mother.

"I understand," her mother said. "Take the Soka University entrance examination. I have actually been saving up because I was also hoping you would attend the university that President Yamamoto founded." Kyoko wept at her mother's compassion.

In the end, Kyoko realized her dream and entered Soka University. Later, she went on to become the leader of the young women's junior high school division, devoting herself to fostering future division members and striving alongside Shin'ichi to raise successors in the movement for peace.

S HIN'ICHI FINISHED SPEAKING. Thinking of the smaller children, he had taken breaks during his talk to hold a lottery and look at the students' calligraphy. Overall, however, it was a solemn guidance session, a genuine life-to-life encounter. Shin'ichi addressed each of the students, including the ones in elementary school, as his equals. He believed that, no matter how young they were, if he spoke to them in earnest, they would listen and respond in like. He did not wish to condescend to them in any way. Believing wholeheartedly in others is the key to nurturing their growth.

Among the participants was an elementary school student named Fumiya Nakao, a fifth-grader who was the smallest in the group and was always making people laugh. He had attended the May 3 Headquarters general meeting that year as a representative of the elementary school division where he witnessed President Yamamoto take the blame and apologize for the obstruction of free speech controversy. The issue had been covered extensively on television and radio, and had even come up at school. Fumiya's classmates who knew he was a Soka Gakkai member had said mean things about the organization in front of him.

Fumiya believed Shin'ichi was working the hardest for the sake of suffering people. He was deeply pained and angered when he saw President Yamamoto forced to apologize at the meeting. *This is wrong!* he thought, and he wanted to do something to help prove the correctness of the Soka Gakkai's cause. But he didn't know what he could do. That is why, when he heard President Yamamoto's guidance at this training session that they should all aim to be the best in their chosen field, that a single lion is better than one thousand sheep, Fumiya felt as though his eyes had opened. Moreover, experiencing Shin'ichi's heartfelt encouragement firsthand, he was electrified. *I need to develop my abilities. I'm going to study as hard as I can!* he thought. This day became an important starting point in Fumiya's life.

With the support of the leaders of the elementary school division, Fumiya entered Soka Junior High School. He then went on to Soka Senior High School and finally the prestigious Kyoto University. He would later join the staff at the Soka Gakkai Headquarters, becoming a warrior of the pen in the cause of kosen-rufu.

"THAT'S ENOUGH TALK about difficult topics," Shin'ichi said. "Let's go outside and enjoy some fireworks. Please relax and have fun." Shin'ichi swayed slightly as he stood up; he was still suffering from a fever. Seeing this, some nearby high school students reached out to steady him. One of the leaders accompanying him said, "Sensei, the damp night air might be bad for you, so maybe you'd better stay indoors."

"I'll be fine," Shin'ichi replied. "I want to be with the students."

We must be prepared to give ourselves completely if we truly wish to foster others.

The students cheered when Shin'ichi stepped outside. The training center had a spacious lawn area from which one could see the dark silhouette of mountains in the distance. Stars sparkled in the evening sky. Using a length of bamboo as a walking stick, Shin'ichi joined the others.

Some of the young people stood around Shin'ichi as they lit sparklers, while others lit them with friends elsewhere in the yard. Speaking to those close by, Shin'ichi inquired about their family situations. Hearing from one student that his parents were not very active members, Shin'ichi said: "That must be difficult. But that means you have to practice that much harder. Just as a single large fireplace will heat an entire room, if you carry out your practice to the best of your ability, the fortune you accumulate will extend to your parents, too. So you must never abandon your faith. Let's make a promise and shake on it."

Shin'ichi then handed the young man a gift for him to give to his parents.

One elementary school student, gazing up at the stars, commented that she dreamed of going into space. Addressing her, Shin'ichi said: "I'd like to experience space travel, too. Did you know that Buddhism teaches that our bodies are like the universe?" Pointing to her head, he continued: "The roundness of our heads is like the celestial sphere, our hair the innumerable stars. Our eyes are the sun and the moon: when they're open, it is day, and when they're closed, it is night. Our eyebrows, meanwhile, are the stars of the Big Dipper.

"The inhaling and exhaling of breath through our nose is the wind blowing through the valleys. The twelve major joints in our bodies represent the twelve months, and all the little joints are the days of the year. The blood flowing through our veins is the rivers—the big arteries are like great rivers and the capillaries are like streams."

THE GIRL WHO SAID she wanted to travel to space listened to Shin'ichi with great interest. "In other words," he continued, "we ourselves are a small universe, and all of us have a splendid palace of happiness within our lives. Faith enables us to enter that palace."

Watching the fireworks display, he then said to the students around him: "Fireworks are impressive, aren't they? But though they are beautiful, they are transient. You may look at celebrities and entertainers and think they have wonderful lives, but just like fireworks, they often burn out very quickly. The important thing is to build a strong self that can never be destroyed. That is the purpose of faith."

Some of the elementary and junior high school students announced that they were going off to explore beyond the edges of the yard and disappeared from sight. Concerned for their safety, a few of the leaders rushed after them. When one of the boys came back carrying a frog he had caught, several of the adults looked on disapprovingly. Shin'ichi, however, smiled and said: "You're very brave. Many of you live in the city, so this is a good opportunity to experience nature. That's why I invited you here so, please, make the most of this occasion."

After the fireworks, Shin'ichi went back to the dining room to encourage members who were relaxing there. He gave them advice about their problems at school and made suggestions about their future course of study. He wanted to speak with each of the students and engrave them in his heart.

Later that night, in the training center lobby, Shin'ichi met with the leaders who had accompanied the members to the center. "They are all great children," he said. "And they are the precious heirs to whom we will entrust the Soka Gakkai's future. We need to foster them with all our might. I would like to name the participants in this training session the Future Group."

Receiving the approval of the other leaders, he added, "With this, the way for victory in the twenty-first century has been opened."

THE NEXT DAY, the leaders told the training session participants about the formation of the Future Group. They cheered, but they looked somewhat serious. Regarding this as a solemn occasion, they vowed in their pure hearts to become capable leaders who would take full responsibility for kosen-rufu and work for the peace and happiness of humankind. It was a fresh departure for mentor and disciples.

The participants visited nearby Lake Ashino and other sights in the morning and then left the training center in the afternoon. Shin'ichi had faith in these young phoenixes of the Future Group. He was certain that they would carry on the baton of mission for kosen-rufu and stand up to make the twenty-first century an age of humanism. At the same time, he resolved to give his life to opening the way forward for these youthful successors.

Shin'ichi planned to name this gathering Tokyo Future Group Number One, to be followed later by Number Two, Number Three and so forth. He also wanted to establish such subgroups in every region throughout Japan in order to initiate a great current for fostering capable individuals.

The next month, on July 23, Shin'ichi attended an inaugural meeting and training session for the Tokyo Future Group Number Two at Misaki in Kanagawa Prefecture.

Additional groups were formed in the Kansai region on September 1, and in the Kyushu region on October 18. The following year, 1971, they were created in the Chubu, Shikoku, Chugoku, Tohoku and Hokkaido regions, as well as in Kyoto Prefecture, thus establishing the Future Group throughout the country.

On May 3, 1971, the First Nationwide Future Group Meeting was held at the Seikyo Shimbun Building in Tokyo. It was a deeply significant day marking the twentieth anniversary of President Toda's inauguration as Soka Gakkai president. In addition, it was exactly thirty years before May 3, 2001—the first year of the new century. For these reasons, Shin'ichi thought it was the most appropriate day for a meeting of the heirs to the kosen-rufu movement. He had enormous hopes for them.

From this year, the annual Headquarters general meeting, which had formerly been held on May 3, was moved to autumn.

SHIN'ICHI AWOKE earlier than usual on the day of the nationwide Future Group meeting. Thinking of the members gathering from throughout Japan, he was unable to fall back to sleep, so he immediately sat down in front of his Buddhist altar and chanted earnestly for the members' safe arrival.

The meeting began just after ten in the morning on the sixth floor of the Seikyo Shimbun Building, with five hundred members in attendance. After stating that he had wished to hold this nationwide Future Group meeting on the significant day of May 3 as a fresh departure toward the twenty-first century, Shin'ichi went on to share his thoughts with the young members. "What kind of leaders will appear in the twenty-first century?" he asked. "Will they be flag bearers of peace or not? The future of humankind hinges on this point.

"The people that I have fostered up until now are currently in their twenties, thirties and forties. Since the new century is still three decades away, it will be too late for them to be the protagonists of the twenty-first century. But you will only be in your forties at the dawning of that age. You will be at the height of your strength and ability. I believe that my most important task is to pour my energy into enabling all of you, whom I trust completely, to develop into truly capable individuals."

Shin'ichi then went on to talk about Wilbur and Orville Wright, the pioneers of powered flight. He said: "The Wright brothers engaged in extensive research and experimentation on flying machines, and finally the day arrived when all their study was put to the test. No more than five people were there to witness their first successful flight. They spent only fifty-nine seconds in the air, going a distance of just 852 feet, but it was a revolutionary feat. It was the beginning of the age of aviation.

"The steps taken to achieve anything momentous are by no means glamorous. In fact, in most cases, they take place quietly and out of the limelight. But such accumulated efforts have the power to change the world. That is why I would like you to study diligently for the sake of your future achievements. I also hope you will study the great life philosophy of Nichiren Buddhism and make it the backbone of your lives."

THE TENDENCY in contemporary society to pursue material prosperity above all else was gradually causing spiritual desolation and decay, which would ultimately lead to society's decline. Shin'ichi believed that spiritual revitalization would be an urgent task for the twenty-first century, and that Nichiren Buddhism was the source of such revitalization. For that reason, Shin'ichi urged the Future Group members to study the teachings of Nichiren Buddhism.

Next, he announced that he would present medals to them as the successors who would carry on the movement to realize world peace and happiness for humankind. "These medals have the image of a phoenix imprinted on them," he explained. "The phoenix is a mythological creature; it is the monarch and most auspicious of all birds." The young members were overjoyed. At the same time, they keenly felt the depth of the mission that had been entrusted to them.

The medals were then passed out to each member, whose eyes sparkled as they opened the box and admired their gift. Shin'ichi said: "This medal represents your vow. I hope that you will devote your lives to your profound mission and never allow yourselves to be defeated. No matter what, the person who is determined to win will do so. This is the formula for victory. And the fundamental source of this power is a sincere commitment to faith. Do your best!"

"We will!" the members called out vigorously.

On the afternoon of the same day, the Soka Gakkai's 1971 Fife and Drum Corps Festival was being held at the Nihon Budokan Hall in Tokyo. Shin'ichi watched the festival with the young phoenixes of the Future Group.

On January 3, 1972, the Twenty-first Century Group was founded, comprised of members from the Future Group and other groups. Shin'ichi wished to create a core group of young people whom he could personally train as leaders of the twenty-first century.

Future Groups were formed during the years in each prefecture until there were sixty-four in total in Japan. Whenever he had the opportunity to meet with the young people, Shin'ichi encouraged them with all his heart.

SHIN'ICHI SPOKE frankly to the Future Group members about the Soka Gakkai's history. On one occasion, he said: "During World War II, when President Makiguchi was arrested by the military government and his disciples were also being threatened by the authorities, many who had previously revered him as their mentor began to resent him and hate the Soka Gakkai. Some of them blamed President Makiguchi and the organization for the persecution they were experiencing, and they cursed their mentor despite all they owed him.

"The leaders at the time all abandoned their faith and the Soka Gakkai collapsed. Mr. Toda, on the other hand, who was arrested together with President Makiguchi, was filled with gratitude, saying, 'In your vast and boundless compassion, you [Mr. Makiguchi] allowed me to accompany you even to prison.' This is the mark of integrity and conviction. It is the mentor-disciple spirit."

Shin'ichi went on to talk about the philosophy of life, saying: "We go through many different periods in life. There are times when we are faced with huge problems that seem like a raging tempest. But it is crucial at such times to courageously press forward, without running away. When you are able to review the experience and take something from it, that becomes the source for creating value in your life.

"For example, let's say you have a leader in the Soka Gakkai whom you really don't like. In such a case, rather than avoiding that person or leaving the organization, it's important to continue carrying out your faith to the best of your ability. And as you do so, if you deeply ponder the way a leader should behave and then put that behavior into practice yourself, you will develop into a truly great leader. In every area of life, experience is a treasure and the mother of value creation."

On other occasions, Shin'ichi played sports with the members, including sumo wrestling and volleyball, and also joined them in commemorative photographs. He threw himself completely into raising these students. The young people profoundly felt Shin'ichi's strong resolve to foster them as the heirs of kosen-rufu in the twenty-first century.

Asako Fukuda was a member of Tokyo Future Group Number Two. She was deeply touched by the sight of President Yamamoto earnestly fanning the smoke of mosquito repellent incense toward the members to protect them from being bitten during the group's inaugural ceremony held in Misaki, Kanagawa Prefecture.

ASAKO FUKUDA'S MOTHER joined the Soka Gakkai with her two children: Asako, who was one year old, and her older brother. But the family was not very active in faith.

When Asako was older, with the support of her aunt, who was also a Soka Gakkai member, she started to recite the sutra regularly. Through her practice, she experienced several benefits of faith, such as overcoming her shyness and learning to speak in front of people.

When she was in elementary school, Asako shared with her friends the joy she felt from her practice. Her friends' parents, however, reacted to this negatively and spread lies about her. Asako was shocked that adults would behave so dishonestly, but a women's division member in the neighborhood told her: "I know you must be hurt, but the only thing you can do now is demonstrate proof of your faith by giving your all to your studies. President Yamamoto is waiting for the growth and development of young people."

Hearing this, Asako felt inspired, and she vowed to

herself that she would gain admission into an exclusive metropolitan high school. That would be her first personal victory.

She studied earnestly and in April 1970, she was accepted to the school of her choice. Three-and-a-half months later, on July 23, she eagerly attended the inaugural meeting for Tokyo Future Group Number Two, for which she had been selected. The mosquito repellent incense Shin'ichi was fanning wafted in her direction as Shin'ichi said: "In the well-known Japanese folk song 'Tabaruzaka' there are the lines, *How can I let this precious body / be eaten by fleas / before I have conquered the world?* Each of you has a very important mission, so I cannot allow you to sit there and be bitten by mosquitoes. I hope you won't become hung up on trivial matters, cause yourself suffering or fritter your life away."

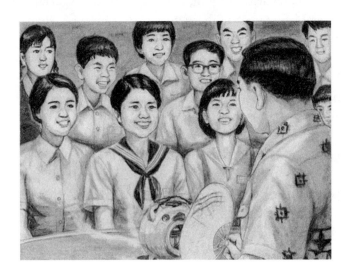

Asako Fukuda felt Shin'ichi's tremendous expectations for them in his words and strengthened her resolve to dedicate her life to the mission of kosen-rufu.

Later, she was accepted into Ochanomizu Women's College, Japan's most competitive and prestigious national women's university. After graduation, she served in various Soka Gakkai posts, such as leader of the young women's division study department, eventually being appointed as chief secretary of the women's division in 2002. Remaining true to her youthful vow, she became a dynamic leader of the new century—the Century of Women.

HARUKI TANIYAMA, who would later become a vice president of the Soka Gakkai, was also inspired by Shin'ichi's guidance in his youth. In January 1973, when he was in his first year at Soka High School, he participated in the inaugural meeting for Twenty-first Century Group Number Two. Every word Shin'ichi spoke on that occasion struck deep in his heart with powerful resonance. He keenly felt Shin'ichi's high hopes for him and the other students.

Shin'ichi said: "My victory will be proven by the number of people I can foster for the twenty-first century. You are all treasures of kosen-rufu and the Soka Gakkai. You are my hope. No matter what hardships you may face, what sadness you may feel, how much you may be criticized or how lonely you may be, please never be defeated. Raise high the banner of the victory of Soka and make the twenty-first century an age when the people triumph. It will be my great fortune if such capable people appear, and my misfortune if they don't."

Taniyama felt as if his life was shaken to its depths. *Despite our youth and inability, President Yamamoto believes in us wholeheartedly and has entrusted us with the future of the kosen-rufu movement, to which he has dedicated his very life,* the young man thought. He was overwhelmed by Shin'-ichi's burning determination, and made a personal vow not to disappoint him.

After graduating from Soka Senior High School, Taniyama entered the University of Tokyo and was later employed by a large trading company, where he was regarded as having a very promising future. But his dream was to someday work at the Soka Gakkai Headquarters and devote his life to kosen-rufu and his fellow members.

Everyone has a unique mission and a unique path in life. Taniyama eventually chose to quit his job in the trading company and go to work for the Soka Gakkai Headquarters. He believed that there was no greater or more rewarding path than the joint struggle of mentor and disciple, even if it meant sacrificing financial comfort, social status or recognition.

He would subsequently take responsibility in such posts as student division leader, young men's division leader and youth division leader, creating a fresh record of victory as a leader of the new century.

Shin'ichi was determined to continue to watch over and support the Future Group members throughout his life. Whenever he met with them, he would offer them sincere encouragement.

TAKESHI YANAI, a member of Kyushu Future Group Number One, later went on to become a doctor. When he was in his thirties, he was working at a university hospital in Yamaguchi Prefecture, aiming to complete his doctorate. After a while, he grew lax in his Buddhist practice and became distanced from the Soka Gakkai. Before he noticed it, he found himself deadlocked in his research as well, and he began to doubt his future as a doctor. He fell into a depressed state and started drinking regularly with his colleagues.

Once you stray from the path of kosen-rufu, the fundamental path in life, you find yourself stuck in a rut and getting nowhere.

When Shin'ichi Yamamoto visited Hiroshima in May 1993, he invited Yanai to accompany him on the trip. Shin'ichi always did his utmost to enable every single member of the Future Group to become a capable person dedicated to the important mission of kosen-rufu. Encouraged by his wife, who was also a Soka Gakkai member, Yanai reluctantly went to Hiroshima to support Shin'ichi's movement.

Everywhere Shin'ichi went during the guidance tour to Hiroshima, he encouraged members with every ounce of his energy, never wasting a single moment. He asked Yanai to help him with preparations behind the scenes. Shin'-ichi wanted to ignite in the youthful doctor the noble Soka Gakkai spirit of working for and serving the people, because that is the true spirit of both medicine and kosen-rufu.

Observing Shin'ichi wholeheartedly striving to encourage members, Yanai felt ashamed. He realized that he had been solely focused on his personal ambitions, and that he had forgotten the vow he had made to Shin'ichi those many years ago as a Future Group member. The gloomy expression on his face was soon replaced by a fresh purpose.

When Yanai went to see Shin'ichi off on his return home, the latter said to him: "You are very talented, so please do your best. You mustn't be defeated."

Those words restored Yanai's self-confidence and gave him courage. He decided to challenge himself based on his Buddhist practice once again. He went on to complete his doctorate and pioneer a new path in humanistic medicine.

The Future Group members were never out of Shin'ichi's thoughts for a moment. Especially when he heard that someone was struggling or having some problem, he did everything he could to encourage them. Sometimes he admonished them with strict compassion, and at others he grasped their shoulders while urging them not to be defeated.

YEARS OF EFFORT and incredible struggle are needed for young shoots to grow into towering trees that can fulfill their mission. They must endure storms and hardships. Shin'ichi continued to emphasize that fact to the Future Group members. At the inaugural ceremony for Tokyo Future Group Number Three, held at the Tokai Training Center in Shizuoka Prefecture, Shin'ichi and the young members worked together to build a path on the not-yet-completed center grounds.

They picked up stones and pulled weeds. When the elementary and junior high school students complained of having sore backs, Shin'ichi said: "Building a path is hard work. Your back and shoulders will ache. But when the path is finished, people can walk along it. I will do my best to build a path for all of you, and I hope that you will do the same for the sake of the future. For that is the great path of mentor and disciple."

On another occasion, he said in a stern tone: "The Future Group's mission is to shoulder responsibility for the Soka Gakkai's future, so you mustn't slacken your efforts. Each of you is a Shin'ichi Yamamoto, each of you is a president. You are my representatives. Please become people who can say, 'As long as I'm here, you have nothing to worry about.'"

Shin'ichi poured his entire being into each encounter with these young people, and his passion, determination and prayer inspired them tremendously. The Soka spirit was thus resolutely passed from mentor to disciple and would be carried into the twenty-first century.

More than thirty years have passed since the inaugural meeting for Tokyo Future Group Number One in June 1970, and the sun of the new century has risen. One after another, the Future Group members have boldly taken their place as champions on the grand stage of kosen-rufu. They have become key figures in all areas of society, holding high the banner of humanism as advocates of peace. Some are educators, others are scholars engaged in cutting-edge research and still others are lawyers fighting for human rights. Some are business people, others are musicians and others are skilled interpreters.

The triumph of his disciples was an enormous source of pride for Shin'ichi, and proof of his indisputable victory. On June 27, 2003, the anniversary of the foundation of the Future Group, Shin'ichi composed the following poem:

The Future Group—
with sights set on the goals of
kosen-rufu and Soka,
capable people
lofty as mountains have emerged.

A SEVEN-STORY BLUE and silver building rose into the clear sky, bathed in autumn sunlight. The modern, cool-toned structure was the new Seikyo Shimbun Building in Tokyo's Shinano-machi. On the afternoon of September 28, 1970, a joyous opening was held with Shin'ichi in attendance.

The new building stood adjacent to the three-story structure that had served as the *Seikyo Shimbun* head office until then. Construction had begun in April 1968 and continued for two years and five months. The building had three floors below ground and seven floors above, with a three-story ell attached. Use of the void slab system made it possible to create large, open interior spaces uninterrupted by numerous support columns on every floor. The building was also equipped with the latest technology for the information age, such as computers and facsimiles.

One entered the spacious lobby on the first floor, which also included reception rooms, conference rooms and an office area. The second floor consisted of offices, with the editorial department occupying the third and fourth floors. The fifth floor contained state-of-the-art computer and communications equipment. The sixth floor was devoted to a large, 5,330 square foot meeting hall, and there were conference rooms and other facilities on the seventh floor. The first underground floor was a large multipurpose area, while the second housed a cafeteria, and the third included a photography studio and the machine room.

The day before the completion ceremony, September 27, marked the *Seikyo Shimbun's* three thousandth edition. With a circulation of more than four million, it was Japan's fourth largest paper, after the *Asahi, Yomiuri* and *Mainichi* newspapers.

Arriving at the new building for the opening ceremony, Shin'ichi said to the paper's representatives who met him: "Congratulations! This wonderful bastion of free speech has been completed. With renewed determination, let's make a fresh departure. To create a good newspaper, it's important to triumph over one's inertia each day. It's a daily struggle.

"We become complacent and unadventurous the moment we are satisfied with our efforts and lose the spirit of trying harder. We must advance continuously. Let us communicate words of truth and justice and a humanistic philosophy from this bastion. Let's transmit messages of hope and courage."

THE OPENING CEREMONY for the new Seikyo Shimbun Building began shortly after half past ten in the large meeting room on the structure's sixth floor. It was attended by *Seikyo Shimbun* staff members, volunteer correspondents, distributors and representatives of the paper delivery staff and the construction crew that worked on the building, as well as members visiting from overseas to participate in a training session. Shin'ichi Yamamoto had suggested that the overseas members attend as an indication of the newspaper's aim to someday be read around the world.

After chanting and reciting the sutra, a progress report was made, followed by remarks from *Seikyo Shimbun* President Kiyoshi Jujo and Executive Director Eisuke Akizuki. Next, in his capacity as the newspaper's publisher, Shin'ichi presented commemorative gifts to representatives of the construction project group. Lastly, everyone joined together in singing the *Seikyo Shimbun* song, "The Pride of Unsung Champions," which had been composed to celebrate the building's completion.

Hearts beating with high ideals,
we have endured many travails over long years.
Words infused with life have great power.
Together, let us blaze
the thorny trail,
for the sake of tomorrow's
shining victory.

Breaking through the gloom of a dark century,
our mission is to illuminate
the proper direction for society.
Together, let us create
a pioneering achievement
for the sake of
an indestructible future.

With the powerful wisdom of truth and justice,
we bear the tidings of kosen-rufu.
As unsung champions,
proudly we sing
an ode to peace
for the sake of a bright, hope-filled world.

Shin'ichi had previously bestowed the title "unsung champions" on the *Seikyo Shimbun* staff. It was an expression of his passionate hope that they would be courageous champions fighting for the people, unafraid of authority and free from the temptations of power and fame. When a newspaper panders to and becomes an instrument of the powerful, it abandons its crucial mission to be a force for social justice. As a result, the people are deprived of their right to know the truth, and the press becomes little more than a deceptive smoke screen hiding the machinations of authority. That is why Shin'ichi believed that journalists needed to stand up as unsung champions and fight alongside the people.

TO MARK the new building's completion, Shin'ichi planted a cherry tree in its forecourt and sat for a commemorative photo with the newspaper's employees. He also toured the building. The editorial office was open and spacious. Shin'ichi wanted the employees to have the best working environment possible in which they could demonstrate their full potential. For the more they did so, he believed, the more they would be able to write articles that would inspire members with hope and courage.

On the fourth floor of the building was a photo exhibit of the history of the *Seikyo Shimbun*. Recalling the events surrounding the launching of the paper, Shin'ichi said to some of the newspaper's executives accompanying him: "I'm very happy that you have these wonderful facilities and that everyone can really enjoy working here. At the same time, we must never forget the difficulties we faced when we were producing the newspaper in that cramped room in Ichigaya.

"The better your working environment and the equipment at your disposal, the more important it is to remind yourselves of the pioneering spirit of those early years. Otherwise, you'll come to take your favorable circumstances for granted, and as soon as you face even a small problem, you'll start complaining. As a staff member, complaining is a sign of defeat and complacency. This is one of my main concerns."

As Shin'ichi toured the new offices, he remembered working with his mentor Josei Toda in the days leading to the paper's inauguration as clearly as if it were yesterday. The first edition was published on April 20, 1951, after Mr. Toda had recovered from the collapse of his businesses and just before he became the second Soka Gakkai president.

Mr. Toda had initially mentioned the idea of publishing an organ paper in August of the previous year, when the Toko Construction Credit Union he ran was forced to suspend operations. Mr. Toda and Shin'ichi had been to a coffee shop in Toranomon, Tokyo, where they had a meeting with a journalist who had learned of the closing of the credit union. On the way back, Mr. Toda said to Shin'ichi with great seriousness: "Shin'ichi, newspapers have unimaginable power in today's world. Publishing a newspaper means having tremendous influence. The Soka Gakkai needs its own newspaper in the nearest possible future. Please think about it, Shin'ichi."

THAT EVENING, after speaking to Shin'ichi about his idea of starting a newspaper, Mr. Toda announced that he was stepping down as general director of the Soka Gakkai. Mr. Toda had decided to resign because he wished to prevent any fallout from the failure of the credit union from harming the Soka Gakkai.

Toward the end of the year, in December 1950, Mr. Toda and Shin'ichi went to a small restaurant near Shimbashi Station. Speaking enthusiastically of his grand vision for kosen-rufu, Mr. Toda said to Shin'ichi, as if confirming the plan:"Let's start a newspaper, a Soka Gakkai organ. We are entering an age of mass media." Despite the dire situation of his own businesses, Mr. Toda's sights were set on the future of the organization as it sailed forth on the vast ocean of kosen-rufu.

On a cold February evening the following year, Mr. Toda announced to Shin'ichi: "Let's get started on the newspaper now. I'll be the president and you'll be the vice president. Let's give this our all!" Preparations for the undertaking thus began at a rapid pace. In March, several members gathered at Mr. Toda's home for the paper's first planning meeting. "This newspaper," Mr. Toda said, "will truly launch our kosen-rufu movement. Let us become, in every arena, champions in the verbal battle for truth!"

Determined to make Mr. Toda's dream a reality, Shin'-ichi wrote in his diary, "Sincerely resolved to develop it [the *Seikyo Shimbun*] into the greatest newspaper in Japan—no, in the world."[2] Several more planning sessions were held, and there were many ideas about what to call the paper— *Bunka Shimbun* (Culture Newspaper), *Soka Shimbun* (Value-Creating Newspaper) or *Sekai Shimbun* (World Newspaper). When the latter was proposed, Mr. Toda laughed and said:" *World Newspaper*? That's interesting. But if we're going in that direction, why not think on a really grand scale and call it the *Uchu Shimbun* (Universe Newspaper)?!"

The title *Seikyo Shimbun* (Sacred Teachings Newspaper) was finally settled on after much consideration. The name brimmed with Mr. Toda's wish to communicate the essential law of the universe, Nichiren Buddhism, to the entire world. And the paper's first edition was published on April 20, 1951.

IN HOPES of making a comeback in business, Josei
Toda was pouring his energies into developing Daito
Commerce, which he had founded in the Hyakunincho
area of Tokyo's Shinjuku Ward. The company's office
doubled as the editorial office that gave birth to the first
edition of the *Seikyo Shimbun*. The building had been a
lens manufacturing plant during the war and its rooms
were huge and bare. Those working inside shivered from
the cold drafts blowing in through the cracks in the walls.

In this shabby space, Mr. Toda wrote articles for the
newspaper at an astounding pace, including one titled
"What Is Faith?" for the inaugural issue's front page. It was
also here that he began his serialized novel *The Human
Revolution* under the pen name Myo Goku, as well as the
"Suntetsu" (Epigrams) column.

About a month after the paper's first issue was published, Daito Commerce moved to the second floor of the
Ichigaya Building near Ichigaya Station in Tokyo. The
paper moved there as well—into a tiny room that could
hold only two desks.

Shin'ichi had also been writing many articles for the
paper. These included introductions of Soka Gakkai
leaders and essays about the lives of such historical figures as Lord Byron, Beethoven and Napoleon. In addition, Mr. Toda would often hand Shin'ichi unfinished
installments of his novel and ask him to take over. This
was Mr. Toda's way of training Shin'ichi to communicate
his ideas to future generations, as well as a sign of Mr.
Toda's confidence that Shin'ichi could live up to his
expectations.

In this way, the *Seikyo Shimbun* was born from the joint

struggle of mentor and disciple, and it would go on to create a brilliant history.

Whenever a story appeared in the media that defamed or criticized the Soka Gakkai based on misunderstanding, it was always Shin'ichi, as the Soka Gakkai's head of public relations, to take action to correct the error. At times he also wrote articles or editorials to refute such errors or attacks and set the record straight. Kosen-rufu is a struggle of words. To remain silent and allow injustice to go unchecked only promotes its pernicious spread.

Those who uphold the cause of good must fight against falsehood and win. If truth is defeated, the people will be cast into a deep pit of darkness.

BOTH MR. TODA and Shin'ichi gave themselves earnestly to writing articles for the *Seikyo Shimbun,* thinking of the newspaper as a personal letter to their fellow members. Initially a single sheet of newsprint printed on both sides, the paper was published once every ten days, with a run of five thousand copies. Though its staff lacked even a professional camera, the paper's pages were filled with interesting and inspiring articles and vividly communicated the Soka Gakkai spirit.

When the Soka Gakkai Headquarters relocated from Nishi Kanda to Shinano-machi in November 1953, the *Seikyo Shimbun* offices moved into the Soka Gakkai Headquarters building. Hoping that someday people around Japan and the world would read the *Seikyo Shimbun,* from the beginning of 1956, the newspaper's fifth year of publication, President Toda began sending complimentary issues of it to ten Asian leaders. These included Indian

Prime Minister Jawaharlal Nehru, Philippine President Ramon Magsaysay and China's Chairman Mao Zedong and Premier Zhou Enlai.

In the letters accompanying these complimentary copies, President Toda expressed his wish that by reading the newspaper, these leaders would gain a deeper understanding of Buddhism and further contribute to the prosperity of Asia. Mr. Toda regarded the *Seikyo Shimbun* as a way of opening the path to friendship and peace in the Asian region.

In August 1957, the newspaper moved to its own building, a renovated two-story structure adjacent to the Soka Gakkai Headquarters. The staff was very happy about this change. In May 1961, ten years after it was founded, new offices were built at a site a short distance from the Headquarters, with three stories above ground and one below. It was here that, for the next nine years, the newspaper would develop tremendously, overcoming numerous challenges in the process of becoming a daily paper.

Now, one year before its twentieth anniversary, the *Seikyo Shimbun* had a brand new building. In the decade since becoming president of the Soka Gakkai, Shin'ichi had not let the newspaper out of his thoughts. Savoring the smell of fresh ink as he looked through the paper's pages each morning, he and his wife, Mineko, would pray for the safety of the *Seikyo Shimbun* deliverers around the country.

A S HE READ the *Seikyo Shimbun* each morning, Shin'ichi Yamamoto thought of the next day's edition, wondering what would be the front-page story, what issue the editorial would address and what kind of articles would be featured. He considered the development of the newspaper, which Josei Toda had poured his entire being into creating, as his personal mission and responsibility. As a result, he sometimes offered direct advice to the newspaper staff, and whenever the editorial department requested an article from him, he always did his best to respond, no matter how busy he was.

When he pondered the future of Japanese society and the progress of kosen-rufu, Shin'ichi keenly felt the gravity of the *Seikyo Shimbun's* mission. Without the paper, it was impossible to accurately communicate the Soka Gakkai's activities, guidance and spirit to the organization's 750,000 member-households throughout the country.

Nichiren Daishonin writes, "It is through the use of words and letters that the Buddha saves livings beings" (WND-2, 6). Accordingly, the role of the *Seikyo Shimbun* in correctly conveying the principles of Buddhism is extremely important. In addition, with the abundance of information available in the modern world, it is not uncommon for people to become so inundated that they cannot actually think about and establish their own sense of values. We therefore need some sort of philosophical standard by which to judge the world around us. The mission of the *Seikyo Shimbun* is to serve as such a guidepost.

Shin'ichi was overjoyed when he imagined the great movement of philosophy and humanism that was about to embark from the bastion of free speech that was the new Seikyo Shimbun Building.

On September 29, 1970, the day after the opening ceremony, an afternoon reception to celebrate the new building was held with more than one thousand guests from various fields and professions attending. Shin'ichi stood at the entrance for more than two hours warmly welcoming each one.

Friendship and trust are born from our sincere encounters with people. Shin'ichi was always firmly resolved to ensure that every person he met fully understood the Soka Gakkai and respected its cause. That is why he took this occasion so seriously.

SHIN'ICHI COMPOSED several poems in honor of the new Seikyo Shimbun Building:

> *The* Seikyo Shimbun *head office*
> *stands majestically,*
> *a melody of journalism resounds.*
> ★

*A vista of Mount Fuji
enjoyed from this citadel of words—
the* Seikyo *head office.*

★

The towering Seikyo *head office,
a bastion
of the mighty pen.*

Shin'ichi hoped that the *Seikyo Shimbun* staff would carry out a noble struggle of words for the sake of truth and justice, and he was determined to stand in the vanguard of that undertaking.

One of the greatest shortcomings in contemporary society is the inability of many to distinguish between right and wrong, between good and evil, as well as the lack of the spirit to fight against injustice. Fundamentally, peace and our humanity must be backed up by the spirit to challenge what is wrong. A peace that acquiesces to rampant iniquity represents the bleak stillness of a spiritual graveyard. Shutting one's eyes to injustice is not tolerance; it is little more than cowardice and apathy. While ignoring wrongdoing may seem the easy way out, in the end it only brings unhappiness to all. The true mission of free speech is to uphold the spirit of justice and challenge inhumanity. Shin'ichi strove to convey that spirit in his poems.

On November 8, six weeks after the completion of the new Seikyo Shimbun Building, some five hundred volunteer correspondents from throughout Japan assembled for a correspondents meeting. This was the second such gathering, the first having been held the year before. Overjoyed that the meeting was taking place in the newly completed building, the correspondents excitedly made their way there.

When Shin'ichi was informed of the meeting, he said to the *Seikyo Shimbun* executives: "Please wholeheartedly welcome all those attending and make it an enjoyable meeting that they will always remember. The volunteer correspondents, together with the delivery staff, play a major role in supporting the newspaper. In addition to their jobs and their Soka Gakkai activities, they make tireless efforts to research and write their articles. It is thanks to them that the *Seikyo Shimbun* has become grounded in the local community and is so loved by its readers."

SHIN'ICHI'S VOICE was powerful as he continued: "The reporting network of the volunteer correspondents throughout Japan is like the network of capillaries of the circulatory system. People tend to pay more attention to major events, which can be likened to the aorta, the body's main artery, but it is the capillaries that sustain life by carrying blood to every inch of the body.

"In the same way, our volunteer correspondents, aware of what's happening in our organization, pick up the news in towns and villages throughout the country. Their endeavors enable the *Seikyo Shimbun* to bring vital, dynamic articles to readers day after day.

"And it is the delivery staff that actually puts the newspaper in readers' hands on a daily basis. The correspondents and the delivery staff are the paper's lifeline. They deserve our deepest appreciation. Those of you at the head office must never forget this." These last words were spoken sternly.

He then went on: "I believe that the efforts of the volunteer correspondents are the true starting point of the *Seikyo Shimbun*. In the beginning, the paper didn't have any full-time staff; Soka Gakkai leaders did all the work. Together with President Toda, some of the directors and I strove hard to write articles.

"I remember when Hiroshi Yamagiwa, who was an academic as well as the Soka Gakkai young men's division leader, had been charged with the task of writing a member's experience for the newspaper. While he was good at writing dissertations, summarizing an experience into a short and interesting article was another matter. He spent many nights working on it until morning. Unable to bear watching him struggle so much, President Toda gave him advice on how to complete the article. But, still, Yamagiwa's final piece wasn't used in the end. Though it was meant to be an experience about overcoming illness, because of his academic background, Yamagiwa had packed too much detail into it and it wound up reading like a medical treatise.

"All of us were working regular jobs and participating in Soka Gakkai activities, and then writing for the paper on top of that. We were incredibly busy, but our fighting spirit filled the pages of the *Seikyo Shimbun,* which is what made it so inspiring. All of the volunteer correspondents have inherited this spirit. This network of volunteer correspondents was established by President Toda, who supported and trained the volunteers with all his might."

The *Seikyo Shimbun* executives listened intently as Shin'ichi spoke.

THE FIRST MEETING of volunteer correspondents had been held in January 1954. A correspondent
had been selected from each of the Soka Gakkai's sixteen
chapters, as well as one each from the young women's
and young men's divisions—for a total of eighteen
correspondents.

At that meeting at the old Soka Gakkai Headquarters
building in Shinano-machi, Tokyo, an explanation was
given of what the job of a correspondent entailed, followed by a question-and-answer session with President
Toda. Lastly, Mr. Toda conveyed his high expectations to
the volunteers, saying: "I am deeply grateful for your
efforts for the *Seikyo Shimbun*. Right now, you are all filled
with fresh determination, but everyone grows lax and falls
into a rut sometimes. In writing articles for our paper, it
is important for us to fight against such an attitude.

"I hope you, our volunteer correspondents, will all be true fighters, true champions. By fighters, I mean individuals brimming with an indomitable spirit to challenge and defeat any iniquitous force that causes people to suffer, individuals who have a constant flame burning in their hearts. If your writing is superficial and concerned only with appearances, you won't be able to refute injustice. Such writing is smug and self-complacent. Only when you are giving your all to writing in order to protect the correct teachings of Nichiren Daishonin and for the sake of the people does the pen become mightier than the sword."

President Toda also announced that to enhance the paper's content, he had invited eleven members from different fields of expertise to be guest correspondents and contribute articles on a regular basis. The January 31 issue of the *Seikyo Shimbun* published the names of these and the eighteen volunteer correspondents. Among the guest correspondents were Senior Director Takeo Konishi; university assistant professor Joji Kanda; writer and author of the novel *Nichiren Daishonin* Kunizo Minato; and twenty-six-year-old Shin'ichi Yamamoto.

In January 1956, two years after the volunteer correspondent system was initiated, regional editions of the newspaper began publication, and in April that year, the number of volunteer correspondents had increased to thirty-three. The following year, 1957, when the Yubari Coal Miners Union Incident occurred in Yubari, Hokkaido, the local volunteer correspondent played an important role. Having surmised the plans of the union leaders the summer of the year before the incident took place, he made a detailed report to the *Seikyo Shimbun* head office, enabling the Soka Gakkai to take appropriate action.

THE VOLUNTEER correspondent's report alerted the Soka Gakkai Headquarters to the fact that the union's persecution of Soka Gakkai members was intensifying. Based on that information, President Toda and other Soka Gakkai leaders were able to discuss the situation thoroughly and take immediate and effective measures as soon as the issue came to the fore.

This particular volunteer correspondent was resolved to be the eyes, ears and legs of the Soka Gakkai. The flame of justice to fight resolutely against the oppressive authorities that sought to harm his fellow members and prevent the advance of kosen-rufu blazed brightly in his heart. It was the spirit of *Seikyo*, the spirit of the volunteer correspondents.

Another correspondent once claimed proudly to a journalist from a different paper that the *Seikyo Shimbun* was the best newspaper around. When the journalist challenged his assertion as being too subjective, the volunteer replied: "I'll tell you why I think so. The guiding philosophy of the *Seikyo Shimbun* is to help people overcome their suffering. It is filled with people's personal accounts of how they triumphed over various difficulties to become happy. There are stories of people who have conquered what were diagnosed as fatal illnesses and of people who have recovered from business failures. The *Seikyo Shimbun* presents a way of life that enables people to overcome any obstacle they may encounter. Does your newspaper offer that? And how many people has your newspaper provided with the strength and courage to go on living? There is no end to the number of people who have gained hope and risen up from the depths of despair from reading the *Seikyo Shimbun.* That is why I can definitely say that the *Seikyo Shimbun* is the best newspaper there is."

The journalist was speechless. The volunteer correspondent had tremendous pride and confidence in the newspaper he was helping create, and that spirit was the driving force of the newspaper's growth.

I N SUBSEQUENT YEARS, with the further expansion of regional editions of the *Seikyo Shimbun,* the volunteer correspondents system was strengthened and regional offices were established around Japan. By September 1970, when the new head office was completed, twenty-one regions, including Okinawa, had their own issues.

After speaking to the *Seikyo Shimbun* executives about the important role of the volunteer correspondents, Shin'-ichi said: "On the day of the correspondents gathering, I have a meeting as well as some other business to attend to at the Soka Gakkai Headquarters, so I will unfortunately not be able to go, but I would like to prepare books and other gifts to present to the participants. And since they are assembling from throughout the country, I think we should have a question-and-answer session or an informal reception where they can get to know each other, as well as take a commemorative photo.

"The correspondents have all taken time out of their

busy schedules to attend this meeting, so as the organizers, I hope you will make every possible effort to ensure that its format and content are the best they can be. Otherwise, you will be wasting the members' time and impeding their advancement. It is very important to make our meetings as valuable and inspiring as possible."

At half past ten in the morning on November 8, the correspondents meeting was held at the new Seikyo Shimbun Building with five hundred participants in attendance. The meeting included the appointment of new volunteer correspondents as well as speeches on the history of the newspaper and the mission of its correspondents, but it was the activity reports that resonated most deeply with the participants.

First to address the audience was Seiji Toyama, a young men's division greater block leader from Kushiro, Hokkaido, who stammered as he spoke. He was employed as an official of the Kushiro Railway Administration, which was then part of the Japan National Railways. He had started practicing in the spring of 1964, and became a volunteer correspondent two years later.

His inspiration for joining the Soka Gakkai was the *Seikyo Shimbun,* which he often saw at the store where he bought bread. Initially, he enthusiastically wrote articles for the paper as a way of showing his gratitude for having discovered Nichiren Buddhism. But when everything he submitted was returned with a rejection notice, he became frustrated and started to distance himself from correspondence work.

He remained active in Soka Gakkai activities, however, eventually becoming a young men's division block leader.

The block he led was about forty minutes by bicycle from his dormitory.

I N TOYAMA'S BLOCK was a women's division member who had lost her husband and was raising their three children on her own. Her children were all cheerful by nature, and her son had been student council president of his junior high school and achieved excellent grades. Studying hard and chanting earnestly, the boy had not only gained admission to the senior high school of his choice but also received a scholarship for his good grades.

Struck by the power of faith demonstrated by the young man, Toyama decided that he wanted to share the story with other members by writing it for the *Seikyo Shimbun*. He visited and interviewed the family, took photos and wrote an article, which he then sent to the regional office. Given his previous experiences, however, he doubted that this one would be printed either.

Several days later, Toyama opened the newspaper and nearly leapt for joy. There was his article in the Hokkaido section of the paper. Large tears fell from his eyes onto the page, and for the first time he felt elation and a sense of mission at being a correspondent.

When we truly fulfill our purpose in life, real joy and happiness well forth from within.

Realizing that he had interpreted the rejection of his articles as the rejection of his personal mission, Toyama renewed his determination. At first, he traveled around on his bicycle gathering material for his stories. In winter, he pedaled his way from place to place, the biting wind stinging his face and turning his eyebrows into icicles. Even with thick wool gloves, his fingers would ache from the cold as he grasped the bicycle handles. Nevertheless, he burned with a fighting spirit to communicate the experiences of his fellow members, who were also struggling in the same freezing climate.

Wherever members were bringing the flowers of actual proof to bloom, wherever joyous members gathered, Toyama was there. Eventually, to cover stories throughout the vast Konsen plain of eastern Hokkaido, he bought a used car. But even with the car, in winter, he often had to make his way through blizzards with temperatures reaching below minus four degrees Fahrenheit to research his stories. On such days, the snow hitting his front windshield would freeze, rendering the wipers useless. This made it impossible to keep the window clear or see the road ahead. The only solution was to pull to the side of the road and scrape off the ice by hand.

ONE NIGHT in the middle of winter, Toyama's car broke down on the way back from conducting interviews for an article he was writing. Stuck in the middle of the wilderness, he was afraid that he might freeze to death. He chanted earnestly inside the car, waiting for someone to come along the road. He was shivering so hard that his teeth chattered.

Just after four in the morning, a truck finally stopped. Toyama felt as if he had escaped death by a hair's breadth. The truck driver took him to the nearest town, where he woke up the car repair shop owner and convinced him to drive out and look at his car.

No matter how challenging the correspondent job was,

Toyama always found meeting with the pure-hearted members to be a source of tremendous joy. His own spirit seemed cleansed by the encounter and he felt fresh courage arise within him. After gathering the material he needed, he would set about composing his article. Often, he would become so absorbed in the task that morning would dawn before he realized it.

At such times, the sound of the *Seikyo Shimbun* delivery staff's footsteps would energize him. *I write articles,* he thought, *but it's because of the delivery staff that others can read them. Delivering the paper day in and day out, in rain and snow, their struggles are much harder than mine.* This thought wiped away Toyama's exhaustion.

By nature, Toyama was not a very articulate person, and he had a difficult time speaking in front of others. But as he continued his activities as a correspondent and interviewing his fellow members, he was able to express himself quite freely.

After energetically delivering his activity report before the volunteer correspondents who had assembled from throughout the nation, he closed his speech by saying: "I think we have entered an age when the struggle of the written and spoken word is going to have a major impact on the development of kosen-rufu. As a pioneer correspondent of that time, I am determined to do my utmost to communicate the Soka Gakkai's true cause. I will proclaim the correct teaching of Buddhism to the very end. Let's work together to create the best newspaper in Japan and the world and write a fresh history of brilliant achievement for our movement!"

The correspondents applauded vigorously.

NOT ONLY MEMBERS of the young men's division but also of the men's, women's, young women's and student divisions were volunteer correspondents. The activities of the women stood out above the rest, and none more than the energetic efforts of one young woman in the Niigata branch office.

In 1956, Yuko Ozawa was the only volunteer correspondent belonging to the original Niigata Chapter. She had just graduated from high school when she took on the responsibility at the encouragement of her chapter leader, who had heard that she had worked on her high school paper.

Ozawa embarked on her first assignment with zest. But when she went to develop the photograph she had taken of the member whose experience she was writing, she found that the subject's head had been cut off from the neck up. The camera must have moved when she pressed the shutter. She was disappointed, but her error only caused her determination to burn even brighter, and she set about studying photography with all her might.

How we react to a failure or a mistake determines our future success or failure.

One year, Ozawa was asked to take a photograph for the New Year's edition of the regional *Seikyo Shimbun*. After giving the matter some thought, she decided to take a picture of the Japan Sea at dawn. She left her house while it was still dark and stood expectantly at the end of the local pier, the icy winter wind stinging her cheeks. Putting up the collar of her overcoat and shivering in the cold, she waited for the sun to rise.

Eventually, the pale light of morning began to fill the

sky. She saw seagulls flying above the waves through the morning mist. Walking out closer to the edge of the pier, she aimed her camera.

At that moment, a voice called out from behind her, "Young lady!" It was a police officer. "Don't be hasty," he said. "Let's go to the police box and talk it over."

"I'm not trying to kill myself," Ozawa replied. "I'm trying to take a photograph."

After she had shown him the camera, the officer sputtered: "Uh, well, I received a report from a fisherman who said he saw a young woman who seemed about to jump into the sea. I'm very sorry. Some people are quick to draw conclusions, which often gets us into trouble." He chuckled to himself as he walked away.

YUKO OZAWA went on to become a leader of the Niigata young women's division, but even amid her extremely busy schedule, she continued to carry out her responsibilities as a volunteer correspondent. She was determined to keep reporting as a witness on the front lines of kosen-rufu.

In June 1964, an earthquake of magnitude 7.5 struck northern Niigata Prefecture. It was a major quake that toppled a four-story concrete and reinforced-steel apartment building. Ozawa lost no time in visiting the area that had been hit and, while encouraging her fellow members, promptly wrote articles for the *Seikyo Shimbun*'s regional edition about how they were surmounting the disaster. These included vibrant reports of a discussion meeting held just two days after the quake at which members encouraged each other, and of young women's division members who sang songs at relief centers to bring joy to the victims. Ozawa also wrote articles on the disaster that were published in the national edition of the newspaper. Members who were worried about the safety of their friends in Niigata were relieved to read these articles, which also drove home to them the greatness of faith.

At the same time, having come to keenly feel the importance of her mission as a correspondent and the immense fulfillment it gave her personally, Ozawa shared her experience with many other young women's division members. As a result, one after another, young women in Niigata began to volunteer as correspondents, their youthful power becoming the driving force of the paper's regional office.

One such young woman was Fumiyo Honda from Sado Island, a part of Niigata Prefecture, who also attended the correspondents meeting at the new Seikyo Shimbun Building.

Honda had joined the Soka Gakkai with her family on Sado when she was in junior high school. After graduating from senior high school, she enrolled in a pharmaceutical university in Tokyo. She passed a national exam to become a licensed pharmacist and started looking for work in the city, but around that time her chronic anemia worsened, and she was forced to return to Sado.

For a while, Honda spent her days moping around. Gazing out at the raging sea off Sado, she felt as if she were a little boat being tossed about on the rough waves of life. Then she received encouragement from Ozawa. Inspired, Honda resolved to make a fresh start in her faith and transform her karma. At Ozawa's suggestion, she also decided to assist the local volunteer correspondents.

OZAWA HOPED that through supporting the volunteer correspondents, Honda would find a way to rebuild her life based on faith. She also felt that Honda would be a wonderful correspondent herself.

Eventually, Honda was able to make use of her pharmacist license and open her own pharmacy. As she helped the local correspondents interview members for the *Seikyo Shimbun,* she began to sense that she was coming into contact with the true radiance of humanity. She spoke to women's division members who were working selflessly to spread the teachings of Buddhism, immensely proud to be residents of Sado Island, with its deep connection to Nichiren Daishonin. She also interviewed men's division members who, while holding high the banner of Soka, had forged a vast network of trust and friendship in their communities by challenging entrenched local customs.

Honda gradually started to feel a strong desire to devote her life to kosen-rufu on Sado, and she couldn't help but think that this was the real reason that her condition had worsened and she returned home. She then became an official volunteer correspondent and demonstrated tremendous ability.

At times she worked under severe time restrictions, given that only one round-trip boat sailed each day from Ogi Harbor, near to where she lived, to Niigata. On one occasion, after interviewing and photographing a member and writing her article, she rushed down to the dock to have it taken to the mainland. But the boat was already pulling away from the dock. Shouting, "Please, take this for me!" she threw the envelope containing the article and film at the boat with all her might. A crewmember who knew her well caught it.

Transportation on the island was not so convenient, either. She even had to spend the night at another young women's division member's home once when she missed the last bus after collecting material for a story.

Honda paid special attention to getting her facts correct. She was particularly careful to confirm names and dates. Accuracy is the lifeblood of a newspaper, and she understood that a single mistake on her part could seriously harm the trust and credibility that so many people had worked hard to build for the *Seikyo Shimbun*.

There were times when the stories or photographs she had gone to great pains to obtain were not printed, but she regarded such cases as tests of her character. Would she allow her disappointment to destroy her enthusiasm, or would she use it as fuel to strengthen her fighting spirit? She was certain that her mind-set would ultimately determine the kind of life she led and whether or not she became happy.

For Honda, her work as a volunteer correspondent was a sort of training ground on which to foster and cultivate her spirit of challenge, and she was grateful for the many opportunities it offered her.

WHENEVER FUMIYO HONDA saw her articles or photographs in print, the pain of all her hardships seemed to disappear instantly. Thinking about how her work was enabling others to know about the activities and experiences of her fellow Sado members, the joy of carrying out her mission as a correspondent filled her heart.

In the meantime, her chronic anemia disappeared, and she took on the responsibility of chapter young women's division leader. Fulfilling her duties both as a leader and a volunteer correspondent was no easy matter, yet she never slackened her efforts.

Learning of the dedicated activities of the Niigata volunteer correspondents, Shin'ichi presented a book to Honda as a representative of her fellow members, to commemorate the opening of the new Seikyo Shimbun Building in September 1970. On the flyleaf, he wrote, *Unforgettable Sado Island / the unity of mentor and disciple.*

Shin'ichi saw the volunteer correspondents as champions in the struggle of words to build a peaceful society—the struggle of kosen-rufu. That is why he had the highest expectations for their activities in regions throughout Japan, and continued to make every effort to encourage them for the sake of their personal growth.

One volunteer correspondent in Hiroshima had experienced the atomic bombing when she was a child. Living with the fear that the effects of radiation exposure could manifest at any time, she joined the Soka Gakkai at seventeen, and later became a volunteer correspondent. When Shin'ichi heard about this young women's division member, who was giving her all to compose articles toward the cause of peace, he presented her with a book in which he wrote, *A great philosophy / fears not even atomic bombs.*

The national correspondents meeting held in the new Seikyo Shimbun Building came to a joyous close. When Shin'ichi received the report about the meeting, he thought to himself: *I will take the lead and struggle along with the members. With the determination of a correspondent and a journalist, like each of them, I will never cease writing articles for the* Seikyo Shimbun, *the bastion of the struggle of words that is kosen-rufu. Let the battle begin!*

That evening, as he was driving through the neighborhood near the Soka Gakkai Headquarters, Shin'ichi looked up at the tall Seikyo Shimbun Building. Against the backdrop of a crimson sky, the paper's flag flew vigorously atop its roof.

NOTES

1. *The Macmillan Book of Proverbs, Maxims, and Famous Phrases,* Burton Stevenson, ed. (New York: Macmillan Publishing Company,

1976), p. 2191. While this quote is widely attributed to Voltaire, research has shown that it was actually invented by a later author as an epitome of Voltaire's attitude. It appeared in *The Friends of Voltaire* (1906), written by Evelyn Beatrice Hall under the pseudonym S. G. Tallentyre.

2. Daisaku Ikeda, *A Youthful Diary* (Santa Monica, California: World Tribune Press, 2000), p. 99.

Index

More on Nichiren Buddhism
and Its Application to Daily Life

The following twelve titles can be purchased from your local or on-line bookseller, or go to the Middleway Press Web site (www.middlewaypress.com).

The Buddha in Your Mirror: Practical Buddhism and the Search for Self, by Woody Hochswender, Greg Martin and Ted Morino

A bestselling Buddhist primer that reveals the most modern, effective and practical way to achieve what is called enlightenment or Buddhahood. Based on the centuries-old teaching of the Japanese Buddhist master Nichiren, this method has been called the "direct path" to enlightenment. (Paperback: ISBN 0-978-9674697-8-2; $14.00, Hardcover: ISBN 0-978-9674697-1-3; $23.95)

The Buddha Next Door:
Ordinary People, Extraordinary Stories
by Zan Gaudioso and Greg Martin

This anthology of personal experiences illuminates how the practice of Nichiren Buddhism has changed people's lives for the better. These first-person narratives—representing people from throughout the country of various ages and ethnic backgrounds—examine the challenges of daily life associated with health, relationships, career and aging, and the ensuing experiences of hope, success, inspiration and personal enlightenment that come about as a result of living as Nichiren Buddhists.

(Paperback: ISBN 978-0-9779245-1-6; $15.95)

Buddhism Day by Day: Wisdom for Modern Life
by Daisaku Ikeda

This treasury of practical information and encouragement will appeal to those seeking a deeper understanding of how to apply the tenets of Nichiren Buddhism in their day-to-day lives.

(Paperback: ISBN 978-0-9723267-5-9; $15.95)

Buddhism for You series
In this oasis of insight and advice on the power of Nichiren Buddhism—which holds that everyone has a Buddha nature of limitless power, wisdom and compassion—readers will learn how to live a life filled with courage, determination, love and prayer to achieve their goals and desires.

(**Courage** Hardcover: ISBN 978-0-9723267-6-6; $7.95)
(**Determination** Hardcover: ISBN 978-0-9723267-8-0; $7.95)
(**Love** Hardcover: ISBN 978-0-9723267-7-3; $7.95)
(**Prayer** Hardcover: ISBN 978-0-9723267-9-7; $7.95)

Choose Hope: Your Role in Waging Peace in the Nuclear Age,
by David Krieger and Daisaku Ikeda

"In this nuclear age, when the future of humankind is imperiled by irrational strategies, it is imperative to restore sanity to our policies and hope to our destiny. Only a rational analysis of our problems can lead to their solution.

This book is an example par excellence of a rational approach."
—Joseph Rotblat, Nobel Peace Prize laureate
(Hardcover: ISBN 978-0-9674697-6-8; $23.95)

Planetary Citizenship: *Your* **Values, Beliefs and Actions** *Can* **Shape a Sustainable World**
by Hazel Henderson and Daisaku Ikeda
"*Planetary Citizenship* is a delightful introduction to some of the most important ideas and facts concerning stewardship of the planet. I cannot think of any book that deals with more important issues."
—Mihaly Csikszentmihalyi, author of *Flow: The Psychology of Optimal Experience,* California
(Hardcover: ISBN 978-0-9723267-2-8; $23.95)

Romancing the Buddha: Embracing Buddhism in My Everyday Life by Michael Lisagor
"*Romancing the Buddha: Embracing Buddhism in My Everyday Life* is…a resource which provides excellent insights into applying Nichiren Buddhism to the difficulties of daily life, including depression, spousal illness, the challenge of raising two daughters and the quest for happiness. An absorbing and inspirational selection of vignettes touched with wisdom, *Romancing the Buddha* is an impressive and welcome contribution to Buddhist Studies reading lists."
—Midwest Book Review
(Paperback: ISBN 978-0-9723267-4-2; $18.95)

Unlocking the Mysteries of Birth & Death… and Everything In Between, A Buddhist View of Life
(second edition) by Daisaku Ikeda
"In this slender volume, Ikeda presents a wealth of profound

information in a clear and straightforward style that can be easily absorbed by the interested lay reader. His life's work, and the underlying purpose of his book, is simply to help human beings derive maximum meaning from their lives through the study of Buddhism."
—ForeWord Magazine
(Paperback: ISBN 978-0-9723267-0-4; $15.00)

The Way of Youth: Buddhist Common Sense for Handling Life's Questions, by Daisaku Ikeda
"[This book] shows the reader how to flourish as a young person in the world today; how to build confidence and character in modern society; learn to live with respect for oneself and others; how to contribute to a positive, free and peaceful society; and find true personal happiness."
—Midwest Book Review
(Paperback: ISBN 978-0-9674697-0-6; $14.95)

The following titles can be purchased at SGI-USA bookstores nationwide or through the mail order center: call 800-626-1313 or e-mail mailorder@sgi-usa.org.

Commentaries on Buddhahood: Lessons on the Writings of Nichiren Daishonin by the Soka Gakkai Study Department
These booklets contain lectures, originally given by SGI Study Department Leader Katsuji Saito for the SGI North America Leaders Study Conference held from July 15–17, 2005, on the following writings of Nichiren Daishonin.
(World Tribune Press; $2.00 each booklet)

"On Attaining Buddhahood in This Lifetime,"
mail order #4901

"The Heritage of the Ultimate Law of Life,"
mail order #4902
"Letter from Sado," mail order #4903
"On the True Aspect of All Phenomena,"
mail order #4904

Faith into Action: Thoughts on Selected Topics,
by Daisaku Ikeda
A collection of inspirational excerpts arranged by subject.
Perfect for finding just the right quote to encourage yourself
or a friend or when preparing for a meeting.
(World Tribune Press, mail order #4135; $12.95)

The Human Revolution, boxed set by Daisaku Ikeda
"A great human revolution in just a single individual will
help achieve a change in the destiny of a nation, and further,
can even enable a change in the destiny of all humankind."
With this as his main theme, the author wrote his twelve-
volume account of Josei Toda's life and the phenomenal
growth of the Soka Gakkai in postwar Japan. Published in a
slightly abridged two-book set, this work paints a fascinating
and empowering story of the far-reaching effects of one
person's inner determination. Josei Toda's awakening and
transformation, his efforts to teach others the unlimited
power of faith, his dedication in leading thousands out of
misery and poverty, the efforts of his devoted disciple Shin'-
ichi Yamamoto—within these stories we find the keys for
building lives of genuine happiness.
(World Tribune Press, mail order #4182; $45.00)

The Journey Begins: First Steps in Buddhist Practice
A pamphlet on the basics of Nichiren Daishonin's Buddhism. Each step is discussed in very basic terms, but each

plays an important role in your practice. For the new member, the points will help you build a foundation in your practice. Return to them again and again throughout your practice to help keep yourself on track and get the maximum benefit from your Buddhist practice.

(World Tribune Press, $1.00 per pamphlet)

[Chinese] mail order #4186
[English] mail order #4138
[French] mail order #4188
[Japanese] mail order #4193
[Spanish] mail order #4139

My Dear Friends in America, by Daisaku Ikeda
This volume brings together for the first time all of the SGI president's speeches to US members in the 1990s.
(World Tribune Press, Hardcover: mail order #4104; $19.95)

The New Human Revolution, by Daisaku Ikeda
An ongoing novelized history of the Soka Gakkai, which contains not only episodes from the past but guidance in faith that we can apply as we grow our movement here in the United States.
(World Tribune Press; $12.00 each volume)

Volume 1, mail order #4601
Volume 2, mail order #4602
Volume 3, mail order #4603
Volume 4, mail order #4604
Volume 5, mail order #4605
Volume 6, mail order #4606
Volume 7, mail order #4607
Volume 8, mail order #4608
Volume 9, mail order #4609
Volume 10, mail order #4610

Volume 11, mail order #4611
Volume 12, mail order #4612
Volume 13, mail order #4613
Volume 14, mail order #4614

The Winning Life:
An Introduction to Buddhist Practice
Using plain language, this booklet gives a quick-yet-detailed introduction to a winning way of life based on Nichiren Daishonin's teachings. A perfect tool for introducing others to the benefits of practice.
(World Tribune Press, $1.00 per booklet)
[Armenian] mail order #4189
[Chinese] mail order #4107
[English] mail order #4105
[French] mail order #4187
[Japanese] mail order #4815
[Korean] mail order #4113
[Spanish] mail order #4106

The Wisdom of the Lotus Sutra, vols. 1–6, by Daisaku Ikeda, Katsuji Saito, Takanori Endo and Haruo Suda
A captivating dialogue on the twenty-eight-chapter Lotus Sutra that brings this ancient writing's important messages into practical application for daily life and for realizing a peaceful world.
(World Tribune Press, $10.95 per volume)
Volume 1, mail order #4281
Volume 2, mail order #4282
Volume 3, mail order #4283
Volume 4, mail order #4284
Volume 5, mail order #4285
Volume 6, mail order #4286

The World of Nichiren Daishonin's Writings, vols 1–4,
by Daisaku Ikeda, Katsuji Saito and Masaaki Morinaka

These books bring to life the teachings and major life events of Nichiren Daishonin through an ongoing discussion between SGI President Ikeda, Soka Gakkai Study Department Leader Katsuji Saito and Study Department Vice Leader Masaaki Morinaka. Revitalize our pursuit of creating happiness and peace with this four-volume series.

(SGI Malaysia, $7.95 per volume)

Volume 1, mail order #1891

Volume 2, mail order #1892

Volume 3, mail order #1893

Volume 4, mail order #1894

A Youthful Diary: One Man's Journey From the Beginning of Faith to Worldwide Leadership for Peace,
by Daisaku Ikeda

Youthful inspiration for people of all ages. Through the tale of the ever-deepening relationship between the young Daisaku Ikeda and his mentor-in-life, Josei Toda, *A Youthful Diary* is a compelling account of both triumphs and setbacks on the road to establishing the foundation of today's Soka Gakkai.

(World Tribune Press, Hardcover: mail order #4101; $23.95, Paperback: mail order #4120; $15.00)